European Economics at a Crossroads

Dedicated to Peter Albin, Don Lavoie, and Larry Moss –
economists who will be missed.

European Economics at a Crossroads

J. Barkley Rosser, Jr.
James Madison University, USA

Richard P.F. Holt
Southern Oregon University, USA

David Colander
Middlebury College, USA

Edward Elgar
Cheltenham, UK • Northampton, MA, USA

Published by
Edward Elgar Publishing Limited
The Lypiatts
15 Lansdown Road
Cheltenham
Glos GL50 2JA
UK

Edward Elgar Publishing, Inc.
William Pratt House
9 Dewey Court
Northampton
Massachusetts 01060
USA

A catalogue record for this book
is available from the British Library

Library of Congress Control Number: 2009940653

Mixed Sources
Product group from well-managed forests and other controlled sources
www.fsc.org Cert no. SA-COC-1565
© 1996 Forest Stewardship Council

FSC

ISBN 978 1 84844 578 9 (cased)
ISBN 978 1 84844 581 9 (paperback)

Printed and bound by MPG Books Group, UK

Contents

Authors and interviewees

Robert Boyer is presently an economist at CEPREMAP (Paris) and GREDEG (Sophia Antipolis). He is known for his work in institutional and historical macroeconomics, innovation and growth analysis, labour markets and wage–labour nexus, international comparisons of capitalisms, European integration and financial crises. He is a major contributor to *régulation* theory which investigates the factors shaping institutional and technological long-term evolutions. His various publications include *The Future of Economic Growth* (Edward Elgar, 2004), *The Productive Models* (with Michel Freyssenet) (Macmillan, 2002), and *Regulation Theory: The State of the Art* (with Yves Saillards, eds) (Routledge, 2001).

David Colander is the Christian A. Johnson Distinguished Professor of Economics at Middlebury College. In 2001–02 he was the Kelly Professor of Distinguished Teaching at Princeton University. He has authored, co-authored, or edited over 40 books and 100 articles on a wide range of topics and his books have been translated into a number of different languages, including Chinese, Bulgarian, Polish, Italian and Spanish. He has been president of both the Eastern Economic Association and History of Economic Thought Society and is Associate Editor for Content for the *Journal of Economic Education*. His most recent books include *Educating Economists* (with Kim Marie McGoldrick) (Edward Elgar, 2009) and *The Making of a European Economist* (Edward Elgar, 2009).

Ernst Fehr is Professor in Microeconomics and Experimental Economics at the University of Zurich, where he is director of the Institute for Empirical Research in Economics. He is also an affiliated faculty member in the economics department at Massachusetts Institute of Technology. He has served as former president of the Economic Science Association and the European Economic Association, and is an honorary member of the American Academy of Arts and Sciences. Ernst Fehr has numerous publications in international top journals including *Science, Nature, Neuron, American Economic Review, Econometrica, Journal of Political Economy* and *Quarterly Journal of Economics.* His research focuses primarily on the proximate patterns and the evolutionary origins of human altruism and the interplay between social preferences, social norms and strategic interactions.

Mauro Gallegati graduated *summa cum laude* in political sciences from the Università di Macerata, and received his PhD in economics from the Università degli Studi di Ancona. He is presently a full professor at the Università Politecnica delle Marche, Ancona. He has held several visiting positions at Washington University, St Louis, MIT, Stanford, UTS Sydney, Santa Fe Institute, Brookings Institution and Columbia University. He has studied with H.P. Minsky and J.E. Stiglitz. In 1996 he founded, with Alan Kirman, the WEHIA conference series and co-founded the International Society for "Economic Sciences with Heterogeneous Interacting Agents." He has published more than 70 articles in economics, history of economic thought, economic history, mathematics, econophysics, complexity and computational economics. His main interests are in agent-based models, business fluctuations and complexity.

Laura Gardini is full Professor in Mathematics for Economic Applications in the Department of Economics and Quantitative Methods at the University of Urbino, Italy. Her main research interests include dynamical systems problems and their applications to the study of economic, financial, social, biological and physical systems.

Geoffrey Hodgson is Research Professor in Business Studies at the University of Hertfordshire. He is editor-in-chief of the *Journal of Institutional Economics.* He has authored over 13 books and over 110 articles in academic journals, and over 70 articles in academic books. His principal academic fields of interest include institutional economics, evolutionary economics, the methodology of economics, the nature of the firm and social theory. His academic honours include Academician of the Academy of Learned Sciences for the Social Sciences, Honorary Life Member of the European Association for Evolutionary Political Economy and past President of the Association for Evolutionary Economics.

Richard P.F. Holt is Professor of Economics and University Seminar at Southern Oregon University, USA. He has authored, co-authored and edited a number of books and journal articles including *A New Guide to Post Keynesian Economics* (Routledge, 2001) and *The Changing Face of Economics* (University of Michigan Press, 2006). His latest books include *Local Economic Development in the 21st Century: Quality of Life and Sustainability* (M.E. Sharpe, 2010) and the edited volume *Post Keynesian and Ecological Economics: Confronting Environmental Issues* (Edward

Elgar, 2009). His research areas include Post Keynesian economics, environmental and ecological economics, history of economic thought, complexity economics and game theory. He is presently working on a book dealing with human rights and the environment.

Cars Hommes is Professor in Economic Dynamics and director of the Centre for Nonlinear Dynamics in Economics and Finance (CeNDEF) at the University of Amsterdam. He is also a research fellow of the Tinbergen Institute and editor of the *Journal of Economic Dynamics and Control*. He received his MSc in Mathematics at the University of Groningen and his PhD in Mathematical Economics at the same university. His current research interests include non-linear economic dynamics; bounded rationality; expectation formation and learning; heterogeneous agent modelling; behavioural finance; and laboratory experiments.

Søren Johansen is Professor of Econometrics at the University of Copenhagen and is best known in economics for his work on cointegration. He has been on numerous editorial boards, including the *Scandinavian Journal of Statistics*, *Econometric Theory*, and *Econometrica*. He is a fellow of Institute of Mathematical Statistics, the International Statistical Institute, and the Econometric Society. He has received numerous awards: in 1997 for outstanding research; as the most cited European economist (1993–96), and the most cited researcher in the world in economic journals from 1990–2000.

Katarina Juselius is an Associate Professor at the University of Copenhagen. She has published extensively on the methodology of cointegrated VAR models with applications to monetary transmission mechanism, policy control rules, price linkages, and wage, price and unemployment dynamics. Her book *The Cointegrated VAR model: Methodology and Applications*, with Oxford University Press, explores these issues in depth. She has served on the editorial boards of several journals, was a member of the Danish SSR, and is a past member of the EUROCORES committee at the European Science Foundation.

Alan Kirman studied at Oxford and carried out his PhD on applying non-cooperative game theory to international trade at Princeton with Harold Kuhn. Hearing that this had no future he moved into general equilibrium theory. However, he then became interested in the relation between micro and macroeconomics and, in particular, how actual markets work. He has held posts at Johns Hopkins, Louvain, Brussels, Warwick, EUI Florence, and Aix-Marseille where he founded the GREQAM, a research group. He is a Fellow of the Econometric Society, was awarded the Humboldt Prize, elected to the Institut Universitaire de France, and is a member of the Institute for Advanced Study at Princeton.

János Kornai studied at the Karl Marx University of Economics in Budapest, Hungary. He also holds a candidate degree from the Hungarian Academy of Sciences. Until 2001 he was a Member of the Board of the Hungarian National Bank (central bank). From 1967 until 1992 he was a Research Professor at the Institute of Economics, Hungarian Academy of Sciences. Kornai joined the faculty of Harvard University in Cambridge, Massachusetts, USA, in 1986 and was named the Allie S. Freed Professor of Economics in 1992. He retired from Harvard in 2002, and in the same year he became a Permanent Fellow of Collegium Budapest Institute for Advanced Study. He is also a Distinguished Research Professor at Central European University.

Joan Martínez Alier has been Professor at the Department of Economics and Economic History, Universitat Autònoma de Barcelona (UAB) since 1975. He has directed the Doctoral Programme in Environmental Sciences (in the option of Ecological Economics and Environmental Management) since 1997, at the Institute of Environmental Science and Technology (ICTA) of the UAB. He was a research fellow/senior associate member of St Antony's College, University of Oxford, and visiting professor at the Universidade Estadual de Campinas (Brazil), Free University of Berlin, Stanford University and University of California (Davis), Yale University, and FLACSO Sede-Ecuador. He is a member of the Scientific Committee of the European Environment Agency. He is also a founding member and has been president of the International Society for Ecological Economics.

Tönu Puu was born in 1936 in Estonia. He was a student of the famous location theorist Tord Palander at Uppsala University in Sweden, where he received his PhD in 1964. He was appointed the Chair of Economics at Umeå University in north Sweden in 1971. Upon retirement in 2001 he moved to the centre for regional science (CERUM) at Umeå University, where he currently works as a guest professor. Puu has published eight books, including *Spatial Economics* (with Martin Beckmann) (North-Holland, 1985); *Nonlinear Economic Dynamics* (Springer-Verlag, 1989–2000); *Attractors, Bifurcations, & Chaos* (Springer-Verlag, 2000, 2003); and *Mathematical Location and Land Use Theory* (Springer-Verlag, 1997, 2003). He has published 115 journal articles and book chapters and has edited two volumes. His published work covers a period of over 45 years in the areas of financial economics, production theory, philosophy of science, spatial economics, oligopoly theory, and business cycle theory. Besides his scientific work, Puu founded the Nordic Baroque Music Festival.

J. Barkley Rosser, Jr. is Professor of Economics and Kirby L. Cramer, Jr. Professor of Business Administration at James Madison University, in Harrisonburg, Virginia. He is also editor of the *Journal of Economic Behavior and Organization*. Among his more than a hundred publications are *From Catastrophe to Chaos: A General Theory of Economic Discontinuities*, 2nd edn (Springer, 2000), *Comparative Economics in a Transforming World Economy*, 2nd edn, with Marina V. Rosser (MIT Press, 2004), and an edited volume, *Complexity in Economics* (Edward Elgar, 2004).

Reinhard Selten won the Nobel Prize in Economics in 1994 with John Harsanyi and John Nash. He is known for his work in bounded rationality and is considered by many as one of the founding fathers of experimental economics. He has a reputation for publishing in non-refereed journals to avoid being forced to make unwanted changes to his work. He is Professor Emeritus at the University of Bonn, Germany, and holds several honorary doctoral degrees. He is a member and co-founder of the International Academy of Sciences, San Marino.

Preface

This is a companion to our *Changing Face of Economics* book (Colander et al., 2004a). In our previous book we interviewed top economists at the cutting edge of the profession, who through their work and stories explained to us how the economics profession is changing. What came out in the interviews is that neoclassical economics is no longer the mainstream orthodoxy, and modern economists are exploring a much wider set of issues with a wider set of assumptions than past economists.

As we looked more deeply into *who* was doing cutting edge work in economics, we recognized that a lot of this important work was taking place in Europe. But for geographical reasons (the three of us teach in America) our previous book focused primarily on interviewing economists in the United States. To make amends, and to continue what had become an enjoyable and informative interviewing process, we decided that it would be fun to supplement that book with interviews of cutting edge economists in Europe. Our thought at that time was the following: we would make the same general arguments about the changing face of modern economics that we made before, but we would replace the United States interviewees with European-based economists.

It did not end up that way. Once we started exploring European economics and talking to European economists in preparation for the project, we found another story going on that was just as important and interesting as the changing face of economics. The other story was that as economics was changing, the European economics academic structure was simultaneously changing in rather substantial ways. What makes this interesting is that the two changes are, in many ways, working against one another. The changes in the European economics profession are reducing the incentives of European economists to do the very work that we describe as cutting edge. It isn't that the top elite in Europe don't value cutting edge work. It's just that they are so concerned with "catching up" with the United States in quantitative measures of research output that they are blinding themselves to the fact that much of the standard work is, at best, pedestrian. All this does is undermine the strengths of European economics by trying to create incentives to "catch up" with the United States on criteria that are backward-looking rather than forward-looking. They are overemphasizing quality-weighted journal articles and losing sight of creative and exciting new ideas that emerge from cutting edge work.

The use of such backward-looking measures is a vice that many of the second tier graduate programs in the United States have fallen into, which essentially makes the work that comes out of these places of little interest in a study of cutting edge work. The main problem with using quantity-weighted measures is that they are not an efficient way of measuring important cutting edge research. By its very nature, cutting edge research often won't get published in the top journals until it has gone through an evolutionary process and been gradually accepted by the profession. Truly new ideas need to go through a period of incubation and then development. It is true that much of the creative work will fail. But the couple of ideas that catch on are what will change economics – not the pedestrian work that often shows up in the journals, even the top journals.

In our view, what is important is having an environment that supports such a process. From our previous contacts with European economists, we believed that the European academic institutional structure, for all its many faults, was supporting such a process better than the United States system and that it recognized and appreciated the importance of plurality in economics, which allows the exploration of a wider range of issues. What we found instead was cutting edge work being undermined by institutional changes associated with expansion of the European Union. They were killing the wildflowers to plant a single hayseed, and in doing so were creating a monoculture. They were planting, row after row, acre by acre, a standard variety of flowers found in the United States.

Our strong reaction against this institutional change led us to change the focus of the book to include a discussion about how these excessive concerns about backward-looking research measures were undermining creativity in research.

THE EVOLUTION OF THE BOOK

Our first task was to get our ideas down. Dave, who had been working on a related project (Colander, 2009), took the lead in coming up with some rough ideas about what was happening in the European economics profession. Barkley, who had been working on histories of economic thought of the various European countries as part of his studies of comparative systems, took the lead in writing about the different traditions. Ric took the lead in drafting a chapter summarizing our views on the changing face of economics in Europe and also worked hard to blend Dave and

Barkley's ideas together (no easy task). Eventually, after much toing and froing, rewrites and further rewrites, we ended up with Chapters 1 and 2.

Once we had these chapters we decided whom to interview. Barkley took the lead in setting up the interviews, and he and Ric made a trip to Europe to start the process. Over the next year further interviews were done, a number of them at a conference that Barkley organized as part of a symposium on complexity for the *Journal of Economics and Behavioral Organization* at James Madison University. We transcribed the interviews, and sent them back to the interviewees, leaving them free to modify them as they saw fit. Finally we decided that we wanted some wise and excellent economists to reflect on the overall project and the future of European economics. We thought János Kornai and Reinhard Selten would be perfect to do that. They both graciously agreed. Since Barkley was going over again to Europe with his wife, Marina Rosser, who is a top economist, they both interviewed Professors Kornai and Selten for this book. These are not the only interviews that Marina was part of. She also participated in the Geoff Hodgson interview. In many ways she should be considered a fourth author.

A note about the order of our names as authors: given our friendship and professional respect for each other we rotate our names with each new book that we do together.

PART I

The Future of European Economics

1. European economics at a crossroads

INTRODUCTION

European economics is at a crossroads. Because of the Common European Educational Policy and the influence it is exerting, the institutions of European academia are changing. Funding and advancement criteria that in the past were considered almost unchangeable are now in play. The result is a jockeying for funds and power. Within this jockeying there is a push by some of the elite of the European economics profession to create a European economics that is both separate from American economics, but is also competitive with it. How the jockeying plays out will play a big role in guiding the future direction of the European economics profession, and more generally, we believe, the future direction of economics.

What makes this all the more interesting is that European economics has arrived at its crossroads at the same time as the economics profession is itself changing; the neoclassical approach based on the holy trinity of rationality, greed and equilibrium is giving way to a less rigid trinity of bounded rationality, enlightened self-interest and sustainability. In a recent book (Colander et al., 2004a) we discussed these changes in economics, and argued that the interesting developments in the profession are occurring at the edge of the mainstream,[1] where innovative cutting edge economists are breaking with old traditions, and are changing the face of economics.

The changes that are occurring in the economics profession are being driven by changing analytic, computing and statistical technology, which allows economists to use much more sophisticated modeling techniques than before. As these technological changes take hold, the profession is opening up to ideas from other disciplines such as psychology and ecology. These technological changes and willingness to accept transdisciplinary exploration[2] have made it possible for the mainstream profession to deal seriously with the proposition that the economy is truly complex – beyond full analytic specification from microfoundations.

We believe the complexity vision marks a significant change in the mainstream vision. While the mainstream still includes work done in the neoclassical "simplicity vision"[3] today those who are doing cutting edge economics are exploring issues that go beyond standard analytic methods. European economics, with its past openness to heterodox thought and acceptance of transdisciplinary approaches, is in many ways in a good position to lead the way in the development of this new work, and thereby play an important role in its future and the direction of the profession.

THE HISTORY AND STRUCTURE OF THE BOOK

To convey the recent developments of cutting edge work to the reader, in our previous book we interviewed a variety of cutting edge economists, providing readers with a sense of the diversity and excitement that is driving this research. We mentioned that much of the cutting edge work was going on in Europe, but for practical reasons (we all live in America), we concentrated on United States economists. Our initial motivation for this book was to expand our previous consideration to give Europe its due as a leader in many of these cutting edge developments.

But as we started to research and talk to individuals in Europe about this project it became clear to us that there was a second interrelated story that was just as important. That second story was the impact of the institutional changes that were occurring within the European economics profession as it moves to a Common Educational Policy. Specifically, rather than adjusting its academic institutions to put Europe at the forefront of the changing face of economics, the European economics profession was simply adjusting its academic institutions to mimic the United States system of incentives. In doing so it was undermining the institutions that allowed cutting edge work to thrive in Europe. Because of our concern with this we changed the focus of the book to include that issue as well. Our goals in this book are to:

1. Shed light on the changes occurring at the cutting edge of the economics profession – how it is moving away from the old style orthodoxy to a much broader and more pluralistic mainstream that goes far beyond neoclassical economics.
2. Consider how the ongoing changes in the European economics institutional structure are likely to affect Europe's role in that transition.

The structure of this book is the following. In the remainder of this chapter we discuss the historical threads in European economics, differences between the United States and European traditions, and explore our concerns about the adoption of United States incentives into European economics. In Chapter 2 we briefly discuss the complexity vision, and why we believe it is the connecting theme of many of the cutting edge developments, both in the United States and Europe. In the next set of chapters we interview economists who we see playing an important role in the changes that are occurring in European economics and who are doing cutting edge work. We discuss with them their research and their views on how the changes in the European institutional structure are likely to affect future cutting edge work in Europe. Finally, in the last two chapters, we allow two leaders of European economics, János Kornai and Reinhard Selten, to reflect on our arguments and the interviews.

HISTORICAL THREADS IN EUROPEAN ECONOMICS

To understand the choices facing European economics today it is useful to understand its history. Here we give a brief history of some of the important traditions in European economics and how they are changing. Throughout the late 1800s and early 1900s the United States was essentially insignificant to global economics. PhD students in the United States had to study two languages, generally French and German, to keep up with global developments. The situation was symbolized by the fact that the founder of the American Economic Association, Richard Ely, had a PhD from Germany. Even in the English-speaking world, the United States was a minor player. Top English-speaking programs in economics were in England, and up until the early 1930s, if a United States economist wanted to succeed they had to spend some time in Europe since that was where the cutting edge work was taking place at that time.

As we will discuss later, during World War II the role of the United States changed, in large part due to an enormous migration of European economists (and many other European academics) to the United States. By the 1960s it was clear that United States economists (many of whom were non-US citizens) dominated the academic forefront of economics. Since then, to study economics at the highest intellectual level, one went to the United States. Its journals dominated, and its universities defined the intellectual cutting edge, which became models for how things should be done in universities throughout the world.[4]

The geographic movement was accompanied by a second major change. Earlier, American economists had to know two languages beyond their own to be considered educated. That changed, starting in the 1960s when graduate schools in the United States required only one other language and then dropped all language requirements completely. Today, to be an economist anywhere in the world one must know mathematics and English; no other languages are required. This movement to English and mathematics as the universal languages of economics fundamentally changed the nature of the competition of ideas in the profession. Mathematics' universality allowed non-English speakers to be able to participate and compete on the global stage of economics, which in turn increased the level of formalism in economics. Economics became a field held together by mathematical tools and models. The interpretation of those models generally involved nuances. Here, non-native English speakers were at a competitive disadvantage, since it is difficult to express nuances in non-native languages. Since English was the lingua franca of economics, the United States and British interpretations dominated.

The rise of English as the sole language of global economics unified aspects of European economics but it also splintered the European economics community. Mathematically oriented economists in Europe became part of the global economics community. Others were to varying degrees removed from it. There was now a two-track development of economics in continental Europe – a global component that was highly mathematical, generally conducted in English, and a local tradition component that differed among schools and countries. The global component used the same approach and focused on the same issues as did United States-style economics. The more autonomous domestic traditions developed in their own ways and reflected the traditions of the particular country.

As examples of this two-track development in European economics we will discuss changes in three nations that have had influential, independent traditions of economic thought within their own languages and also have had some global influence: France, Germany and Italy. Of course other non-English-speaking European nations have had important influences on global economic thought, including such countries as the Netherlands (long wave theory and Tinbergenian econometrics), Sweden (international trade theory, public economics, capital theory, parallel Keynesian macroeconomics), Switzerland (Lausanne School general equilibrium theory), Austria (Schumpeter and the Vienna School of "Austrians"), Spain,[5] Hungary (Kornai and actual socialist economics), Russia (Kantorovich and linear programming), and outside Europe, Japan stands out.[6] Our focus on France, Germany and Italy should be seen as examples only.

FRENCH ECONOMICS

Probably the nation with the strongest continuing set of national schools of thought, with original work still done in the local language, is France. Of course, it is probably prouder of its language than are most nations and has made official efforts to enforce scientific communication being carried out in French (with little success). There is some irony in this as France is arguably the most important global source of orthodox mathematical neoclassical economics, deriving from Cournot and Walras. France provided post-World War II transplants to the United States such as Gérard Debreu. His work reflects the deep tradition of abstract rationalism dating from Descartes (if not indeed from Aquinas) that would manifest itself in the ultra-formalistic Bourbakist School of mathematics in the mid-twentieth century, out of which specifically Debreu came.

Even while French economists were making important contributions to what would become global economics, France was also a fountainhead of numerous heterodoxies, including several of the important schools of socialist economic thought.[7] In his final book, Friedrich Hayek (1988) would identify Saint-Simon and the rationalistic French approach to economics as the source of what he labeled "the fatal conceit", the idea that through central planning societies could rationally order and manage themselves.[8] It is therefore not surprising that some of the most vigorous ongoing theoretical Marxian economic thought is occurring in France, with Gérard Dumenil and Dominique Lévy both ensconced at CEPREMAP.[9] This institute also houses Robert Boyer, widely viewed as the founder and main figure in the *Régulation* School. Another distinctively French school that is related to the *Régulation* School is the Conventions School, led by Olivier Favereau at the University of Paris-X-Nanterre. Yet another is the circuitist branch of Post Keynesian monetary theory, whose most prominent figure is Alain Parguez of the University of Besançon. While increasingly these schools have begun to publish their work in English language outlets, most of their key work was originally done in French. Important French-based journals such as *Revue Economique* and *Economie Appliquée* continue to publish many of their papers in French as well.

GERMAN ECONOMICS

Another great center of independent economics traditions is Germany, although its history has been substantially different because of World War II, which generated a profound discontinuity in its intellectual development. Much like France, Germany was also an early center of neoclassical economics, with Alfred Marshall borrowing heavily (often without attribution) from such mid-nineteenth-century thinkers as Heinrich Rau, who first drew supply and demand curves in the form now firmly entrenched in English language principles of economics textbooks. Indeed, as already noted, German was often a language learned by English-speaking economists, at least before World War I, and the German higher education system profoundly influenced the American system. While neoclassicism would be reinforced by the early Austrians, notably Menger, the Historical School came to prominence after the unification of Germany and would serve as the fountainhead for the Old Institutionalist School in the United States. Of course, Germany was an even more important source of socialist economic thought than France; Karl Marx did most of his writing on economics in German though he lived as an exile in England.

These strands were decisively broken by Germany's defeat in World War II, partly due to conquest and partly due to death or emigration of many German intellectuals. While the Social Market School (Müller-Armack, 1947) would emerge in the immediate post-war period (in Freiburg particularly) using the German language, the dominance of English would come much more swiftly and thoroughly in German economics than in most other European countries.[10] In that regard, there has been less preservation of older traditions and more acceptance of the American intellectual hegemony, despite a distinctive pattern of hierarchy in German higher education that imitates the guild system structure of master-journeyman-apprentice. Werner Hildenbrand exemplifies this tradition. He is a top German economist writing in English who was highly influential within the American-dominated post-war neoclassical orthodoxy. This master-journeyman-apprentice system is now breaking down in various ways, with German academic institutions becoming more like United States academic institutions. This is being driven by returning European economists trained in the United States, and a new system of nationwide faculty evaluation that essentially reproduces the United States incentive system.

As these changes are going on in Germany, the influence of German economics is still being felt globally. For example, the development of behavioral and experimental economics has been most advanced in German language countries, even as most of this work has been carried out and published in English. While substantially paralleling what one finds in the United States, researchers such as Werner Güth and Ernst Fehr have been somewhat more willing to stand further away from orthodox ideas than their American counterparts, with the example and influence of evolutionary game theorist and behavioralist, Reinhard Selten, playing an important role. In recent years, research institutes such as the Max Planck Research Institutes, have become centers of the newly emerging distinctive German approaches in evolutionary, behavioral and experimental economics, adding to this tradition and developing complexity theory. Other German universities have managed to develop alternative approaches; for example, Bielefeld University houses work in non-linear macro dynamics with economists such as Willi Semmler, Peter Flaschel and Herbert Dawid. Similar to France, we still see a two-track system in Germany but with a larger willingness to accept American influence.

ITALIAN ECONOMICS

During the period from 1890 to 1920, Italy was arguably the leading center of abstract, mathematical economic thought and development of theoretical neoclassical economics. Italy also played an important role in the development of ideas that influenced economics globally. The most important figure was Vilfredo Pareto, although he wrote much in French while located at the University of Lausanne in the French-speaking part of Switzerland. Others included Enrico Barone, whose work on the Ministry of Production was inspired by Walras and Pareto, which led to the famous and long-running Socialist Controversy. Italy's prominence at this time even led non-Italians to publish in their journals, such as the Ukrainian-Russian, Eugen Slutsky (1915), whose equation is the foundation of standard indifference curve analysis.

Besides Barone's work, Italy would also foster a more radical strand of socialist economic thought led by Antonio Gramsci. Mussolini's rise to power in 1922 forced his followers into exile, the most important of whom was Piero Sraffa who moved to Cambridge, England. For half a century Cambridge University would be the center of the development of the most important Italian school of economic thought – the neo-Ricardian school represented by the work of Sraffa. Although they had adherents in Britain and the United States, today the school is most forcibly defended in Italy. Its high cardinals are Pierangelo Garegnani of La Sapienza in Rome, who controls Sraffa's papers, and Luigi Pasinetti of Catholic University in Milan.

This neo-Ricardian school has directly spawned another generation of economists who have used the strong Italian mathematical tradition to make Italy one of the most important centers in the world of complex, non-linear dynamics, and of interacting heterogeneous agent modeling – both strains of work that are playing an important role in the development of modern complexity theory. A protégé of Pasinetti's in Milan, Domenico Delli Gatti, has co-founded with his longtime co-author, Mauro Gallegati of Ancona, the increasingly influential Workshop on Economic Heterogeneous Interacting Agents (WEHIA).[11] Together they have developed insights of Hyman Minsky and have trained a large number of practitioners to this approach who are now in many locations in Italy. They have also been working closely with a leading developer of econophysics, Rosario Mantegna of Palermo. There is also the multi-dimensional chaos group at Urbino led by Laura Gardini. Evolutionary technological models of firms have been developed by Giovanni Dosi, now at one of the institutions in Pisa.

Italy has also become a favorite place for important heterodox,

English-speaking economists to migrate to, with such figures as the late Richard Goodwin and more recently Samuel Bowles in Siena. You also have Axel Leijonhufvud in Trento, whose presence there with K. Vela Velupillai has made Trento a world center of computable economic theory. It has been joked that in the world of complex and heterogeneous agents' economics, Italy is virtually a Third Continent after North America and the rest of Europe.

PAST EUROPEAN ECONOMICS AS THE SEEDS FOR MODERN ECONOMICS

We could continue our overview of specific countries, but we believe the above examples should make our point: European economics is vibrant and intellectually alive. It has much diversity and creativity that has not been allowed to develop in the United States. The reason why Europe has this more eclectic approach to research is not because European economists are somehow different from economists in the United States, but because of historical reasons. Each of these various economic traditions remains distinct because of different linguistic and historical traditions.

These traditions are not distinct from global mainstream economics. In combination these traditions were the seeds of modern United States economics, which in turn has become modern global economics. Since, during, and after the world wars, many top European economists went to the United States either as faculty or graduate students. As Paul Samuelson pointed out "the triumphant rise of American economics after 1940 was enormously accelerated by importation of scholars from Hitlerian Europe" (Samuelson, 1988, p. 319). Examples of such scholars who came to America and strongly influenced American economics include Richard Musgrave, Abba Lerner, Franco Modigliani, Tjalling Koopmans, Gérard Debreu, John von Neumann, Oskar Morgenstern and Jacob Marschak, just to name a few. It was the ideas of these European economists, pushed to the United States because of the political strife in Europe, that served as the foundation for what is now modern economics.

European economics was severely hurt by the departure of these and other stars, and it is only now recovering. But it continues to be held back by its university institutional structure, which for top economists pays far less than do United States academic institutions and is burdened by a stifling administrative bureaucracy. Because of these problems European schools have had a difficult time holding on to top notch economists. Those top global economists who chose to stay in Europe, such as Jacques

Drèze, were drawn there by lifestyle considerations rather than by pay or influence in the profession.

Continental European economists were also held back by the language barriers; many wrote in their home language. As we discussed above, in the 1950s this was far less of a problem, as the definition of a scholar included the ability to read other languages. However, as the language requirements of PhD's in economics decreased, it became more of a problem. European ideas expressed in any language other than English, no matter how good, did not get a hearing.[12] The situation started to change in the 1980s as more and more non-native English-speaking European economists began to write in English, and by the 1990s, with the influence of the European Union integration throughout Europe, English had become the common language of what can be called global economics. At that point continental graduate programs in economics began to be taught in English, and research began to be written in English. It was the acceptance of English as the common language that has made it possible to talk about a global economics profession. This has led to the recent push to energize the European economics profession, and make it into a center of global economics rather than an appendage to a United States-dominated global economics. The trick here for European economics, we believe, is integrating itself with global economics, but keeping its diversity represented historically by the traditions of different countries.

UNITED STATES AND EUROPEAN TRADITIONS IN ECONOMICS

Let us summarize our argument so far. There are a number of differences between traditional European and United States economics that reflect their different institutional, cultural and linguistic traditions. Because of language and institutional differences among countries that we described above, European economics includes more diversity in its economics than does United States economics.

It is this diversity that places traditional European economics firmly at the cutting edge of global economics. In fact, it was the work in European countries that we had in mind when we argued in our last book that Europe was a leader in the cutting edge work in economics. The diversity of European economics is important to us because we view the economics profession as a complex system of multiple competing ideas. For that system to maintain vigor, diversity of ideas is necessary. Its development is best seen through a biological model of competition, in which the institutional environment allows some ideas to develop and others to die.

The strength of a complex system is in its diversity as much as it is in any particular idea. The seeds for modern complexity economics, which involve a serious reconsideration of some of the core assumptions of the general equilibrium model, did not find a fertile field in the United States. The payoff was too long for the United States institutional structure which advanced researchers who publish quickly. But they could continue to exist in Europe because of its institutional structure that placed less emphasis on quick publication.

Another way to put our argument is that the European profession is a bottom-up profession, while the United States is more top-down. Thus, Europe has Italian economics, Swedish economics, German economics, and French economics (and often, university-specific traditions within countries themselves) – all of which differ. These traditions can survive in Europe, but they have a hard time expanding globally because the language of global mainstream economics is English and mathematics only. In United States economics, where a small group of interrelated top schools dominate, and set the research agenda for the entire United States economics profession, it was much harder for these alternative traditions to survive. The house journals of the elite schools, such as the *Quarterly Journal of Economics* (Harvard) and the *Journal of Political Economy* (Chicago) have become the top journals of global mainstream economics; the elites at these schools control the American Economic Association with its journals. Essentially, as opposed to being a highly competitive structure, the United States economics profession is a tightly controlled oligopoly, in which economists at a few schools dominate the entire profession and are in charge of all the primary journals. All ideas are thus filtered through a small group of very bright, but highly interrelated individuals. The result is that diversity in the United States is weeded out, unless the internal group of editors favors that diversity. The spread of a single output metric – quality weighted journal article publications – quickly spread the control of this small group of schools to lower-ranked schools, as they hired the graduates of the top schools as professors.

The institutional structure of United States graduate education further embedded the mono-culture. Specifically, the United States graduate programs all have two years of course work, followed by two or three years of seminars and work on the dissertation. It has a national job market in which schools hire instructors and professors from the entire United States, rather than just from schools in their geographic proximity. Though this creates some efficiency, it also encourages the development of a mono-tradition where professional work that does not conform to the norm is killed off. Publication metrics of success focus solely on journal articles published in journals controlled by the oligopoly. Other aspects of an economist's output, such as writing books[13] or advising government, or simply providing new insights for other economists to think about are given little or no weight in hiring and promotions. With the acceptance of the journal publication metric as the primary way to evaluate performance, the power of a small group of individuals who control the journals increases, and competition decreases. Diversity disappears, with schools such as Virginia, Notre Dame, UCLA, and Maryland giving up their heterodox traditions.[14] Because of the control of the journals by a small group, and the development of a quality-weighted journal metric, the control becomes self-fulfilling. Competition of ideas decreases.

We are not arguing that this group of elite United States economists is malevolent or do not have the best interests of the profession at heart. These are brilliant economists who want to further economic thinking and who are committed to developing economics as a science. Many of them are also committed to diversity of opinion, as we discussed in our last book. And a number of the elite have worked hard to promote and encourage diversity, as long as that diverse work meets their scientific standards. The problem is not motivation; the problem is with the institutional structure and the lack of competition within that structure. Ideas outside the standard set of ideas at the top schools do not have an opportunity to develop to the level where decisions can be made whether or not they meet the criteria as set by the elite. Over time the genetic gene pool of ideas is reduced, and the result is a rather bland economics – rigorous but often far from exciting or insightful. There are of course differences in approach. For example there were Keynesian, monetarist, New Classical, and New Keynesian approaches in macro, and structural and formalist approaches in micro. But, over time these different approaches are soon blended into a single approach by the top-down United States structure. Thus, over the last decade differences between Chicago, Harvard and MIT have declined, as all become combined into a single mainstream global economics, with a newly emerging orthodoxy, in which a small group of elite economists decide what type of ideas are acceptable and publishable in the top journals and what should be considered outside the purview of mainstream economics.

It is our concern about the American structure of economics that makes us so anxious about the recent developments in Europe. We see traditional European economics as a type of untainted island, which has allowed non-standard ideas to exist and develop. It provides the basis for what might be called a variety of heirloom economic ideas. Language and institutional differences mostly protect these heirloom ideas, because they did not have to compete on a broader European or global stage. They were further protected by the European labor market institutions. Because there is little hiring competition among different countries, diversity has remained. While clearly there is an important strand of European economics that takes part in mainstream global economics debates, this strand is the exception.

The result is a much more diverse field of economics in Europe than in the United States. Different countries have different traditions, but in almost all the traditions, researchers worry less about publication and more about other things. This sometimes means that their research focuses on deep abstract ideas in economics or looking at practical applications. At other times it might mean exploring ideas that appear to have very little to do with economics. Despite or perhaps because of its many problems, Europe tends to be a better incubator for ideas that have not been followed up by global economics. They provide a seed pool of diverse ideas for research (Colander et al., 2007–08). There is also a cultural acceptance and even an expectation that professors take a more active role in policy debates than in the United States. Professors often become public intellectuals and enter into public debates, consult with governments, hold public office and take a much broader approach to economics than their United States counterparts.

With the development of the European Union and the Common Educational Policy, all that is changing now. As we will discuss below, these changes are resulting in the imposition of a United States-type ranking system in Europe. The result is a push to make economics in Europe look like an adopted twin of the United States. We don't want to give the impression that all these changes are bad. Some of them are very positive. They are leading to merit-based competition, replacing cronyism in the allocation of jobs with competitive job markets. But instead of creating an environment within which these ideas can fairly compete, they are being placed into an environment created by the United States. Those who do not toe the line have little chance, regardless of how good they are, of success. So while we strongly favor fair competition, we see a perverse competition actually developing that undermines the strength of the traditional European economics profession.

A CLOSER LOOK AT UNITED STATES AND TRADITIONAL EUROPEAN ACADEMIC ECONOMICS INSTITUTIONS

To better understand the advantages and disadvantages of these changes let us look more closely at the distinctions between the economics profession in the United States and Europe. A good way to begin is with Bob Coats's list of distinctions between Europe and the United States economic programs (2000). According to Coats, compared with traditional European economics, the United States has:

1. greater proneness to fashion;
2. less tolerance of heterodox ideas;
3. greater homogeneity across economics departments;
4. more highly developed graduate education programs;
5. greater emphasis on technique and less emphasis on applied theory;
6. less hierarchical organization of departments, with individuals free to pursue independent research at a much earlier stage;
7. more competitive labor market and higher mobility;
8. less involvement in public policy debate;
9. lower status of academics in society.

This list fits our perceptions of the differences between European and United States economics, and so provides a good place to start examining them.

What explains these differences? First, in our view, a large part of the explanation can be found in the different institutional structures in Europe and the United States, which can be characterized in the following way:

- European schools tend to be public and many have civil service rules for promotion.
- United States schools are a combination of public and private, and even the public schools have specific rules governing promotion and tenure that require specific research output.
- United States schools have a unified job market; European schools have a much more fragmented job market.
- Coinciding with this is the generally higher salaries for academic economists in the United States than in Europe, which have helped to enforce the American global dominance in the profession since World War II.
- Research incentives are much clearer in the United States; they involve a metric of quality weighted journal publications and citations. European incentives are much more diffuse.
- European schools are organized by countries and languages whereas the United States has a common language, and similar schools.

We believe that the different institutional structures, and the incentives toward research that they encompass, lead to many of the differences that

Coats notes. For example, consider the greater degree of engagement in public policy debates in Europe as compared to the United States. Most United States academics have little incentive to become involved in policy; advancement and promotion depend almost entirely on journal publications. Academics in Europe have research embodied in journal publications as only one of their goals, and numerous European economists play a role advising government on policy.[15]

A second important difference that can be explained in terms of incentives and institutional structure is the greater openness to heterodoxy in Europe as compared to the United States. In Europe mainstream economics is broader and more pluralistic. While the center of the United States and European professions may be identical, the deviation is wider. Since advancement depends on a wider range of activities in Europe, and less on a single metric than in the United States, Europe tends to have more diversity and openness to different ideas. In the United States less diversity can be attributed to the quality-weighted journal article metric which gives a small number of journal editors (those at the highly rated journals) a central role in determining which ideas are important. If those editors have similar backgrounds, as they generally do, with most of the editors coming from a small set of schools, a stranglehold on thought occurs. Academics in Europe are freer to work on a variety of different approaches than academics in the United States, because country differentiation and the lack of a unified job market allows these pockets of heterodoxy to develop. This allows Europe to place less emphasis on conformity than one sees in the United States.[16]

As the European economics profession changes in response to pressures for it to become more like the United States, it is alienating and undermining the work of those European economists whose work does not fit the United States mold. The diversity of traditional European economics, which is one of its major strengths, is being undermined. Those who are considered part of the European mainstream are now being pushed into the heterodox periphery without necessarily choosing to be in this status. What is occurring reminds us of the story about European forests told by James Scott in *Seeing like a State* (1998). He discusses the push in Germany at the turn of the century for "scientific forestry" and efficiency, which involved planting and harvesting mono-crop forests, while clearing useless underbrush and less valuable trees. The result was *waldsterben* – the death of the German forests, due to disease, lack of soil replenishment, and the killing of many of the aspects of the forest that gave it life. We see the European push in economics to adopt its policy as a type of *ecosterben*, which will have equivalent disastrous long-run effects.

What we believe is lacking is the recognition that the more eclectic assessment system in Europe has both costs and benefits. On the one hand it leads to less published research (Kirman and Dahl, 1994) since social factors play a larger role in advancement. Much of the discussion of research in Europe and reforming European economics has focused on this aspect. On the other hand, what have not been focused on are the benefits of this more eclectic assessment system. That eclecticism allows pockets in which cutting edge work can be nurtured and advanced, avoiding the fads and conformity that characterize the United States assessment system. This is especially true about cutting edge work that is more exploratory and might not lead to immediate publication. Thus, the European assessment system provides incubators for new ideas, which is why we believe that Europe is at the forefront of much cutting edge work. To modify the reassessment system in a way that eliminates these incubators undermines the most important strength of European economics.

DIFFERENCES IN EUROPEAN AND UNITED STATES INCENTIVES AND INSTITUTIONAL STRUCTURES

Let us now look more closely at how the institutional and incentive structures of Europe and the United States affect their research. European academic researchers' incentive systems for advancement tend to be more informal, political and social than incentives facing United States researchers.[17] This means that European assessments have often been vague and idiosyncratic by school and country; they rely on multiple subjective elements, and it is often difficult to determine precisely what they are.[18] In European economics, doing good work, impressing higher-level professors, measures of publications and citations, and positively interacting with other professors are all important. This continues to hold widely even as the system moves into flux, with many schools now imitating the United States system.

While all these elements are important, the United States incentive system gives greatest emphasis on quantitative measures of quality-weighted journal publications and citations.[19] It is this emphasis that we see leading to the differences in United States and European economics. Because measures of journal publication output have become key elements of judging a researcher's contribution, United States economic researchers focus their research more on "journal publishable research" than European economic researchers.[20] Publishability of one's research affects all aspects of economic research in the United States, including choice of research topic and research methods. It leads economists away from asking big questions – and to focus on areas of research where data readily exists that can be condensed to a 30-page double-spaced paper (papers longer than 20 journal pages are difficult to publish in a journal, so research topics that take longer than that to explore are discouraged).

The focus on journal publishability is pervasive and it starts early on in graduate school. In recent interviews with United States graduate economics students, Colander (2006) found an enormous concern about publishability of research. Consistent with this focus, United States graduate students have almost abandoned full-length dissertations, and replaced them with three-essay dissertations, so that the essays can be adapted into journal articles quickly. He also found that students differentiate various types of papers that they write on the paper's usefulness for advancement. For example, some of his interviewees distinguished a job market paper from a journal article paper, which in turn was distinguished from a dissertation essay.[21] Graduate education in the United States has adapted to the United States assessment system by focusing on preparing graduate students to become efficient journal article writers, rather than preparing them to become general researchers. In its attempt to make European economics competitive with United States economics, it is this system that European economics is attempting to copy.[22]

In overview, the "European style" of research has significant advantages, and our fear is that the recent changes in the incentive structure of the economics profession in Europe will undermine those advantages. One of those advantages is its pluralism. Unlike the United States, where working on non-standard ideas has generally meant being alienated sociologically from the mainstream, in Europe there was a more pluralistic tradition, which allowed for researchers to work on some of the cutting edge ideas of the profession. There are still many different traditions in Europe as we have mentioned – Italian, French, Swedish – but these traditions are fading and are being blended into global economics. Despite this push toward a global blending, the most distinctively local traditions have continued to flourish within the local language journals and outlets. Having said this, we are concerned about the future of European pluralism as pressure mounts to copy the incentive system of the United States.

THE GLOBALIZATION AND REINVIGORIZATION OF EUROPEAN ECONOMICS

As we stated at the beginning of this chapter, European economics is undergoing change, and there is a push in Europe to adapt a United States metric of output to create a research-oriented European economics. The problem with doing so, we believe, is two-fold. First, any specific metric will create perverse incentives, and introduce the same problems that characterize United States economics. Second, the use of a United States centric metric unfairly burdens European economists because it does not fairly recognize the European-based original work. So the problem we see is that instead of creating a system of incentives that builds on the strengths of European economics – its diversity and creativity – and thereby putting itself into a position to leapfrog United States economics into a place where it is the center of a new economics, it is instead choosing a model that will strongly push it to be a second-rate carbon copy of United States economics. Our view is that Europe can, and should do better. By doing so, it is not just European economics that benefits, but the overall economics profession.

With so many Europeans making up global economics, it seems only natural to suggest that the way forward for European economics is to repatriate some of these Europeans and simply to shift the geographic center away from the United States. We agree that such a change is going to take place in the future. But changes along these lines will be slow and difficult. The reason is that European academic institutions have enormous bureaucratic problems; they have inefficient funding mechanisms, advancement criteria, and far less in terms of endowment than United States institutions. They tend to be state financed and subject to myriad state regulations. Many European academic institutions suffer from the notorious Eurosclerosis, and are being chocked off by the bureaucracy and restrictions on meritocracy. Making such institutions effectively compete with the United States is difficult; it requires either changing the system, or setting up new institutions outside the standard system.[23]

It is that Eurosclerosis that the elite in the European economics profession are trying to escape as they push European economics to adopt United States metrics for advancement. To do so, they are creating a set of new global economic programs in Europe, which are designed to compete with United States programs. These programs, which include schools such as Boconni, Bonn, the Stockholm School of Economics, Tillburg, Pompeu Fabra and Toulouse on the continent, and the London School of Economics and UCL in England, have graduate economics programs taught totally in English, and have structures almost identical to United States programs. The same books are used, the same courses are taught, and the same approaches developed. Even Oxford and Cambridge are changing their systems to be more like the United States (Colander, 2009).

In many ways we applaud these changes, and we certainly agree that European academic institutions are in need of major change. (This is not an especially novel position; we have met few economics professors in

Europe of any persuasion who do not agree with that assessment.) Our concern is not with the need for change, but with the nature of the change being advocated. We feel that there is a better way for reform to take place that advances change, but that also builds on some of the strengths that the European system still allows today. The problem is that in an attempt to institute clear and fair standards, Europe is giving up judgment about what is good and what is bad. European economists should be willing to make these judgments; they should not become mired in quantitative metrics of publications. Unfortunately the reform doesn't seem to be doing this. Instead, as we have mentioned, Europe seems to be adopting a United States metric that measures quality and output on the basis of established English-speaking journal outputs which means that they are based on measures that heavily favor United States geographically controlled journals.

In short, economics in Europe is replacing what are admittedly problematic standards with quantitative standards highly biased toward United States, English-speaking measures, which are as flawed as the standards they replace, especially for judging a field in flux such as economics. For that reason we find this push to adopt US-centric publication metrics dangerous for both the *broader economics profession* and for the strengths that European economics currently has. In our view, instead of making European economics a true competitor for United States economics, even if successful, it will simply make European economics a second-rate version of United States economics. We see this push toward US institutional standards as undermining some of the very strengths that European economics has over United States economics: specifically its (1) openness to diversity of thought; (2) its encouragement of the *development of ideas* rather than the *development of journal articles*; and (3) its role in hands-on policy.

The problem is that the output measure used in the United States – quality-weighted journal articles – are not good measures for the contributions economists are making to the work that will change economics in the future. Such quantitative measures work better in a static profession which is most concerned with dotting i's and crossing t's of existing work. In such a static world the ideas that guide today's economics will be the same ideas that guide future economics. If this is what you want, then these quantitative measures work reasonably well. However, when the structure of the profession is a complex system and there are competing ideas that are "in play" as in the economics profession currently, in which the paradigmatic structure of ideas is changing, such backward-looking measures of output and significance of research tend to miss the swings, and encourage the pedestrian: you get lots of i's dotted and t's crossed, but you don't get a new language developed. We believe that *the appropriate metric of a complex adapting field must be forward-looking*, which means that judgments must be made about research with less weight on where it is published. Somehow, the system must have the ability to say, "this is good work" independent of publication in "top journals" because too often those top journals shy away from such innovative work until it becomes popular, at which time it is no longer cutting edge.

Europe's previous system for judging research, for all its faults, had that ability. Judgments were made. That led to lots of waste, but it also led to a few pockets of excellence that were separate from the mainstream. The huge benefit we see with this pluralism was that Europe became an incubator for the ideas that are becoming the new basis of modern economics. Experimental economics took off in Europe with distinctive differences from the United States. Europe has been in the lead in agent-based modeling, and non-linear dynamics, cointegrated VAR, and general to specific econometrics, to name just a few of the ideas at the cutting edge of modern economics that are likely to become the mainstream ideas of the future. These ideas are only now gaining acceptance in the mainstream journals. If European economists had been facing United States incentives, most likely they would not have worked on these cutting edge ideas, and those who worked on them would not have succeeded to the degree that they did. But, as we noted in our last book, many of these new ideas were germinating and growing in Europe. European economics is very successful at the cutting edge precisely because researchers don't have to worry about mundane issues like "what's my journal publications ranking going to be". Instead, they seem to worry more about ideas than do researchers in the US.

The United States incentive system's failure to use judgment for the majority of researchers has led to fads and has encouraged pedestrian research. What we mean by "fad" can be seen by considering the recent developments in modern macroeconomics, which have been described by Robert Solow as a "rhetorical swindle on itself, and on its students" (Colander, 2006, pp. 235, 236). Solow continues

If you pick up any 'modern macro' paper, it tells you it will exhibit a 'micro-founded' model that will then be used to study this or that problem. When the model turns up, it is of course the representative-agent, infinite-horizon, intertemporal-optimization-with-conventional-constraints story with its various etceteras. This model has no valid claim, except by reiteration, to be 'micro-founded'. Basic micro-theory tells you no such thing.

Solow further states that the common story why this happens is that

. . . it is technique-happy aficionados who grab the initiative and defend it behind walls of mathematics. This view gets some support from the students who say their macro courses are all abstract mathematics, and it puts them off. But the mathematics is not that hard, nor is it that beautiful. The students master it, just to pass their examinations; and then they go off to work on a more interesting branch of economics. Maybe that's the point: it drives away all but a high-morale in-group that is enough to keep the sacred flame burning.

We agree with Solow in this judgment of modern macroeconomics, even though that work has provided innumerable articles. We suspect that many, if not a majority, of United States economists agree with Solow as well. They just don't say it.[24]

This discussion of macroeconomics is relevant because most European macroeconomics did not take part in this modern sterile macro revolution. Instead, some began working on a quite different macro theory and macro econometrics which provides a new foundation that will be influential for the next twenty years.[25] This alternative cutting edge macro has been incubated in Europe for some time, and was able to avoid the "modern" macro fad that happened largely in the United States. The development of this cutting edge work occurred because European researchers did not feel a need to jump on the "modern" bandwagon. In the United States articles matter, and when the Solow-types retired from the profession there were too few macroeconomists committed to common sense in the economics profession to change it.[26]

SOME REALISTIC PROPOSALS

Let us now review our argument and give some ideas about the type of policies that we believe it leads to. The central argument is that a vibrant economics profession requires a competition of ideas, and the United States incentive system has led to an oligopolistic control of ideas by a small interrelated set of individuals. For historical reasons Europe has avoided that control, which has made it a more attractive place to explore alternative ideas; Europe has been an incubator for ideas. The current movement to adopt United States dominated journal metrics is likely to undermine that incubator role.

We are not arguing against metrics, although with a profession as small as economics, we question the need for rigid quantitative metrics. When one considers that the economic profession is actually a collection of a large number of subdisciplines – public finance, micro theory, cross-sectional econometrics – it is not clear that a rigid publication metric is helpful. When one knows the people working in the field, one can informally judge their knowledge and contributions. Shared judgments can be made about what is good and what isn't, and such judgments should be made far more often than they are. The reality is that journals have become an inefficient method of scholarly communication, which takes place much more through working papers posted on the internet. Journal articles are tombstones marking ownership, not methods of spreading ideas. The internet is making journal publishing obsolete, and making alternative means of scholarly communication far more effective. There are bottom-up metrics that are developing to consider this work; such metrics are based on accesses, downloads and on-line "comments". Any forward-looking metric should include such measures. Metrics that don't include websites, blogs, and even traditional books, are missing important elements of scholarly communication. The primary research metric should be: "Do good and interesting work in economics that advances our understanding of the economy".

If one decides to use quantitative metrics, as we suspect will be done, the metric should be much broader than just journal articles and should include other elements, including teaching and books. The use of quantity weightings based primarily on past citations should be significantly reduced and replaced by either no weights, or a set of weights that are adjusted which doesn't put Europe in a competitive hole.

The *Journal of the European Economic Association* hoped to become one of the top six journals, but it has not achieved it, not because it is of lower quality in its reviewing process, but because it started later. Its lower rank is recognized by researchers, and its position becomes self-fulfilling as the best papers are sent to the highest ranked journals, and lower ranked journals get the rejects. This is furthered by the fact that journals have proliferated, and have become very expensive, meaning that libraries are not buying new journals. This means that new European journals are at a significant competitive disadvantage relative to the established United States journals, and even to the journals that are part of the journal collections that are sold to libraries as a whole. Any ranking metric used by Europe should take that reality into account and develop methods to offset it. One way would be to use research money from the European Union to make all European economic journals freely available to libraries throughout the world for a period of ten years. Subsidizing all European journals for a limited time period would give them a chance to develop and compete. We argue that such a use of research funds may be more effective at advancing European economics than using the same funds for traditional research.

A second policy that Europe could follow is to bias European metrics toward European journals. There are many metrics of journal publication, and the one that seems to be favored by the European Economic Association is the one that is most biased against Europe. This favored metric is far too concerned about past quality, and not enough concerned with future quality and diversity. If one is using weights, one way is to give no quality weights whatsoever in ranking methods (Coupe's ranking) or alternatively to give European-based journals double, or triple, weight in the metric used for European funding decisions. This would encourage Europeans to publish in European journals and build them up. Such an alternative weighting system for European scholars should not continue forever, but instead be part of a planned phase-out over a ten-year period.

Another method that European journals might use is to establish journals that have "invited peer review" papers. Journal publishing is a game of chance – all the more so if you don't know the editor – which makes it difficult for young scholars to take chances. They go with "safe" papers dotting i's and crossing t's. To offset this problem editors can choose promising young European researchers and invite them to publish a paper on a subject in the European journal. The papers are still peer reviewed, but the presumption is that the paper will be published, and the writer will have a chance to respond to reviewers. This is essentially how some United States-based journals, such as the *Journal of Economic Perspectives* and the *Journal of Economic Literature* work. The fact that they rely on invited papers has not led to any lowering of their quality weights and importance. It is also how other journals informally work, since editors often "encourage" economists whose work they find interesting to submit papers to their journals, although this clearly only helps a smaller set of younger economists who have some level of recognition or contacts already.

More radical methods might be to have an outside team of experts examine the papers and judge them independently as a contribution, rather than basing the "value" of a paper on where it was published, or to establish a system of open reviewing in which all papers submitted for publication, and all reviews of those papers, are open for examination by others. *Economics E-Journal* has adopted that policy. There are many more ideas, but these should give the reader a sense of our approach, which is to not take any specific metric too seriously, to use many metrics, and to temper all metrics with judgment.

CONCLUSION

Let us conclude by putting our thesis bluntly. The economics profession is best thought of as a complex system in which ideas compete. A thriving profession has an ecology to it that has many competing ideas, all as part of the mainstream. That leads to cross-fertilization and a pluralism of ideas, which keeps the profession healthy. The United States system has become a monosystem, which is very efficient at producing articles, but which involves eliminating the diversity that is necessary for a complex system to thrive.

Traditional European economics has been an incubator for ideas in economics, and has helped keep diversity within economics. The recent attempts to turn European economics into a United States type mono-system so that it can score better on an arbitrary and almost meaningless ranking metric are likely to destroy that diversity, and instead of allowing Europe to leapfrog the United States, by cultivating the ideas it has developed in its incubators, will kill those ideas, and make them into a second-tier set of United States-type programs.

NOTES

1. In that book we identified "mainstream" as a sociological category associated with the ruling elite of the profession, while "orthodox" is an intellectual category and "heterodox" is both anti-orthodox and alienated from the mainstream. These arguments have triggered some controversy and discussion (Callari, 2005; Garnett, 2005; 2006; Gordon, 2005; Hodgson, 2005; Davis, 2006; Lawson, 2006, and Dequech, 2007–08). See Bateman (2007) for a broader view of the book.
2. There is a lot of discussion recently of how one is to describe research that involves more than one discipline. Transdisciplinary is different from multidisciplinary, which is applied to situations where you have persons representing different disciplines working together. It is also different from an interdisciplinary approach which involves the integration of the ideas of different disciplines. We favor transdisciplinary to describe the new developments at the cutting edge of economics, which implies a more thoroughgoing and profound interaction between the disciplines leading to some type of transcendence. See our article, Colander et al. (2004b).
3. Simplicity is a matter of degree; all agree that the economy is highly complex – the question is whether light can be shed on these issues by using standard analytical techniques, or whether one must go beyond them and employ new methods such as agent-based modeling or non-linear dynamics.
4. A particular irony here involves the German system. On the one hand, American graduate higher education was originally modeled on the German system of the late 1800s. On the other, the Germans retained certain practices that did not migrate to the US. One of these was the practice of obtaining a Habilitation after the PhD before one can become a professor. This extended the period of effectively serving as the apprentice of a master, although this system is now finally apparently breaking down.
5. Spain is a country that rapidly adopted English language economics after Franco, but Spanish is a language with strong ongoing work in various heterodox schools such as Marxism, Post Keynesianism, and the *Régulation* School, although most of this is in Latin American countries such as Mexico and Argentina.
6. Japan has a strong ongoing tradition in its own language, with evolutionary Schumpeterianism, industrial organization, growth theory, and Marxism all strong within the language. For a history of Japanese economic thought, see Morris-Suzuki (1989).
7. The term "socialism" apparently originated in Britain, being initially popularized by Robert Owen. However, both "nationalism" and "communism" are of French origin.
8. Given the strength of this socialist tradition, it is perhaps appropriate that France also has one of the stronger traditions of libertarian Austrian economics as well, led by Pierre Garrouste at the Sorbonne-related institute ATOM.

9. CEPREMAP has long been associated with the Commission Général du Plan, the agency that formerly engaged in France's indicative central planning. Thus, it is not surprising that it hosts more leftist economists than other institutes. Quite recently there has been a controversial move to enfold CEPREMAP into a broader entity.

10. One symbol of this has been a greater willingness in Germany than in most other European countries to actually change the names of old, established journals from German to English. Thus, the famous *Zeitschrift für Nationalökonomie* is now the nearly anonymous *Journal of Economics*, and while its original name is still there as a subscript, the oldest German journal, *Weltwirtschaftliches Archiv*, has become the undistinguished *Review of World Economics*. These journals only rarely publish any papers in German any more, and the new *German Economic Review* has never done so to the best of our knowledge. See Berndt (2003) about how the US influence has overwhelmed the German language, social market tradition of Müller-Armack.

11. It has since been renamed the Economic Science of Heterogeneous Interacting Agents (ESHIA).

12. Britain, of course, did not have that problem, and remained more integrated into United States economics than continental economics. Britain was, however, hurt by the low pay and lower level of research support of its professors compared to those in the United States, with the same general story holding for its former, English-speaking colonies such as Canada, Australia, New Zealand, India, Pakistan and Bangladesh, none in Europe of course.

13. An example of the downgrading of books in the eyes of US academic economists has been the case of the removal of the graduate program from the economics department at Notre Dame University, where, among other complaints, members of the department were held to be publishing too many books and not enough articles in top journals (McCloskey, 2003).

14. The one significant group to develop separately from the mainstream was public choice, which has led a nomadic existence, beginning at Virginia, moving to Virginia Tech, and finally to George Mason (with some side wanderings to Arizona and other outposts), mainly on the power and perseverance of its leaders.

15. This contrasts sharply with the view expressed by one prominent European economist, Jacques Drèze (Dehez and Licandro, 2007, p. 298), who argues that US economists have more policy influence than European ones because the Chair of the Council of Economic Advisers (CEA) sits in on cabinet meetings, whereas there is no automatic mechanism for European economists to sit in on crucial decision-making meetings of the European Commission in Brussels. Aside from the issue of whether CEA chairs really have much influence on US policy (Stiglitz, 1998), the involvement of European economists in policymaking has continued to be at the national level rather than at the Europe-wide level, and at that level there is good reason to believe that it has been stronger than at the national level in the US. It is understandable that a founder of the European Economic Association and a trans-European, indeed international, research institute such as CORE in Louvain, Belgium, would focus on the Europe-level of this issue. But we contend that at the level that still dominates most policy, the national (except regarding monetary and some regulatory policies), European economists have the greater degree of real influence than do their American counterparts.

16. Despite the more pluralistic nature of the European economics profession, there is nonetheless a large heterodox group of economists in Europe who feel quite alienated from the mainstream. This shows up in the post-autistic movement (Guerrien, 2002) which began in France, but which has a significant following in Britain, and the larger number of Post Keynesian and Marxist economists in Europe than in the US, as well as other groups of economists in various countries that see themselves as outside the mainstream. Having said this, if one compared the average economist in Europe with the average economist in the US, say an Italian, German, or Portuguese economist with an economist from California, Maine or Iowa, the work that the European economist would be doing would be likely to come from a broader range of approaches than the

economists in the US, and the European economists would not be considered to be outside the mainstream of European economics, though the US economists would be considered to be outside the mainstream and be considered heterodox. One aspect of this that should be recognized is political and ideological, a greater willingness in Continental Europe to question laissez-faire ideology than in the US or Britain.

17.	The differential assessment system in Europe and the US is explainable; in the US, there has long been an integrated labor market; in Europe, there was not, so in Europe there was less need to develop a generalized ranking system to compare researchers across borders. An important reason for this difference was that, until recently, European economics was fragmented by different languages and national borders, and a different promotion system that was based less on publications and more on subjective judgments that would develop over time. The smaller markets meant that all top economists in a country would meet. They could know one another personally, discuss with each other, and be able to come to an independent judgment about each other's work. Assessments based on quantitative output measures, such as publications, would matter, but they would be only one element in the subjective judgment. With the development of a common educational policy and a common language, the structure of European economics is now in the process of change, albeit slowly.

18.	We present just one example. In Britain, judgments about who was good guided placements rather than publications, with this done through established "old boy" networks. This meant, for example, that until recently, it was considered unnecessary to get a PhD in order to get a job, and in fact the getting of a PhD meant that the researcher was not considered good enough to be hired in the market; as Britain integrated its profession with the US profession, that is no longer the case. Indeed, today British economics may have become more "American" than American economics, slavishly following outdated orthodoxies being abandoned in the US.

19.	At the highest levels in the US, advancement depends more on judgment and expectations of future research, not measured research. This happens because the future stars of the profession – those in the running for the John Bates Clark Medal – often receive offers and tenure at young ages, long before they have developed a large publication record, although most go on to become stars and publish a lot, making the expectations arguably correct. These are self-fulfilling expectations; once one is classified as a star, it becomes easier to publish, making it difficult to determine causality. This subjective evaluation system for stars based on expected publications is an important element of the US system because it allows for a turnover of the elite, and for new ideas to enter into the scheme. As one gets down to economists who are good enough to get tenure at a top school, but are not leading candidates for the John Bates Clark Medal, one finds that measures of publications matter a lot, and young US economic researchers focus enormously on publishing in top journals.

20.	The measures of publication are continually evolving, as researchers learn how to game the existing measures. The need for publications has led to an ever-increasing number of "peer-reviewed" print journals (publications that count for tenure and promotion). With the development of the web, print journals are becoming increasingly inefficient for communicating research among researchers (Colander and Plum, 2004), although many of these journals are increasingly becoming essentially electronic journals for all practical purposes, with their electronic versions available prior to their print versions and what most people access and read.

21.	A major professor at a top university tells students to spend all their effort on developing the job market paper, which demonstrates one's cleverness, one's technical prowess, and can be easily presented in the 45 minutes one has for a job market talk, and essentially to ignore the other two essays in the dissertation. Another aspect of the changed attitudes regarding dissertations is the trend for students to co-author on each other's thesis chapters, including even the job market paper, as well as open co-authoring with the major professor on such chapters. Arguably this follows actual practices in publishing, but it moves further to eviscerate the traditional concept of a dissertation, which in principle should be publishable as a coherent original book.

22. Tönu Puu (2006, pp. 31–2) has nicely summarized our view of the contrast between European and American approaches to academic economics over the last several decades from the perspective of contrasting "university cultures," and what we fear the new changes are undermining:

> "European university culture, until the 1960s, heavily depended on seminars, where various members of the staff, working with entirely different topics, communicated their results. For that reason the staff members had to keep a broad perspective on their disciplines. Relatively little was regarded as being worth publishing, and national and local 'schools' were established, which made visits to other environments really interesting.
>
> We tend to look down on the previous generation as they published relatively little. This fact, however, does not imply that they worked little or were less creative. It might just signify that they were more choosy about what they regarded as being significant enough to merit publication.
>
> After large scale production ideals from the US overtook the European style, everything is produced for immediate publication, even the relatively insignificant ideas. If it is publishable, it is not insignificant, and the number of journals will expand to allow ever-increasing publications. The number of journals, which has exploded accordingly, conveniently provides for the space. We still have seminars, but we read already published or accepted papers, which we do want to criticize, and we hardly expect anybody else at the department to understand our whole message. Travel and change of department only results in new personal relations, not new ideas; it may be that we would urgently need more interdisciplinary scientific fora in the future just in order to provide for encounters with the unexpected ideas we need to secure creativity."

23. This is beginning in some places with the new, EU-supported, university established in Bolzano in the German-speaking part of Italy as an example. Courses there are taught in three different languages: English, Italian and German.

24. In interviews Colander (2007) carried out with top United States students, there was much questioning and doubt about this approach. But those who chose to do macro had to go along with it because the only way they could publish in acceptable macro journals was to go along. Those who refused were shunted to the side.

25. These ideas are developed in Colander's *Post Walrasian Macroeconomics* (2006).

26. This is not to say that these ideas did not have importance, and did not move macro ahead. This work is precisely the type of work that cutting edge economists should be doing, and we agree that the Nobel Prizes awarded for that work are warranted. Cutting edge work pushes the frontier, and the macro frontier needed pushing. Our point is that the majority of the idea content of that work was in its initial formulation, and that the almost total focus of macro publishing on that idea is wrongheaded and should have been seen as wrongheaded by the majority of the profession. It does not take a rocket scientist to see that macro is much more than representative agent models, and that a whole variety of methods should be explored, but have not been because of the institutional incentive structure in the US. It is for that reason that much of what we consider cutting edge work in macro is taking place in Europe.

2. The complexity revolution in economics

INTRODUCTION

Imagine for a moment that one were looking at the economics profession in England in 1890. One would say that Alfred Marshall, with his blend of historical and analytical economics was the economics of the future; Walras's and Edgeworth's more mathematical approach would be considered minor players. Now fast forward to the 1930s – Marshall is seen as a minor player, while Walras's and Edgeworth's mathematical approach has become the foundation for Samuelson's cutting edge economics. Now imagine economics in 2050. Much of what is currently done in economics will not be cited or even considered. Some parts of economics, which today are considered minor, will be seen as the forerunners of what economics will become.

The point of this comparison is to make clear, which we mentioned in the last chapter, that to judge the relevance of economic contributions one must be forward-looking. One must have a vision of what economics will be in the future, and judge research accordingly. Current journal publication and citation metrics don't do that; they have a status-quo bias because they are backward-looking, and thus encourage researchers to continue research methods and approaches of the past, rather than to develop approaches of the future. They are useful, obviously, because they show activity, but they are only part of the picture, and must be used in conjunction with specific knowledge of the researcher – what they are trying to do, what their vision of the future is, and how they see their work fitting in. Articles dotting i's and crossing t's, even those that are cited relatively often in the short term, are far less important than articles that strike out in new directions. These are the ones that will change the direction of economics and be remembered in future history of economic thought texts.

So our argument is that any system of assessment of literature has to be based in a judgment about the future direction of economics. If one doesn't, one is, by default, choosing the judgment that the current approach in the profession will continue. We have a definite view of the future of economics – there will be more acceptance that the economy is complex, and the profession, over time, will adopt ever more technical, mathematical, analytical and statistical tools to deal with it. Models based on a priori assumptions will decrease, and will be replaced by empirically driven models and assumptions. Behavioral economics will expand; experiments will become part of the economist's tool kit, as will complex technical tools such as cluster analysis, ultra metrics, and dimensional analysis. This increasing complexity will be accompanied by a division of labor; theorists and statisticians will be become more and more specialized, but they will be complemented by economists who have a broad overview of where economics is going, and who are trained in applying economics. Economics will stop trying to answer grand questions such as, is the market preferred to command and control, or is the market efficient, and answer smaller questions such as, what structure of market will achieve the ends that policymakers are trying to achieve.

Since the term 'complexity' has been overused and over-hyped, we want to point out that our vision is not of a grand complexity theory that pulls everything together. It is a vision that sees the economy as so complicated that simple analytical models of the aggregate economy – models that can be specified in a set of analytically solvable equations – are not likely to be helpful in understanding many of the issues that economists want to address. Thus, the Walrasian neoclassical vision of a set of solvable equations capturing the full interrelationships of the economy that can be used for planning and analysis is not going to work. Instead, we have to go into the trenches, and base our analysis on experimental and empirical data. From there *we build up*, using whatever analytic tools we have available. This is different from the old vision where economists mostly did the opposite, by starting at the top and then building down.

The complexity vision is not only what we believe connects the various research threads that will be the future of economics; it is also what we believe provides the best way to look at the economics profession – we see the economics profession as an evolving complex system that has competing forces operating at all times. It is a profession that can only be understood as a system in constant change and flux.

DEFINITIONS OF COMPLEXITY

Taking a complexity vision does not require choosing among the many specific definitions of complexity.[1] But it is probably useful for us to note the most relevant views that are being bandied about in economics today. Three such views seem the most pertinent to us: a general view, a dynamic view and a computational view. The general view is the most useful one for thinking of the evolution of economics as a discipline; the computational view is starting to become influential as a research methodology, and the dynamic view is relevant for both concerns. But a more general definition of a complex system is given to us by Herbert Simon:

> Roughly by a complex system I mean one made up of a large number of parts that interact in a nonsimple way. In such systems, the whole is more than the sum of the parts, not in an ultimate metaphysical sense, but in the important pragmatic sense that, given the properties of the parts and the laws of their interaction, it is not a trivial matter to infer the properties of the whole. In the face of complexity, an in-principle reductionist may be at the same time a pragmatic holist (1962, p. 267).

Simon then goes on to emphasize how this definition leads to a focus on the hierarchical structure of systems, with Seth Lloyd identifying Simon's view as one of his 45 definitions, labeled "hierarchical". Simon emphasizes that he is drawing on older literature, particularly general systems theory (von Bertalanffy, 1962), which he sees as including the work of economist Kenneth Boulding with cybernetics (Wiener, 1948), and information theory (Shannon and Weaver, 1948). Of these, cybernetics can be seen as a foundational form of our second variety of complexity, dynamic complexity, while information theory can be seen as a foundational form of our third variety, computational complexity.

The emphasis on the problem of the whole and the parts raises two issues that are central issues in economics and more recent approaches to complexity. One is clearly the problem of the relationship between micro and macro in economics, with this formulation calling to mind the old problem of Keynes's "fallacy of composition", although Walrasian approaches to macroeconomics have attempted to avoid this problem through its assumption of representative agent models. The other is the phenomenon of the apparently spontaneous "emergence" of higher order structures out of lower order ones, an idea much emphasized by many at the Santa Fe Institute (Crutchfield, 1994), as well as by Austrian students of complexity (Lavoie, 1989), also sometimes labeled "anagenesis" (Boulding, 1978; Rosser et al., 1994).[2]

Simon's general definition also has the virtue of being close to the original meaning of the word "complex" as found in the *Oxford English Dictionary* (OED, 1971, p. 492) where it is first defined as "a whole, comprehending in its compass a number of parts", from the Latin "complectere", meaning "to encompass, embrace, comprehend, comprise." Among its partial synonyms is "complicated", although, as Israel (2005) points out, this comes from a different Latin root, "complicare", meaning "to fold together" or "interwoven" (OED, 1971, p. 493). Israel takes the strong position that this latter is a merely epistemological concept while the former is fundamentally ontological, complaining that such figures as von Neumann (1966) mistook them as identical, although this is arguably an overly strong position.[3]

Finally, a virtue of this general definition is that it also encompasses one of the current cutting edge areas of economics, the behavioral and experimental approaches. Many who follow these approaches do not consider the complexity view to be all that relevant to what they do, with Kenneth Binmore and Matthew Rabin expressing such opinions in their interviews in Colander, Holt, and Rosser (2004a, 2004b). However, at the foundation of behavioral economics is the concept of *bounded rationality*, introduced originally by Herbert Simon. It is not just Simon, but many since who have seen complexity as implying that rationality must be bounded (Sargent, 1993; Arthur et al. 1997), and thus is lying at the foundation of behavioral economics.

The second definition is of dynamic complexity, which is arguably the most widely used form in economics, even though this is not per se on Lloyd's list of 45 definitions. Rosser (1999) has codified this as "broad tent complexity" and draws on Day (1994) for its definition.[4] "A dynamical system is complex if it endogenously does not tend asymptotically to a fixed point, a limit cycle, or an explosion" (Rosser, 1999, p. 170). Rosser then draws on the criticisms of "chaoplexity" by Horgan (1997) to argue that this broad tent view contains four successive approaches based on non-linear dynamics:[5] cybernetics (Wiener, 1948), catastrophe theory (Thom, 1975), chaos theory (Dechert, 1996), and "small tent" complexity. This latter is identified with approaches coming initially out of Brussels (Nicolis and Prigogine, 1977), Stuttgart (Haken, 1983), and the Santa Fe Institute, with Schelling (1971) being another predecessor. This approach emphasizes dispersed and interacting, heterogeneous agents (Arthur et al., 1997; Hommes, 2006).

Arthur et al. (1997, pp. 3–4) provide a summary of this approach through six characteristics: 1) dispersed interaction among heterogeneous agents;[6] 2) no global controller in the economy; 3) cross-cutting hierarchies with tangled interactions; 4) continual adaptation and learning by evolving agents; 5) perpetual novelty; and 6) out-of-equilibrium dynamics with no presumption of optimality. This approach is seen as implying bounded rationality, not rational expectations, as noted above.

Finally we come to our third definition, that of computational complexity. While advocates of this approach emphasize its greater degree of precision, we shall also keep this to a more general level, as there are many different varieties of this concept, with arguably over half of the 45 definitions listed by Lloyd constituting one or another of its varieties. Many of these definitions are derived from the already-mentioned information theory of Shannon and Weaver (1948), for example Solomonoff (1964) and Kolmogorov (1965), which eventually boil down to descriptions of the minimum length of a computer program that will describe the information or system (Chaitin, 1987) or some variation of this (Rissanen, 1989).[7] However, a harder line view is that a system is only truly computationally complex if it is not computable at all (Blum et al., 1998).[8]

Advocates of this approach (Albin with Foley, 1998; Velupillai, 2000, 2005; Markose, 2005) argue that its greater precision makes it a superior vehicle for scientific research in economics. It must be admitted that there is some truth to this. Nevertheless, the vast majority of research in economics that identifies itself with complexity tends to be more of the dynamic variety just described. Furthermore, this definition is certainly less useful when we consider the question of the economics profession itself as a complex evolving system. Here we consider that the first two definitions provide a more useful construct for analysis than this admittedly challenging and substantial view of complexity, which we expect has the potential for important future research in the area of economic complexity.[9] Not only is the economics profession a set of hierarchies, but it also evolves through a set of local interactions among dispersed networks of influence.

WHAT DO WE MEAN BY CUTTING EDGE COMPLEXITY WORK?

The actual work that we are calling cutting edge involves a number of fronts, and the people working on those fronts have varying degrees of connection to the broader complexity approach. Along with this, and interacting with it, is a new openness to ideas from other disciplines. The new complexity economics is also increasingly a transdisciplinary economics. More specifically:

- Evolutionary game theory is redefining how institutions are integrated into the analysis.
- Ecological economics is redefining how nature and the economy are viewed as interrelating in a transdisciplinary formulation.
- Behavioral economics is redefining how rationality is treated.
- Econometric work dealing with the limitations of classical statistics is redefining how economists think of empirical proof.
- Complexity theory is offering a way of redefining how we conceive of general equilibrium and economic dynamics more broadly.

- Agent-based computer economic (ACE) analysis is providing an alternative to analytic modeling.
- Experimental economics is changing the way economists think about empirical work, with this being the principal method by which behavioral economics is studied.

These are changes that are ongoing, and which have, in varying degrees, entered into the mainstream. As that has happened, there have been a broader set of changes in how mainstream economics sees itself. Modern economics is much more willing, it seems today, to accept that the formal part of economics has limited applicability, at least as currently developed. It is also far more willing to question economics' special status over the other fields of inquiry and to integrate the methods of other disciplines into their methods.

CHARACTERISTICS OF CUTTING EDGE WORK

Now let us turn to our judgment of the main characteristics of cutting edge work. In most textbooks today one gets the impression that economics has not changed that much during the last 50 years. Essentially, one learns the neoclassical paradigm that develops a simple analytic deductive model, sometimes called the Max U model. There are many variations of this simple model, Walrasian or Marshallian, for example, but in almost all cases the microeconomics taught in these texts is some variation on the Max U model; it focuses on efficiency and optimization, assuming agents are rational, selfish, and are operating in an environment that arrives at a unique equilibrium.

The Max U model has been explored to death and, from a cutting edge view, is no longer of much interest. (That doesn't mean it doesn't still have considerable importance, and relevance, and that there are still many practical applications that warrant research; it is just to say that from a cutting edge standpoint, we've pulled about all we can from it.) That is why a major part of the new cutting edge work is going beyond these assumptions; while it does not deny the usefulness and insight provided by that model, it does not see a model based only on these assumptions as sufficient, and is therefore pushing the envelope on each of those assumptions. Some examples of how cutting edge work is questioning these neoclassical assumptions would be the following:

- Expanding the meaning of rationality to include a much broader range of agent actions that reflect actual actions; in the new approach, individuals are purposeful (incentives still matter) but are not necessarily formally rational. The new research considers the behavioral foundations of actions, using experiments to determine what people actually do, rather than simply basing their arguments on what people rationally should do. Also the work in game theory by such economists as Peyton Young (1998) is pushing rationality to its limits to demonstrate the importance of the expectations and information environment in people's decisions. The cutting edge work that is being done here is going beyond the traditional accepted definition of rationality, with extended versions of Herbert Simon's bounded rationality increasingly accepted.

- Other cutting edge researchers are moving away from a narrow view of selfishness. While textbook economics generally presents a view of agents who care only about themselves, the new work is trying to come to grips with the more realistic sense of individuals who, while they are self-interested, are also social beings, concerned about others and deriving happiness from interacting with others.

- Cutting edge researchers are moving away from the assumption of a unique equilibrium, and are dealing with much more complicated systems that have multiple equilibria, path dependency, and no clear-cut answer. A complex economy does not have a single equilibrium; it has many basins of attraction, and the question researchers ask is, which basin is sustainable? In this work equilibrium is not a state of the economy; the economy is continually in flux.

Combined, these changes can be summarized as a movement in economics from a textbook economics of *rationality, selfishness, and equilibrium to a new economics of purposefulness, self-interest, and sustainability.* Cutting edge work is work that is helping to move that transformation along.

CHANGES IN RESEARCH METHODS

Another aspect of cutting edge work is a change in research methods that can serve as a catalyst for many changes in the profession. For example, advances in computing technology have led to new approaches, such as agent-based modeling that allows economists to analyze complicated systems, with much more complicated interactions. Instead of assuming optimal behavior, economists are using lab, field and natural experiments to determine what people actually do. As economists have started to use these new techniques they are taking notice of institutions, since the incentives embodied in those institutions are often central in understanding people's behavior.

This change is being accompanied by a change in the deductive nature of economic reasoning. The new work is based much more on empirical inductive reasoning, and far less on pure deductive reasoning. As this is happening, the mathematics being used in economic analysis is becoming less the Bourbakian mathematics of "theorem-proof", and more applied mathematics, which is designed to come up with answers about policy issues, and not just talk about general issues. Set theory and calculus, which come to definite results, are being replaced by game theory, which seldom comes to a definite conclusion independent of the precise structure of the game. For example the work on auctions combines insights from game theory with experimental results, and which are then used in practice. Similarly, information economics is used in designing efficient algorithms for search engines.

THE LACK OF IMPACT OF CUTTING EDGE WORK ON MODERN MACROECONOMICS

Interestingly, these cutting edge changes in micro theory toward inductive analysis and a complexity approach have not occurred in macroeconomics. In fact, the evolution of macroeconomic thinking in the United States has gone the other way. By that, we mean that there has been a movement away from a rough and ready macro theory that characterized the macroeconomics of the 1960s toward a theoretically based analytic macro theory based on abstract, representative agent models that rely heavily on the assumptions of equilibrium. This macro work goes under the names new Classical, Real Business cycle, and the dynamic stochastic general equilibrium (DSGE) theory, and has become the mainstream in the United States.

In part, this development in macro is understandable. As the new work has demonstrated, the macro theory that was prevalent in the 1960s claimed a much stronger theoretical foundation than was warranted, and many of the conclusions it came to were not supported by either empirical evidence or theory. However, while the new theoretical models have done a good job in eliminating the old theory, it is less clear as to what the new theoretical work has added to our understanding of the macroeconomy. At best, the results of the new models can be roughly calibrated with the empirical evidence, but often the calibration of these new models is no better than any other model, and the only claim they have to being preferred is aesthetic – they have micro foundations. It is a strange micro foundation – a micro foundation based on assumptions of no heterogeneous agent interaction, when, for many people intuitively, it is precisely the heterogeneous agent interaction that leads to central characteristics of the macroeconomy. This is essentially the insight of Keynes regarding the fallacy of composition, now persisting mostly in Principles textbooks, even if the old example of increased efforts to save leading to lower savings may have been overdone.

In our view, the interesting cutting edge work in macro is not in the theoretical developments organized around representative agent micro foundations work, but in the work that is going beyond that and viewing the macroeconomy as a complex system. In this work, one sees the macroeconomy as being endogenously organized. The issue is not why there are fluctuations in the macroeconomy, but instead, why is there so little instability where complex interactions intuitively should generate chaos. In this view, the thought that one could develop a micro foundation of macro without considering the feedback of the macro system on the individual is beyond belief. While it may still make sense to push analytic macro theory as far as one can, to see whether it will provide any insights, in the short term, such analytic extensions of analytically solvable pure theoretical models based on assumptions that are far from reality offer little hope for policy guidance. In the absence of a pure theoretical foundation, macro policy is best based more on statistical models that pull as much information as possible from the data. Empirical macro precedes theoretical macro.

CONCLUSION

When we first made the above arguments about complexity nearly a decade ago, they were far more controversial than they are now. During that time, economics has changed and become more open to all the approaches we have suggested constitute complexity economics, so that now, it is becoming more and more, just economics. We are not saying that the movement to the complexity era is going to be smooth, or that the work is without problems. We recognize much of it has serious problems that require a lot of work and weeding out. For example, some areas, such as experimental economics, have even become fads, and an ever-increasing number of economists are including experimental work in their research. Such fads will require a weeding out, and a far more careful specification of what is an acceptable experiment and what isn't than currently exists (Binmore and Shaked, 2010; Fehr and Schmidt, 2010).

Other work, such as ACE modeling, still has problems getting published because it doesn't fit well into a journal format, and it is very difficult to figure out precisely what we are learning from these models. Similar problems exist for the craftsman approach to econometrics discussed in Colander (2009), in which the econometrician interacts with the data and makes judgments while doing the analysis rather than working as a technician who is applying specific methods to data analysis. How does one judge the judgment? These issues will be debated over the next decade, and tentative answers will be arrived at. Once they are, the true cutting edge economists will no longer be involved; they will have moved on to other problems. And this is the way that it should be in an ever changing, dynamic and evolving profession.

NOTES

1. Quite famously, the MIT physicist Seth Lloyd provided (at least) 45 definitions of this concept (Horgan, 1997, p. 303, footnote 11).
2. This approach can be seen as preceded by the British "Emergentist" School, which arguably first emerged in Mill (1843).
3. See Rosser (2004b) for further discussion. It can be argued that what Rosser (1999) calls "structural" complexity is really more this "complicatedness", with Pryor's (1995) model of the US economy fitting this category (not one of Lloyd's definitions). However, this structural approach is quite congruent with Simon's view.
4. While Day originated this dynamic definition of complexity, he is also aware of the older views and in a more recent contribution (2007, p. 57) notes one of the other OED definitions: "a group of interrelated or entangled relationships".
5. It is generally argued that dynamically complex systems must be non-linear, although not all non-linear systems are complex. However, Goodwin (1947) showed that coupled linear systems with lags could exhibit what are described as complex dynamics, although the normalized equivalent of such a system is nonlinear, and Turing (1952) used such systems to develop his idea of *morphogenesis*.
6. While it is generally argued that all this contradicts general equilibrium theory, Arrow in his interview in Colander et al. (2004a, p. 301) argued that "One of the things that microeconomics teaches you is that individuals are not alike. There is heterogeneity, and probably the most important heterogeneity here is heterogeneity of expectations. If we didn't have heterogeneity, there would be no trade. But developing an analytic model with heterogeneous agents is difficult." This reminds us that while current macroeconomists like to describe their models as being "Walrasian", their assumptions of representative agents with rational expectations are far simpler than the assumptions in the Arrow–Debreu general equilibrium framework. Curiously, some of the greatest criticisms of the Arrow–Debreu general equilibrium framework have come from its own developers, as with the Sonnenschein–Mantel–Debreu Theorem (Debreu, 1974).
7. Velupillai (2000, 2005) discusses the relationships between these different definitions.
8. In such cases the program is of infinite length, that is it does not halt. A fundamental source of this may involve problems associated with the incompleteness concept of Gödel (Lewis, 1985). An application to general equilibrium is due to Richter and Wong (1999).
9. Rosser (2007) provides a more detailed discussion of the debate between the second and third of these two definitions of economic complexity. A further development of the computability argument has been to say that markets themselves are fundamentally

algorithms, and that market systems themselves are evolving through higher and higher levels of a Chomskyian hierarchy (Chomsky, 1959; Mirowski, 2007), thus bringing the argument back somewhat again to the Simonian perspective. This argument could also conceivably be applied to the economics profession as well.

PART II

Conversations

3. Alan Kirman

This interview took place on 16 May, 2008, in Harrisonburg, Virginia

How did you get interested in economics?
It's a weird story. I went to Oxford and studied law and geography. After that I became a high school teacher, and I did that for four years. When I was working as a high school teacher I went to some evening classes run by the *Workers Education Association*, which is associated with the cooperative movement. They organized evening courses for anyone who wanted to go to them. I got interested in economics there, and I thought rather than continuing as a high school teacher for the rest of my life, I would like to do some economics. At that time, however, there were no taught master's courses in Europe.

Then I saw an advertisement for a program run by Johns Hopkins University in Bologna, Italy and it said SAIS, School of Advanced International Studies. They had a diploma in International Economics, Law and Politics that you could apply for. They gave me a scholarship. There were very good people there – some of the founders of the European Union. The person I took microeconomics from was Ira Scott, who came from the University of Minnesota. He wrote a letter for me to get into Minnesota, and said that if I was interested in going on in economics, I would be accepted there. I went there as an innocent graduate student, having done almost no economics, and zero mathematics. I didn't know what a derivative was. So I appeared in Minnesota, and was assigned Hugo Sonnenschein as my advisor (*laughter*).

So I went to see Hugo, and he told me that I could not do economics without having a degree in mathematics. Since this was not a possibility, he said don't worry about that; you can do it in parallel with your graduate courses in economics. I didn't point out that I actually hadn't had any economics before either (*laughter again*).

Anyway, he said that I must get myself up to being able to do real analysis. There were six courses considered necessary, but he said just do the second, fourth and sixth courses. My first course in calculus was a disaster; it started with integration, which was explained as the inverse operation of derivation, which was covered the previous semester, which I hadn't done. I did make it through the program. To pay my way, I was a teaching assistant to Jim Henderson, so I was a teaching assistant in microeconomics, which I also didn't know much about. It was also very cold in Minnesota, and about half way through the year, I went to see Hugo, and told him that I came to study economics because I was interested in economic phenomena, and it doesn't seem this is a central issue in Minnesota. I said that I'd like to learn about things like inflation and unemployment. Hugo, who was always very kind to me, said no, no, no. Macroeconomics is about wisdom, Alan, and what you can learn at your stage is microeconomics; that's technical stuff. You can't learn wisdom. So I carried on, but I said that I was going to try to go somewhere else. So I looked around and Princeton offered me a fellowship, in part because I had published an article in the *National Banking Review* with Wilson Schmidt (1965), one of my former professors in Bologna, who became Undersecretary of Treasury in the United States.

At Princeton I didn't have to teach, and I concentrated on learning and starting research. There were only 12 of us in the PhD program. But by the time I got there Hugo had somehow corrupted me and I began to think that what he was doing was quite interesting. So when it came time to choose an advisor, I chose Harold Kuhn, who was half in the mathematics department and half in economics. So, like an idiot, I went to see him and told him that I was interested in doing a thesis with him. He took me on board. Harold was a wonderful teacher, and he taught me very basic things, which were essential later on. He said, "economics is all about maximizing concave functions on complex sets, and then looking at the first order conditions, sometimes second order conditions – that's all they do, really. So don't worry; they dress it up in fancy spaces and make it look more complicated, but that's the essence of what they do. There are also some rather interesting things you might want to do, which are possible, but don't let people try to persuade you that this is very high level mathematics; it's far from the frontier." That was very wise. The more I moved on, the more I recognized the importance of that. It gives you a good perspective when you get people who try to impress you with pure mathematics.

Princeton was great for me; I had some great teachers and some great fellow students like Orly Ashenfelter, Jim Heckman and John Pencavel.

After you graduated from Princeton, what did you do?
I took a job at Johns Hopkins University, which had a very nice department. It was small and very broad. It had Peter Newman, Carl Christ, Jurgen Niehans, and some young people. The summer before going there, I went to a workshop out in California on game theory, and I had long talks with Werner Hilderbrand, who invited me to come to CORE in Belgium for a year; he said we could work together. Johns Hopkins gave me a year's leave, and I started working closely with Werner and with a variety of people at CORE, and I just felt better over in Europe than I did in the United States. So I decided to stay.

Many see your early work at being focused on general equilibrium theory. Would you describe your work as highly orthodox at that point?
I don't think so. My thesis was on applying non-cooperative game theory to international trade (Kirman, 1971). All the sensible people that I had met in the profession explained to me that there was no future in non-cooperative game theory, and that international theory was two goods, two people and two factors, and you don't start with the *n* stuff. Otherwise, you can't do diagrams (*laughter*).

Fritz Machlup explained to me how international theory would not become mathematized like other branches of economics and certainly all the people in game theory saw the future of game theory in cooperative game theory at that time. They said that I had done a nice thesis but that I should get out of it. I was also interested in fairness and social choice (Feldman and Kirman, 1973; Hildenbrand and Kirman, 1973). So it's not true that I became a formal general equilibrium theorist. I was never good enough mathematically to become a really powerful general equilibrium theorist. Yes, I wrote some papers and two books with Werner on pure general equilibrium theory, so we did make progress in that area and I also worked on the mathematical structure of Arrow's theorem with Dieter Sondermann. With Jean-Michel Grandmont and Wilhelm Neuefeind we even wrote a paper as a joke on GE theory, one of the few jokes to be published in a major economics journal (Kirman and Sondermann, 1972; Grandmont et al., 1974; Hildenbrand and Kirman, 1976, 1988).

But I've always been interested in both abstract theory and real world markets. For example, when I was at Johns Hopkins, I had a student write a paper on prices in grocery stores in downtown Baltimore and the suburbs of Baltimore. What we found was that prices were higher in the black downtown areas than in the suburbs. So my interest has always spanned both abstract theory and the real world.

Would you say that you still have a general equilibrium soul even though you moved away from it?
No, I don't. But neither do many others who worked on general equilibrium, such as Werner Hilderbrand, who was much more into it; he was Debreu's protégé. I think one of the reasons for this is the Mantel–Sonnenschein–Debreu conclusion that you cannot talk about either stability or uniqueness (Mantel, 1974; Sonnenschein, 1972; Debreu, 1974). That result undermined the plausibility of general equilibrium theory. You ask: how do you get in that equilibrium position, and you cannot be sure that you will do so even though you impose all these restrictions on individual behavior, and yet the latter are what people like to refer to as sound microeconomic foundations. But those sound microeconomic foundations don't come, as we find in other sciences, from observations about how people behave, and then trying to use those observations as our basis.

I recognized this when I wrote the papers "The intrinsic limits of economic theory: the Emperor has no clothes" (Kirman, 1989a) and "What or whom does the representative agent represent?" (Kirman, 1992). We have built all this careful structure on these microeconomic foundations that you cannot extend to the macroeconomy. So for me, the basic problem at that point was the aggregation problem: how do we actually move from the behavior of individuals up to the behavior of the aggregate. In other words, what we require is that aggregation imposes some structure at the aggregate level from the structure we place on individuals. At the same time, you were getting all these attacks on the very assumptions that we make about individuals arguing we should look at how individuals truly behave. So, economists also started to feel the pressure from the behavioralists.

A third aspect of the problem was the notion that individuals interact directly among each other, and not only through the market. That's why back in the 1970s I wrote an article on stochastic graphs, applying it to the problem of the core (Kirman, 1983; Kirman et al., 1986). I argued that it seemed silly to assume that all coalitions could form. Surely there is a structure out there that says only certain people are open to forming coalitions with other people. So supposing we put limits on who could actually form coalitions with whom. Then what is the chance that we could still get all these theorems? I think that was the first time that stochastic graph theory was used in economics.

Was there any structure to the development of your thinking?
No, I don't think there was. Some people have a clear vision of where they are going. I didn't. I went from problem to problem. One of the problems that interested me the most early on was the question that if I live in a world and I've specified the world with the wrong model, how does the system work? I remember talking with Jerry Green, who was at CORE then, and he wrote a little paper on this idea with Ken Arrow, that was never published. I had a slightly different idea, because I thought of what might happen if individuals got the model wrong, but their empirical observations fit sufficiently well to make them believe they got it right. And if you allowed them to learn from what they are observing, would they actually converge to the true model? Or will they learn to be happy with the wrong model? The idea is that they can learn about the wrong model, and confirm their belief in it, and only if something from the outside shook the whole system would you actually know that you had the wrong model. A lot more has been done on this now, but at the time people didn't think like that.

Was this the paper you presented at the Mathematics Research Center at Wisconsin in 1974 that some think was the opening shot for your later approach? How was it received?
There was strong resistance to that paper (Kirman, 1975), which was rejected by *Econometrica* on the ground that the individuals in the model used least squares learning. But least squares learning people should know that the error terms wouldn't satisfy the assumptions under which it is appropriate to use least squares learning. So instead of thinking of least squares learning, as we think of it now, as a useful learning process, at the time it was thought of as being econometrics, and therefore it had to satisfy econometricians. So it was not the idea of the paper that made it unacceptable, but rather that the learning procedure was not thought to be a reasonable approximation at that time. So I put in generalized least squares so that it would not bother the econometricians so much. Now, however, least squares learning is very widely used.

You were at CORE in Louvain, Belgium for three years. What led you to leave?
CORE was owned by three universities, two of which were splitting up and one which was going bankrupt. They had a long argument about how CORE was going to continue. The job I had was half-time researcher and half-time professor at the school that was going bankrupt. They were not going to continue financing my position at CORE. They said I was welcome to stay, but it was as a full-time professor. At that point the University of Warwick offered me a job, so I went there.

Did you think of going back to the States?
Not really. In part it was because I didn't hear anyone from the States
yelling, "We want you" and it was in part because I didn't explore options
– perhaps because I didn't want to discover that no one really wanted me.

*Did you think that you would be losing something by staying in Europe
rather than going to the United States?*
Yes, I thought that if my main ambition was to make it in the profession,
I should be in the States. I had the sense that the United States was taking
over the profession. You could see people in Europe who received a lot of
respect, but all the weight was moving to the States. But it also depends
on your view of yourself. If you don't think that you are that important,
it doesn't really matter where you are. I didn't see myself as one of the
movers and shakers of economics.

Was Warwick different from CORE?
It was. CORE was a place where people were doing abstract research –
operations research, game theory, and so forth, and high-level researchers
such as Gérard Debreu and Bob Aumann would come through. It was a
home for mathematical theorists. Warwick is a regular department full
of different people, from John Williamson, an institutional international
trade theorist, to Avinash Dixit. It was a very different environment. I
spent a lot of time at the Mathematics Institute at Warwick in part because
I liked the people there, and in part because there were some ideas floating
around on how to deal with the problems that I was interested in. I had
already met Hans Föllmer who was a mathematician at the University
of Bonn who had published a paper on interacting agent models back in
1974 (Föllmer, 1974). David Rand, who was at the Mathematics Institute,
said that all this is about spins, and that's really interesting, because at the
aggregate level, what you get depends on the interaction of these spins.
You can't simply look at a particle and generalize to what will happen
at the aggregate level. After three years of Warwick I was offered a one-
year visitorship at Marseilles, and there was a small group of people
there whom I found interesting. Provence is a nice place, and I asked
myself, where would I like to bring up my kids? In Coventry, England,
or Provence? After I was there for one year, they offered me a permanent
job, and we created a group called the GREQE in 1982. We organized
the World Congress of the Econometrics Society to try to get us inserted
into the mainstream of the profession. That worked reasonably well, but
overall in France we felt isolated in a sea of people who didn't seem to
understand what we were doing, and who felt that we were a threat to their
peaceful academic environment.

Then I got an offer to go to the European University in Florence, where I went for eight years but I kept my position at Marseilles, and went back there later.

You've been active in one of the topics of this book, standards in European economics, for a long time – going back at least to 1989 when you worked on the economic financing of research in Europe with Mogens Dahl (Kirman, 1989b). How have you seen things developing, and where do you see them going?
That's a huge question. The idea in our work on evaluating economics departments was simply to find out what was going on – how much research was going on, and to give a very primitive ranking. It was not supposed to be a very sophisticated comparison of where there was a lot of activity and where there wasn't. I think people have later come to the idea that you need to flesh this out more. At the time of our study the amount of real activity in what you might call quantitative economics was concentrated essentially in the United Kingdom and a few places in continental Europe. It was mainly being done by people who had come back from the United States.

There were a number of local schools of economic thought that were thriving at that time, but they didn't really figure into our evaluation since our interest was in more standard economics. So we didn't include the work by Pierangelo Garegnani and Robert Boyer; these were very special schools that didn't seem to have much desire to communicate with the rest of the profession. There were a number of these special schools in Europe at that time. In the last 10 years or so, what you could call global economics – mainstream United States economics has grown enormously. This has basically been in the image of United States departments. The mainstream in Europe has been filled up with departments whose goal is to be like United States departments as they see them. I don't think they see American departments as they really are; they have an idealized conception of American departments.

Over this time, how did you see European economics evolving?
I think there has been a big increase in nebulous mainstream economics, which is an imitation of what's going on in the States, although there are exceptions to that. People like Ernst Fehr and company are doing work that will be considered far ahead in behavioral economics of most of their counterparts in the States.

Why do you think that this is happening?
There has come to be a view in Europe that you have to toe the line. I get a sense when I am talking that they would prefer that I don't push my

criticisms of general equilibrium too hard because that will undermine the status of real, serious economics. There came to be a European consensus in top programs that serious economics was standard neoclassical economics. Any other approach was just done by people who were a bit flaky.

We've heard that many of these global European departments are more orthodox and more narrow minded than many of the United States departments. Is that your perception as well?
I think that is accurate. It's a combination of two things. First, some of these places have specialized a lot, so they have a very focused idea of what it is they want to do. An example is Toulouse, which has specialized in a very particular part of economics. They've built up a reputation for a highly technical approach, although the leading economist there, Jean Tirole, is actually interested in a wide range of ideas. The people just underneath him are narrower and take a much more conservative approach to economics. Many of the departments that are trying to emulate United States departments are much purer than the pure. Their criteria are very narrow; that's true of many departments in England as well. I think that that's a lack of self confidence. That's why they develop all those ranking measures and go far beyond what people in the United States do. These ranking measures have become an industry in Europe. Instead of looking at what a person accomplishes you look at what the referees of those journals think about what he does, and that's your criterion.

Why do you think that happened?
In part it is because people became enamored by the very mathematical people like Werner Hildebrand and company. They thought if you can use all this mathematics, it must be serious. I don't think that Werner would agree with that. They thought that what mattered was to prove results. By that they meant you could prove them for examples – these results are really theoretical in any general sense – because you have such specific assumptions on the example that it makes it into what Werner called a Mickey Mouse Model. Werner would say, "what does this theorem mean, in a Mickey Mouse model – you make such strong assumptions – everyone has Cobb–Douglas preferences – you have this amazingly restrictive production set and then you prove a theorem? What do you mean by this theorem? It is just an example."

What many European economists today don't recognize is that in the States, the role of a mathematical economist has declined. If you went on the United States market as a mathematical theorist today, you wouldn't have a lot of success. As a graduate student I gave a talk at Rochester on unequal treatment in the core – a pretty abstruse subject. There was a young man there who thought it was interesting, and decided to do his thesis on that topic. That young guy was Jerry Green, who became one of the most prominent theorists in the US and was later Provost at Harvard. Jerry did very well in the job market; he was a hero for working on such subjects (Green, 1972). At that time you could do well as a mathematical economist. In the States, at least at the top schools, that has disappeared, and in Europe there is the illusion that mathematical economics is the way ahead, and that things based on sound micro foundations is what one must do. But I kept hearing all these signals, except from the freshwater macro sect, that that was wrong.

For example with Christopher Zeeman at the Mathematics Institute at Warwick, we organized a whole series of conferences, including one on mathematical economics. We had the very best people there, like Hugo Sonnenschein, Robert Aumann, Herbert Scarf, Gérard Debreu, and the prominent Princeton mathematician, John Milnor, and a whole series of other wonderful mathematicians. After the first morning session, I think it was Milnor who held up his finger and said that this whole thing is based on a misunderstanding. We know that you guys can do mathematics, but we're interested in the economics. We'd like to join in with our mathematics but we don't really want you to talk to us about the mathematical problems, but economics. That really made me think that something has gone wrong, when we are trying to persuade mathematicians that what we are doing is mathematics.

This sounds similar to the first meeting of the Santa Fe Institute where the physicists were astounded by the approach the economists took.
Absolutely. So that is the sort of thing that led me to think that what we should look for are explanations of economic phenomena and that we should spend a bit less time just pushing our models. Mathematician friends, like David Rand and Hans Föllmer, said what is really interesting is the passage from the micro to the macro level. The simple aggregation process that economists use didn't make sense to them. That idea kept coming back to me – the idea that you should have simpler individuals, who obey simple rules, and are not in contact with everyone else – was the way to go.

Is that view best expressed in your "Ants and Recruitment" paper (Kirman, 1993)?
Again, it wasn't a conscious decision to embrace heterogeneous interacting agent models. Let me explain to you where the Ants story comes from. I directed a foundation for a wealthy elderly lady in the South of France, which had a lot of distinguished people come through. Because I was a

director, I used to go to these workshops, and one workshop was on social insects. That was a wonderful workshop, and two entomologists came and explained about the phenomenon of ants' behavior that I explain in that paper. They said that by solving difference equations they could obtain the asymmetric solutions that they observed. I said that that can't explain why every now and then, it flips. That's how I became interested in that particular problem.

The person who gave me the insight into the simple stochastic process was Hans Föllmer whom I met at a workshop in Germany shortly after I heard this talk. I asked him if it might not correspond to some type of stochastic process, and not just a deterministic model. Hans said that we could easily develop a model for that. He actually developed the underlying stochastic process. I wanted to have him as a joint author, but he refused because the mathematics was too elementary. He felt that the mathematical contribution to the paper was not very deep. The underlying idea that you could get this constant switch was intriguing. At that point I got the idea that we had the wrong notion of aggregate equilibrium. Our equilibrium was always convergence towards something – the preferable notion for aggregate equilibrium is of a system always changing (Kirman, 1997).

Since you seem to share some of our concerns, it makes us wonder how you became involved with this work on ranking.
I think the real reason was that when I turned up at the European University Institute in Florence, they had a collection of extremely good graduate students who were faced with no course work. They had come out of undergraduate work and the attitude was, once here, you just do your thesis. You don't need any more education. There was no pressure on the people in the department to publish. So we thought we should change that. First, we would collect a few people who would do research and actively publish. Second, they would be asked to give these students courses. There was a lot of opposition to that. The German authorities told us that they wouldn't send us any more students if we made them take courses and have exams. But finally, that was all settled.

The interesting thing was that the European University Institute, which wasn't ranked at all in these department rankings, suddenly moved to the top in Italy. It was the best department in a few years. I asked myself how that could possibly happen in a country like Italy where there is a long tradition of economics. That's what started the interest in the project. We said, let's have a look at what is really going on in these universities. Then the European Commission was very interested, since they were putting a lot of money into these research programs and they wanted to have some idea about what the market facing them looked like, and which people were active and which weren't. It wasn't intended to be a very careful ranking (Dahl and Kirman, 1994; Lubrano et al., 2003).

In one sense you are pushing mainstream economics, and in another you are pushing against the mainstream. People who were doing research were doing fairly technical work – formal models – and were comfortable with general equilibrium theory. On the other hand, you had a lot of the heterodox European economists saying "no we don't have equilibrium and that you need to take interaction into account". And then some mainstream economists switched over to the heterodox side, adopting many of their ideas. What we hear from the heterodox economists is that "the mainstream is coming and stealing all our ideas". What's your view of their reaction?

I'm not a real academic. If I had been reading all these people, maybe I would have gotten the message. I didn't get that message because I was unaware of their existence. If you asked me what heterodox economists were doing, I really didn't know and still don't have an idea. I still cannot tell you what the *Régulation* School is really about. Perhaps, I just haven't spent enough time with their work. The only person where I saw the same ideas expressed in verbal terms was in Hayek, who seemed to have a strong sense of this, but he somehow mysteriously came to the conclusion that one had to leave things to the market. But Hayek really saw it functioning in a way that I had in mind – people who were rather isolated from each other getting together, but not having all the information in their hands (Hayek, 1948). Hayek has nice quotes about that.

Hayek had a whole group of followers – the Austrian school – that were around; did you follow that literature?

No, I didn't. One of the reasons was that in my university, Marseilles, there is a group of people who consider themselves to be Hayekians but who, for want of a better term were almost neo-fascists. At least, let us say that they had strong political views about the primacy of the market. That put me off so that I kept away from it.

You are one of the rare foreigners to have actually become a part of the French academic establishment. How did you manage to do that, and how do you see French economics progressing?

I believe there is a huge struggle going on now in France right now, and the current government is playing a role in it. France has a very strange system where you have research groups structured around research areas or topics, rather than around departments or universities. That causes a great deal of conflict. So a big issue being faced now is how these research groups are trying to keep up with what is going on in the world. And what is their identity? The Toulouse group is following the approach that the way to do so is to publish in the top United States journals. Our group, GREQAM, has a broader sense – let's get interesting people together. But it is a struggle in the French system because of the way appointments are made.

There is a tremendous resistance from various groups. There are a lot of people who are simply anti anything theoretical. But there are also many people who are pushing the idea that we should just accept the criteria of publishing in top journals. I don't see that as the key. But I do see as the key that people should show some concrete signs of real research activity. When I looked at all the people in France who had published in a journal that is actually registered by EconLit, which is 684 journals, 40 percent had never published more than one article in any of those journals.

But EconLit rules out many French journals doesn't it?
Yes, it rules out many of them. I'm not saying that it is an unbiased sample; it is a biased sample – but somehow not to have published in any of those journals in ten years is quite an achievement. You really have to want to be hidden.

Let's admit that my criteria are biased. But now let me ask the following question: what is the median publication of all the people in that group who have published one article? What do you think it is? You're right, it is one. The majority of economists publish one article, and that is enough under our current system. After that people don't bother any more. The distribution is very strange – some people have a huge number of articles, but they are a small proportion. So if there is a real academic life in France in economic research, for the great majority of people it certainly is not in that world where you are trying to publish in the top United States, or even any other international, journals. So the question is: is there life? And is it a different sort of life? The answer for me is that there's not much life, but there is a little bit of this different sort of life which is local. You're obviously trying to defend these people. Your man in Besançon who is cited in your paper (Alain Parguez); I asked all my colleagues at GREQAM, and none of them knew him. They said, oh, who is that? And yet you cite him in an article where you are talking about European economics in general, which means that he will be much more famous than he ever would have been (*laughter*).

Let's talk a bit about where economics is now. What is your view of the recent developments in game theory? Has it become the dominant paradigm in economics?
I don't think that it has, even though if you look at game theory books, you might think that it has taken over from standard optimization. I don't think that is really true. If you look at the formal structure of non-

cooperative game theory, they are still looking for a fixed point, and that fits the standard maximization model. The philosophy behind it is very important, because it starts from the opposite view to that of perfect competition, where no one is interacting with anyone else, except through the market. In game theory everybody is interacting with everyone else, and consciously doing so. I think that's the real insight.

How about evolutionary game theory?
For me, evolutionary game theory is a bit of an illusion in the following sense. What I think people are really interested in is not the true analogy with evolution. They are more interested in saying, "let's say we can establish what we mean by fitness by some fixed criteria. Fitness is just the payoff in this matrix. We have all these people playing the same game. We then increase the proportion of those strategies which do well. Then, we are going to see if that converges to something." People saw this just as a way of selecting equilibria. Firstly it was a way of showing how things could have arrived at an equilibrium. Secondly it asked the question, did the learning process select out a particular equilibria? It doesn't seem to me that evolutionary game theory is really talking about adaptive behavior, which is what I think is interesting – how do people adapt and learn. Evolutionary game theory is much more mechanical than that. You can reinterpret it by saying that people learn to adopt better strategies, but for me that's not satisfactory. All I see evolutionary game theory as having added is a plausible story of how certain rules develop. Those ideas are around even amongst the most neoclassical people.

Think of Lucas; you can't get a more standard macro person than Lucas, and yet Lucas wrote clearly that he didn't believe that people optimize. He thought that people use rules and come to use the rules which work best for them. Once they have done that they behave as if they are optimizing. But that is very questionable; it says that the learning process is very fast, and the environment is very static while you are learning. If the environment is one in which other people are also learning, it's not so clear that you are ever going to converge to anything through that process. So the idea that everyone is optimizing because they have learned to use the best rules, only works in a relatively static world. The same issue exists in game theory. If people are learning to use strategies, and other people are learning at the same time, it's unclear whether the environment will remain in, or converge to, a fixed state (Brousseau and Kirman, 1993).

So where do you see economics going in the next 25 years?
My feeling is that the whole notion of complex systems will become central. That means that you have to turn economics almost inside out. Instead of

thinking of interactions, and the influence of agents on each other as marginal – externalities – which have to be incorporated into the analysis, they should be central phenomena, and the central question of economics is coordination, not efficiency. The first part is that we should do less building from isolated individuals; we should look at the system, and the interaction among people. Agents in such models can be much simpler in that environment. Once you take that position, you can have very simple rules for individuals. In the standard model informational requirements are simple since all individuals need to know about are the prices. But they make quite sophisticated decisions. Here the idea would be that people have more local information but that they choose in very simple ways. The second part is that we should give up the axioms we impose on individuals' preferences for mathematical convenience, and focus on models with agents with simple rules that seem to correspond to what people actually do. The next step is thinking about how people actually do develop the rules.

For me, at least, neuroeconomics, even if only about 5 percent is directly relevant for economists, has one important message – and it doesn't seem to be the message that people are conveying. People have the idea that you are going to be able to relate specific parts of the brain to different specific decisions, a sort of twenty-first century phrenology. That, for me, is not what it is about at all. For me what is important is the notion that the brain itself is a complex system, and, in some moods, certain networks get activated, and then in other moods, other networks get activated, and we may switch from one to another. This means that you won't have the sort of consistency from one moment to another that we try to impose on our agents. Neuroeconomics really tells us that people behave in different ways and will make different, and possibly contradictory, decisions in different circumstances.

Do you see economics remaining a separate field, or do you see it becoming part of a transdisciplinary social science?
I think we benefit a lot from transdisciplinary work. Even though people resist econophysics, and don't like neurology; all of those things are giving us insights into economics. If you stick to the idea that the goal of economics is to understand economic phenomena, then it seems to me that, you will be driven to transdisciplinary social science. But if you say that, too many economists would react negatively. They will insist that the goal of economics is to publish papers in good journals, and then it is a different story. At that point many people in economics departments with a good reputation want to say that we shouldn't tell this to young people because the young people will go around trying to understand economic phenomena and won't get ahead and publish and move us up in the rankings.

Let's now switch to European economics. Where in Europe is top research being done?

There are some young, interesting guys doing work in game theory. I think there are some good game theorists around Europe doing interesting things in places like Bonn and Mannheim. There is a small group in Italy who work on political economy models, but they became somewhat more conventional, which I think is not especially promising. Some of the editors of *Econometrica* have been situated in Europe, so in some sense the profession has seen them as top rate. Ernst Fehr is doing some innovative work in neuroeconomics. He was at Vienna where it is said that they didn't want to give him tenure, so then he moved to Zurich and really found his niche.

Europe allows these niches to develop. For example, Bonn became a center for mathematical economics because there was an older professor named Krelle who was there. He was not a great economist, but he wanted to build up Bonn. He wanted to hire only people who were all better than him. That's not an attitude that you always find. And he put together an excellent group. But if I had to look around, I would say that there are all kinds of wonderful niches in Europe. University College London has a good group. The financial markets group at LSE has interesting things going on. However, one of the problems in Europe is that we don't have this tradition of rich patrons who will invest money in research and universities. Of course, there are exceptions, like a certain number of endowed foundations and centers and colleges at Oxford and Cambridge, and there is the recently established Grantham Centre on climate change and environmental research at the LSE under Nick Stern. This is an example of a privately financed institute which is a world leader in its field.

Where would you like to see European economics going?

It's difficult for me to answer these questions because I'm a person who never had a clear forward vision. At the present time we hear a lot about the role of markets in the economy. I think that one good place to start would be to combine analysis of data – how markets really function – with theory – and to try to understand how changing the rules changes the way in which markets function, and how rules in markets develop endogenously (Kirman et al., 2000; Kirman and Vriend, 2000), I think that would be very productive. I always have this idea about one very good thing that we should do and we never do, which is to say to all undergraduates, at one point in their career, you have to collect some data and then analyze them. Not data that has already been collected, but data that they collect themselves. Then you will learn about the difficulties of economic phenomena, and you will understand that data is much messier than you thought when you started collecting it. They should try to ask some sensible questions about this data, and see if they can come up with some explanations of what they observed. I think that would be a good exercise for any young economist.

A specific area of study concerning markets is that they can only work if there is trust. Rules can only do a certain amount of work, and what is very important is the interpersonal connections in markets. I think that networks within markets are a fertile field of study. In work that I did with Jernej Copic and Matt Jackson (Copic et al., 2009) we found that clusters of people, or, in our case, journals which cite each other, developed, and we give a method for finding those clusters. As a last remark in this context, I am depressed by the fact that in the United States one has moved away from a scholarly approach to economics where people learned a foreign language, and people had to have read the predecessors in the history of economic thought. Instead of replacing that with something useful, we just teach them more technical models. I would prefer having students work with data, posing questions and trying to answer them.

One of the arguments in the book is that when the United States switched to rational expectations in macroeconomics, Europe did not, which from a complexity perspective seems to give an advantage to Europe. Something in Europe prevented the mechanistic approach to rational expectations from catching on. Do you agree with that, and if so what prevented it?
I agree with that insight. It is probably due to a strong Keynesian tradition that held sway. I think that it is also due to the rationing tradition in macroeconomics that never developed in the United States (Malinvaud, 1977; Gérard-Varet et al., 1990). Somehow, that alternative tradition made it much harder to get people to swallow the assumptions necessary for real business cycles. It was sold through the United States by an almost religious fervor among supporters. That never developed in Europe. But how it actually took over in the United States is still a mystery to me. There were so many of the people in power who were opposed to it.

Another of the arguments we make in the book is that for all its faults, the European system created more people who were primarily interested in understanding economic phenomena than in the United States. We used you as an example. Would you agree with that?
I think the one thing about the European system is that it had a great deal of tolerance. The German system was ideal for that, because the German professor had his assistants and his little empire. A German professor who had ideas, such as Reinhard Selten, could construct around him an interesting group of people, and then he could do his thing. So in that sense, I think you are right. But it also has negative aspects.

You've been active as a leader in the European Economic Association (EEA). Do you think that it is serving a useful purpose in defining a distinctive European economics?

I would say that it is not serving such a useful purpose although it has certainly grown in size. Initially, both Werner Hilderbrand and I didn't want to become members, because we said that they were just trying to build a second rate American Economic Association (AEA). Did we need this? Later, I did join and became a Fellow. I still think that there is too strong a tendency to be like the Econometric Society or the AEA and to not carve out its own niche.

Why doesn't the EEA and the Royal Society in England allow more heterodox groups to take part?

We proposed a special session at the Royal Society, and they didn't want it. I think they are more conservative than the AEA in the United States, and it's once again a question of professional self-confidence. If you are not sure of yourself, then you don't want to expose yourself, and let the big boys from the United States come over and say, "That's pretty flaky". That's probably why the *Journal of the European Economic Association* hasn't established its own identity.

If you look at the *Journal of Political Economy*, it's a house journal, but it has an identity given to it by its editor. Even the *Quarterly Journal of Economics*, which is extremely incestuous, has its own identity. What identity does the JEEA or the EER have? I don't see any. The *American Economic Review* seems more open-minded than the two European journals.

Did being in Europe hurt your career?

There are two ways of answering that – an honest way and a dishonest way. The dishonest way is to say that if I had gone to a good United States university, I could have been more prominent and such ideas as I have had would have had a better reception. The honest answer is that given the way I am, and given the fact that I am a very lazy person, what has happened often is that I have found some interesting ideas, which people have liked, but which I didn't really push hard and sell in the right way. If I had wanted to move up I could have done it in Europe or the United States. It is purely a question of character. I just didn't have the drive to do so. You have to put a lot of effort into pushing your ideas if you want them to succeed. If you don't market your ideas, you don't get customers. But I don't feel in any way resentful about that. I think that was a pure consequence of the way I behave and the way I would flip around from topic to topic. I didn't do the things one is supposed to do from a professional point of view because I'm too lazy, and also because to work that way isn't so much fun. It's much more fun exploring new issues.

In many ways, that's what makes you such an interesting researcher. The people we talk to whose research we respect a lot are doing it for fun. They jump around a lot. It's fun. When we talk to economists whose focus is on publications, the fun is lost and so too is much of the value of the research. Much is not worth reading. The contradiction we see with your views is your concern with all these people who are not doing any research. It's probably good that they are not doing any research; they are not cluttering up the journals with papers that really wouldn't be worth reading. A good teacher is not necessarily a good researcher and vice versa.

Let me give you the opposite opinion. Why should a guy like me who is so lazy and unmotivated be so critical of this mass of people not doing any research work around me. The answer is that I don't think that they are doing a good job by their students. If they were being good teachers, I would have no problems with that. But the fact is that they want to have zero evaluation both of their teaching and of their research and this means that their activity gets no focus. And yet regularly in promotion committees and national committees you hear that someone is a very good teacher. When I ask, how do you know that, the answer is that "people tell us". When I ask why they don't have an evaluation system of teaching along with research, I'm told that you can't evaluate teaching. My sense is that too much of their teaching is just the same thing they taught before. Too often they simply read old notes, until the papers become so yellow that you can't see the print (*laughter*).

So my objection to these people is that early on in their lives they get tenure, and they get a position for life at 29 or 30. This person is called a teacher and researcher – I just have the feeling that these people should be doing something other than six hours of teaching a week. I think that's the killer in the French system. All universities are supposed to be the same, so everyone has the same job. You don't have some universities that are research oriented, and others that are teaching oriented, and we should have. It should match the students with the universities to best serve their needs. The matching process in France today leads to 60 percent of the students dropping out because we have open admissions. This is a terrible waste.

There is this myth around that all universities are the same, and the consequence is that universities are populated by professors whose main activity is academic politics. One of their main aims in life is how to get academic jobs for their students who often never should have had doctorates. You think I'm exaggerating. But I have sat in meetings where the selection committee deliberately meets late in the game, when all the good candidates are gone, so that there will be less competition for their internal candidates. It's much less embarrassing pushing the internal candidate when all the good candidates are gone. That's a caricature, but it has much truth to it. If you are an insider, the chances of getting a job at a university on average are 18 times higher than an outsider with equivalent qualifications, and at some universities it is 40 times. That doesn't seem right.

Speaking of France's students, what's your view of the Post-Autistic movement?
It is a complicated story, because the people who initiated the movement were students at the École Normale Superieure and these are the crème de la crème of the French higher education system. They were complaining that they were getting mathematics, not economics, from their courses. Unfortunately, their movement was taken over by a whole group of economists who used it to protest against anything mathematical or technical. So that movement became a type of Trojan horse for economists who want to criticize but who don't understand what they are criticizing and who don't have anything to replace it with.

Any final comments?
I think there is a need to see economics as a profession devoted to trying to understand and explain economic phenomena. We should be extremely catholic in whom we let in, but there should also be a resistance to people trying to make some radical change too fast, but not resistant to the point of killing the profession. We want openness but with some skepticism. I think that's the way the profession should develop. As Buz Brock once said, 'Keep your mind open, but not so open that your brain falls out'. We should never forget that it is about economics. Finally, the most dreadful thing in our profession is self-satisfaction. So many economists actually believe that they understand how the economy works. I see my colleagues making statements that are in my view totally unfounded. Then in a few weeks, they will be telling you something totally different.

Let me close with one last story. I think we should be much more humble about what we understand. The Bank of England kindly gave me a fellowship and they allowed me to observe people on the trading floors of the foreign exchange market (Kirman, 1995). I went there and I watched the traders, and they would tell me why they did what they did. I asked the head of the trading floor why he allowed me to ask the traders questions, because I was most likely, through my interruptions, to lose them and the bank a lot of money. He said, "We like you asking questions.

You see we have quite a few economists coming through here, and all the others spent all their time telling us what we should be doing. What you've done is trying to find out what we do. That's a new approach; we haven't seen that before and we appreciate it."

4. Ernst Fehr

This interview took place on 21 September, 2007, at MIT

You have been successful in the economics profession even though you started over in Europe and have remained there. Do you think you would have done better in the United States?

Initially I stayed in Europe for personal reasons because I was always interested in topics that were not in the mainstream of economics. When I studied economics, I always read a lot of psychology and other related fields. Even before behavioral economics was on the table, I had the impression that economics was too narrow in capturing what was going on in human behavior. But I didn't have a way to express it. So I learned all the standard economic tools – optimization, game theory – and got excited by game theory because it increased the opportunity to model things that could not have been modeled before. But still, I thought that economics could not capture important issues such as fairness or emotions. I think what really changed my whole career path was when I came into contact with experimental economics. I saw this as a tool to really show important, yet neglected things to economists, and not just talk about them.

In some sense you could say that my work started with a rejection. In the late 1980s I wrote a paper about fairness that got rejected everywhere. It was a theoretical paper where I placed fairness into the utility function. One important implication of the model was that workers are willing to accept unfair wages if they subsequently have the possibility to punish greedy firms with low effort choices on their part. I remember that one referee at the *American Economic Review* said that it is totally implausible that people care for fairness within the firm but not at the market stage, when they accept or reject wage offers. Without facts it is, of course, hard to argue against this. Just about that time I discovered experiments, and I saw experiments as a way to change the debate from a battle of *beliefs* to a battle of *facts*.

It should also be said that I had a different view than the mainstream experimentalists. Experimental economists in the late 1980s and early 1990s were convinced that all this fairness stuff plays no role in markets. They were overwhelmed by the competitive double auction results documented by Vernon Smith (1962).

I approached experiments from a totally different angle. I grew up in an intellectual milieu where people didn't believe that much in the empirical relevance of perfect competition models. These models were too much of an abstraction. For example, the assumption that firms are price-takers is empirically wrong for most markets. Vernon Smith's experiments changed my mind, and I was very much impressed by his results because they showed that markets can converge rapidly to the competitive equilibrium even in the absence of price-taking. His experiments showed that many of the unrealistic assumptions of perfect competition models are not needed to achieve competitive prices and allocations. My own experience that one is willing to change deeply held views if clean and rigorous experimental evidence calls them into question, this led me to believe that experiments are a wonderful tool for generating scientific progress.

Do you consider this difference in the basic view of the market a major difference between United States and European economists?
In Europe people were faced with strong union power in almost every country, whereas in the United States, unions play almost no roles at the national level. In Europe there was always a much higher willingness to accept social norms as a driving force of behavior. For example, even standard neoclassical economists, such as Assar Lindbeck, were always convinced that social norms are important. In the United States it is only in recent times that economists such as Paul Krugman have started speaking of the importance of social norms, for example, in his *New York Times* columns. He never did it when he did his academic work. But of course, we now also have the evidence from many experiments that social norms do play a role in economics, which makes it easier to believe in their importance.

The funny thing is that my rejected theory paper was the blueprint for my first experiment. I got money for a project, and we developed an experiment based on the model. We were fascinated that effort was posi-tively correlated with wages, so that the gift-exchange hypothesis seemed to be confirmed (Fehr et al., 1993). In addition, we found that subjects in the role of workers indeed accepted very unfair wages but at the same time they responded to such wages with a low effort level. Thus, here we had the evidence that refuted the argument of the *American Economic Review* referee. This was when everything started. We were really lucky in terms of timing. Our paper entered the scene right when there was a battle going on between mainstream experimental economists and behavioral economists. So what now looks like a happy marriage between experimental and behavioral economics was a vigorous battle in the late 1980s. Vernon Smith criticized behavioral economics. His argu-ment was that all these behavioral anomalies play no role in markets. I didn't believe Smith's argument but thought that it opens up a whole new research agenda.

What he held as a strong belief, I saw as a research agenda. This led me to conduct all these competitive market experiments, in an attempt to study the relevance of anomalies in competitive markets. We showed that fairness did matter in such markets, and I believe that our results turned around a lot of people in the experimental economics commu-nity. For example, people such as Dan Friedman strongly believed that anomalies play no role in competitive experimental markets (Friedman and Rust, 1993). Then they saw that it did matter in the experiments, and as honest scientists, they changed their views when they saw the evidence. I remember in the early 1990s when you went to an Economics Science Association conference, and you had a paper on fairness, you had no people in the session. If you had a session on auctions, you had a full session. Five years later everyone went to fairness and social preference sessions.

What effect did Matt Rabin's paper (1993) in the American Economic Review *have?*
Economists are very different from other scientists. In economics if you find an empirical result and don't have a model, then economists discount the empirical fact. It is the other way around in physics, biology or chem-istry. There the empirical facts have much more weight – they come first. Then they start coming up with theories.

We had a paper submitted to *Econometrica* back in 1993 which was on reciprocity as a contract enforcement device (Fehr et al., 1997). That paper was initially rejected because there was no theory behind it. Then, Rabin's theory came along; it was not a theory that can be easily applied, or that you can use to make good quantitative predictions, but it is a theory that guides your intuition because it gives the notion of reciprocity a precise meaning. So even if it doesn't help you in making quantitative predictions, it allows you to interpret the empirical observations in terms of a precise definition of reciprocity.

Has your movement toward publishing in Science *and* Nature *reflected your sympathy with the natural sciences approach to empirical work?*
It was that, but I saw it also as an opportunity for Europeans to get into journals that are not controlled just by Americans. Honestly, the *Quarterly Journal of Economics, Journal of Political Economics, Econometrica,* and the *American Economic Review* are all controlled by Americans. Except for the *Review of Economic Studies* all these major journals are controlled by American editors.

But aren't a lot of the "Americans" actually Europeans who are in the United States?
It was different in the early 1990s, but it is increasingly that way. It is not that people are deliberately biased; it is more that an editor who sees a paper well presented by someone he knows looks at it differently than a paper from someone he doesn't know and who comes from an "unknown" school. It is human nature, not bad will. It is just the social distance that matters. I thought that by publishing in *Nature* and *Science*, I could influence economics not only from the inside, but also from the outside. It also gives me a chance to reach other sciences. Biologists are very interested in what we were doing. They submit regularly to *Science* and *Nature*, and I thought, why shouldn't I?

In 2000, there was a conference in Austria, organized by two well known mathematical biologists, Martin Nowak and Karl Sigmund. There was a *Nature* editor there, and I didn't know anything about *Nature* or *Science* at this time. I learned at the conference that they reject at least 80 percent of the manuscripts that come to them without even reviewing them. After the presentation of my work on "Cooperation and Punishment", I asked an editor who was sitting at my table during lunch time whether he would be willing to consider it for the review process. He said yes, I should submit a Letter to *Nature*. I didn't know what a "Letter" meant. I thought that a "Letter" is just a tiny, unimportant, note. I later learned that a Letter to *Nature* is a big thing – it is a serious scientific report which confers a lot of prestige in the natural sciences. In fact, most natural scientists never publish a "Letter to Nature". Not knowing that, I thought that the editor's suggestion was ridiculous and I told him that I want to publish an article. However, an article is a very special category in *Nature*. Articles are reserved for papers that document a real "breakthrough", papers that are exceptionally important. Thus, the *Nature* editor looked very strangely at me. I guess he must have thought that I was very immodest. Only later did I learn that my behavior was probably quite inappropriate. Interestingly, when I submitted our paper two years later it did end up as an article in *Nature* although I had submitted it as a "Letter to Nature" (Fehr and Gächter, 2002).

If you had been in the United States, would you have made the same career choices?
I don't think I would have made the same career choices if I had been in a United States PhD program. For example, had I gone to MIT they put a lot of emphasis on technique, so you learn a lot of technique the first two years. Then there is a lot of applied micro. I most likely would have ended up as a standard applied microeconomist, and probably would never have had the freedom that I had in Europe to cross boundaries.

So you would agree that there is a major difference between the non-United States style programs and the United States style programs.
Yes, there is a big difference. At the University of Vienna, we did not have a PhD program at all. I was completely on my own. Nobody helped me. I had very few interactions with my so-called supervisor. I was extremely frustrated during the years of my dissertation because of the tension between my broad interests and the narrowness of neoclassical economics at that time. And in addition my supervisor graded my thesis with a 2 (in Austria grades go from 1–5 with 1 being the best and 5 being the worst) and told me that one could, in principle, also grade it with a "3". But because he wanted to be nice to me he gave me a "2". That is the downside of the European system. You are basically left alone. There was not much push on publication either. My view is that a kind of mixture of the European and United States programs would be ideal.

Today, top students demand behavioral economics; so MIT had to give in and add something to attract some top students who strongly expressed a demand for behavioral economics. It is a bit strange that departments have to respond to these desires and demands by students instead of anticipating them.

It is interesting that experimental and behavioral economics was not generated in the top departments. It was generated elsewhere; for example Dick Thaler was at Cornell, and Vernon Smith was at Arizona, and Al Roth was in Pittsburgh. To me, the economics profession in the United States is in some sense similar to the European soccer league, where the big clubs suck up all the talent that was developed elsewhere. It is not quite that way, but it is sometimes close.

Is Reinhard Selten the originator of the approach you were following?
I think Selten's influence was big at some level and weaker at another level. Selten was very influential in game theory and the concept of sub-game perfection was a real breakthrough. In addition, he strongly encouraged the study of bounded rationality and I am sure that this also left a mark on the profession. However, he did not have that much influence on behavioral economics and the substantive issues that were studied in experimental economics. Later on he also was important because he won the Nobel Prize and he made it very clear that experiments are important for the science of economics. Also, whenever you had to apply money to run experiments, you could say that Selten said it is important to pay subjects according to their decisions in the experiment. I think that Selten was less helpful for young people in his own laboratory because he didn't help his own people to publish successfully in top journals. He had more the older European view that you don't have to publish very much.

He had this view that if something is important, it will turn out to be important. He once told me the interesting story about his paper on the chain store paradox that he had submitted to the *American Economic Review*. The AER would have accepted it, but he had a bounded rationality story attached to it; the AER editor said, cut out the modeling part and we will publish the other part – the paradox. He said no, and sent it elsewhere (Selten, 1978). It is true that this paper became famous. But I nevertheless think his work would have had an even larger effect if it would have been published in the top journals. Some good ideas don't have that many followers, and they don't have the impact they deserve because they don't get the multiplier effect of the good journals.

Can you talk about your decision to stay in Europe?
From 1994 onward I was in Zurich. In 2001 and 2002 I received offers from the United States. Princeton, Berkeley, NYU and MIT also asked whether I would be interested to join their econ department. If I would have gotten an offer in 1996 or 1997, I probably would have been more tempted. But by 2001, I noticed two things. First, all my successes up until that time I had accomplished while being located in Europe. Second, the basic funding for the type of research I am doing is better at my university than at a United States university. The reason is that Switzerland is a rich country with well funded universities. They gave me funds to conduct experiments and promised me that if my research was successful, that it would become permanent. Grants usually run out, and you don't always have time to apply for a new grant. So it was a funding issue. There was also the time associated with investment in a new program. It takes a lot of effort to build up an infrastructure for the conduct of experiments. When

I moved to Zurich, I had a large drop in publications during the first two years because I was focused on building up the infrastructure for experiments. I just didn't want to experience a similar drop again.

Is Zurich changing its doctoral program, and if so, why is it doing it?
Yes, it is. We want to have a more regular program. Currently it is all very compartmentalized because we have this chair structure, which brings in a totally different social dynamic. For me, it was perfect, because I had resources that I could productively use. But I also recognize that there is a lot of slack. In economics, the system has changed. The Habilitation is no longer required; it is now called piecewise Habilitation, which involves five journal articles [the Habilitation being the post-doctoral award for major research formerly required in German language universities for a professorship]. But there is also the patronage issue. Before I came to Zurich the amount of inside hiring was enormous. Bruno Frey was very important in moving toward forbidding insider hiring at Zurich.

Does that mean that Zurich is now hiring on the European job market?
Yes, but also on the US job market; we basically have only a few Swiss left in our economics department.

Is the program taught in English or in German?
All our seminars in economics are in English. This has occurred in the last five or six years.

In regard to your publications, your early work is in German, and then in the late 1990s, it moved to English. Your German language papers seem a bit more radical (Fehr, 1985).
Yes, that's true. I have a left-wing past, and I consider myself someone who thinks that society should help the poor. I view the income distribution in the United States as a scandal. My early work reflected that view. I still have those views. For example, the tendency to think of all unemployment as voluntary is in my view untenable (Fehr, 1991). At least some of the unemployment is reflecting real constraints on people's actions and can thus be qualified as "involuntary". Basically that was the impetus for my gift exchange work. Efficiency wage models have always been criticized from a contract theoretic viewpoint by saying that one can always find a clever contract that does away with the incentive problem and the involuntariness. For example, by just charging an entrance fee the labor market can clear. This is a very powerful criticism. The answer to this argument was credit rationing, but while it is quite likely that many unemployed workers are credit constrained, the argument is not cogent for the

following reason. If workers cannot afford to pay for entering an efficiency wage job the entrance fee still clears the market. We also don't say that the market for helicopters does not clear because many people cannot afford a helicopter. Likewise, if some workers cannot afford to pay an entrance fee, we have a social problem but we may still claim that the market clears.

I think the fairness argument provides an answer. If workers view it as unfair that they have to pay for access to an efficiency wage job, they cannot commit to not shirk once they have the job. The preference for fairness is, in a sense, like a commitment to retaliate in terms of subsequent shirking. Rational employers will anticipate this commitment and will thus not charge entrance fees. Employers may not even be willing to employ workers who offer to pay an entrance fee because they anticipate that once they have the job, workers will retaliate by shirking.

How did you connect to Sam Bowles and Herb Gintis?
In the 1970s and 1980s I read some of their work and found it interesting. Then, in 1996 they got some money from the MacArthur Foundation for an inequality and a social norms project. I was part of that, which brought me into contact with the anthropologist, Rob Boyd. That opened up a whole new element in my studies which I could never have previously imagined.

In one of the earliest meetings, I gave a presentation at the MacArthur Foundation about the ultimatum game and about our cooperation and punishment results back in 1996, I think. Although the papers weren't published until 2000 (Fehr and Gächter, 2000a; 2000b; 2002), the results were there earlier. Rob Boyd was so excited that he convinced Joe Henrich, who just left for the Peruvian Amazon, to conduct the ultimatum game with the Machiguenga, a tribe in the Peruvian jungle. Joe got completely different results compared to everything before. Then, Rob Boyd had this idea that we could collaborate with anthropologists, teach them a little bit of game theory and how to conduct experiments, and convince them to conduct experiments on social preferences in different parts of the world. I still remember the meeting at UCLA where Colin Camerer, Catherine Eckel and I taught the anthropologists experimental economics; Rob Boyd taught elementary game theory. This collaboration was a fascinating event and we all thought and hoped that it will have a significant effect on anthropology in the long run. We introduced quantitative experimental methods into anthropology that are a powerful tool for their research. The project turned out to be very successful in my view (Henrich et al., 2001; 2004).

There is a difference between anthropologists and economists. Anthropologists get excited if they observe that people behave differently in different cultures. Economists only get excited if they can explain the differences. The economists were interested in other issues, such as: what is the degree of market integration in the society, and what are the gains to cooperation in that society. It turns out that both these aspects are good predictors of how people behave in the ultimatum game. So the higher the degree of market integration and the greater the potential gains from cooperation in a society, the more egalitarian offers proposers make in the ultimatum game. Indonesian whale fishermen, the Lamalera, face a severe "nonconvexity" as it takes many people to catch a whale. However, they found ways to establish cooperation in whale hunting, and the whole society is built around this cooperation. Also, when they catch a whale there are elaborate social norms specifying who gets what.

One irony in the results is that the most primitive group – the Michguenga of Peru in the Amazon rain forest were the most "rational" in a conventional economic sense. Another irony is that a recent paper in *Science*, Jensen et al. (2007) replicated an experiment of Falk et al. (2003) with chimpanzees and show that chimps behave like *Homo economicus*. They don't reject unfair offers. This adoption of social preference experiments in primatology (for example, Burkhart et al., 2007) is also extremely exciting as it promises a deeper understanding of the evolutionary roots of human sociality.

Is economics going to remain a separate field?
This depends not only on economics, but also on the other social sciences. Today, in labor economics, they basically do a lot of sociology. They have very powerful statistical tools, but are also very atheoretical, which is a mixed blessing. So clearly economics is expanding, but I don't think that this will just generate a bond. I think that many sociologists are extremely hostile to economics. However, compared to the other social sciences, economics is the most dynamic social science, because many of us were willing to import insights from other disciplines.

In my seminars given to sociologists, they like my work on social norms, but they dislike it when I criticize sociology as having no anchor, no unifying theoretical framework. My argument is that economics has been hooked on the wrong anchor (that is selfishness), and sociology is without an anchor (Fehr and Gintis, 2007). They have 20 different paradigms and they can't agree. They don't seem to find productive ways to remove disagreements and embark on a ship that brings cumulative increases in knowledge.

Is economics losing its anchor? Is the work that you are doing turning economics into sociology, or at least anthropology?
Jon Elster (1989) has the notion of local mechanisms or local explanations, and I believe that in the end many insights from behavioral

and experimental economics will belong to this category of knowledge. Economists will be willing to go beyond the current mainstream paradigm when we have evidence that bounded rationality or non-standard motives play a role. Currently, there is still some resistance, but that resistance is decreasing. For example, Oliver Hart recently came to me and suggested that we do an experiment to examine his work on contracts as a reference point, which basically imports behavioral ideas into contract theory. Fairness and normative legitimacy are creeping into contract theory (Fehr et al., forthcoming). My impression is that the "big" guys in economics are much more open to new things than the middle ground.

In recent interviews with graduate students we found that students felt that rational choice did not hold economics together (Colander, 2007). What did hold economics together were the empirical methods. Is that consistent with your views?
I think there has been a very healthy change in the last twenty years which has to do with the shift from theory to empiricism. Basically, the biggest losers in terms of prestige and reputation in the profession are the theorists. They were the kings of the discipline in the 1970s and the 1980s, and empirical economists were looked down on. The earlier sense was that only those who were not bright enough to do theory did experiments and empirical work; that has changed. Today, empirical work is much more respected and sometimes gets much more attention than theory.

The problem with game theory is that the tools are just too flexible. The theoretical tools and logic alone just don't impose enough discipline. My friend Klaus Schmidt once said: "Give me a real world contract and I give you an appropriately chosen extensive form game whose equilibrium 'predicts' the existence of the contract." This enormous flexibility is a blessing and a curse; it demonstrates that further progress can only be achieved through a close interaction between theory and empirical evidence.

If that is the case, where is the anchor in economics today?
That's a good question. I think that we strive for parsimonious, rigorous, theoretical explanations; this distinguishes us from psychologists. Let me give you an example. Competitive market experiments show that people behaved as if they were self-interested but the ultimatum and public goods games (Fehr and Gächter, 2000b) indicate that many people care for fairness and cooperation. Economists want a theory that provides a unifying explanation of these results whereas psychologists are much more willing to accept two different theories to explain these "contradictory" results. We have now social preference models which can account for both these results. These theories may not capture every detail in the data but they do

capture big patterns. When I met psychologists and showed them my competitive market results (Fischbacher et al., 2009), they tended to say, well, your results are not surprising because competition primes subjects to behave competitively. This explanation basically boils down to assuming the preferences you need in order to "explain" your results. But of course, what disciplines this kind of reasoning, and prevents it from becoming arbitrary? This problem is also a reason why I don't like the argument that everything is context dependent. That view lacks any grounding. In this regard, I really like the strong theoretical emphasis of economics and our desire for unifying explanations. It distinguishes us a lot from biologists and psychologists, and provides us with a normative anchor. It is something we strive for.

Probably your most influential paper is your 1999 Quarterly Journal of Economics *paper with Klaus Schmidt, "The Theory of Fairness, Competition, and Cooperation". Can you comment on it?*
I think the greatest value of that theory is that it shows that you can provide a relatively parsimonious explanation of a diverse set of facts within one framework. Having said this, we write in the paper, that inequality aversion is but one of several non-selfish motives. At that time I felt that the most important non-selfish motive was intention-based reciprocity – a desire to respond to kind intention with kindness and to hostile intentions with hostility. When we wrote that paper, I was convinced that this is the strongest among the non-selfish motives. Now, I am surprised about how much evidence has been provided for inequity aversion. A recent paper in *Nature* (Dawes et al., 2007) gave people random incomes, and then let them punish or reward each other, so there can't be reciprocity. The paper shows that people rewarded and punished just to change the income distribution, so there was straight inequity aversion. So now I am more confident that inequity aversion is an important element in our social concerns. But it is only one element among others.

How do these ideas relate to the debate about multi-level evolution?
I think that there is a lot of confusion in this debate, and I am also guilty of not distinguishing sharply enough between the proximate level and the ultimate level. The evolutionary biologists make this distinction. An ultimate explanation concerns the evolutionary function of a behavior or a trait. For example, people have sex with each other because they like it, but that is not the ultimate evolutionary function. The ultimate evolutionary function of sex is reproduction. In the same sense you can distinguish between a proximate reason why people engage in reciprocity – that is their motives and the ultimate reason. I believe that their motives are often

non-selfish. But it could be that the evolutionary forces behind non-selfish motives are mainly driven by repeated game interactions. Biologists have termed this evolutionary force "reciprocal altruism". It is very plausible that repeated interactions had an important influence on our behavioral traits and motives. However, I am skeptical that this is the whole story because Rob Boyd and others have shown that reciprocal altruism is a limited force in sustaining cooperation in large groups. But we see a lot of cooperation in large groups, so I believe that we need an additional explanation for large group cooperation (Bowles et al., 2005). *Homo economicus* is an inherently proximate notion. I don't think you should apply *Homo economicus* to the ultimate level. *Homo economicus* is a statement about people's motives, and not a statement about evolution. The experiments show that people have other motives, and that's why I am comfortable in criticizing the concept. It is more complicated with regard to the evolutionary explanation. It is much harder to assess the relevance of an evolutionary mechanism that was operative 10 000 or 50 000 years ago where you don't have data. All arguments have to be indirect and there is a lot of uncertainty about the conditions under which our species evolved.

How do you feel about the criticisms of your 1999 paper?
I have no problem in admitting that inequity aversion is just part of the story; in fact I said so long before the paper was published. In a 2003 *Economic Inquiry* paper, we even provided data indicating that the inequity version may not be the most important social preference (Falk et al., 2003). But I would also say that it is a key paper that provided a rationalization of broad patterns of behavior that look very different at first instance. The paper showed, in particular, how it is possible that social preferences play no or little role for equilibrium behavior in certain competitive situations while in strategic interactions these preferences can be decisive. Also, the paper showed that seemingly innocuous institutional details – which play no role when everybody is selfish – can be decisive if some people have social preferences.

When I teach these models, I emphasize that they are about social comparisons; people compare themselves with what others have and do. Empirically, we know very little about those comparisons; thus, equality of material payoffs is almost surely in many situations not the relevant reference point or not the only relevant one. But you have to start somewhere. I think the right way to go is to have a tight interaction between theory and experiments. So everyone is invited to come up with a better theory. It is very hard to do. You have to find a balance between complexity at the individual level and at the aggregate level. My model was partially successful because it is simple at the individual level. In contrast, Rabin's reciprocity model has, to my knowledge, never been applied to any real data set; it can't be applied. It's just too complicated at the individual level. Rabin's model provides powerful conceptual insights but it is very hard to productively apply it to empirical data.

How did you come up with your model?

That was a funny thing. Klaus Schmidt comes from a very different tradition than I do. He was a graduate from Bonn, where game theory and contract theory played an important role in teaching and research. Long before we wrote the paper I once had a conversation with him and he expressed an almost visceral opposition against changing the utility function. This was considered to be something bad in the profession, since you could explain everything if you allowed changes in the utility function. However, Klaus also saw the powerful experimental regularities that called the self-interest hypothesis into question. And he also saw that we now have new tools to empirically test different formulations of the utility function. He invited me to come to Munich to brainstorm about developing a theory. In our meetings the idea of inequality aversion emerged.

Our contribution was not so much to invent this utility function because Loewenstein et al. (1989) had already proposed something similar. The real contribution is, first, that we show that there are important interactions between a heterogeneous population of selfish and inequity-averse agents and the institutional environment. A minority of selfish agents can induce a majority of inequity-averse agents to behave as if they were completely selfish. Likewise a minority of inequity-averse agents can induce a majority of selfish agents to behave as if they also had preferences for inequity aversion. It is the institutional environment that determines which behavioral type dominates at the aggregate level. Sometimes it is the selfish type, in other environments it is the inequity-averse type. And second, we can integrate behavior that looks totally selfish and behavior that looks cooperative into a unifying account within one model. Our model is not the only one that can do the latter. For example, the Bolton and Ockenfels (2000) model also achieves this. Where these two models differ is in regard to punishment. In the Bolton and Ockenfels model, you can't explain why people punish defectors. If I care just for my relative share, I don't care about what happens between me and a specific other individual in a group of *n* individuals. So I also don't care about the payoff difference between me and any specific other individual, implying that there is no reason to target punishment toward a defector. In Fehr–Schmidt, that is not the case.

In our interview with Herb Gintis, Herb said that "Ernst Fehr is the leader" (Colander et al., 2004a, p. 98). How are you their leader?

Herb is known for his exaggerations. I think the altruistic punishment of free riders came as a surprise to them. I believe it is a fundamental aspect of society; it has many implications. For example, it has implications for the normative legitimacy of the welfare state, and the reaction to people taking advantage of the system. It is across the board. People don't like others who take something from society and give nothing back. Back in the late 1990s Herb Gintis and Sam Bowles applied this idea to explain why the United States welfare reforms implemented under Clinton were so popular. They argued that Clinton's welfare reforms introduced an element of reciprocity into the system, helping those who cannot help themselves but refusing to help those who could contribute to society but are just too lazy to do so.

What is your view about the argument that with sufficient repetition and learning the ultimatum game converges to the sub-game perfect Nash equilibrium?
There is no evidence that this is true. It is pure speculation. There is evidence that the public goods game unravels if it is played finitely often. But that is one of the facts that can be explained with social preference theory. In the theory a small minority of selfish people can cause a large majority of cooperative people to defect. It is an incorrect inference to infer from the unraveling of the public goods game that people are selfish. If that were the case, then they would not be able to reach nearly 100 percent cooperation if they are given the opportunity to punish free-riders (Fehr and Gächter, 2000b).

Moving on to broader topics: one of the arguments we make in the introductory essay is that heterodoxy in Europe has a different meaning from heterodoxy in the United States. Do you agree? Or more specifically, do you consider yourself mainstream or heterodox?
Europeans overall have somewhat different views of how the economy functions. The average European economist has perhaps also a different view on human nature. Historically, they have been more willing to take into account other forces such as social norms.

Why?
In the end, I believe that the society in which we live shapes our preferences to some extent, and we don't have a good empirical grip on how this happens. Actually, I believe that this is one of the most exciting questions to tackle in the next few decades – to understand how social arrangements affect our preferences.

One of the points we make is that European economics, because of the different languages and culture, was far less centralized, and that a wider diversity of views was allowed.

You're right; Europe is still very compartmentalized. This has good and bad features. There is a lot of provincialism in Europe, but most people in the United States only speak English, and this limits them to those ideas that have been expressed in English.

What role do you see the European Economic Association playing in the process?
I think they are bringing in some aspects of the United States culture, but they don't want to just do this. I think that they want to strengthen European economics, and not make it a copy of American economics. They want to have as rigorous methodological standards as the United States in theory and empirical work. It is Jean Tirole who went into psychology and economics; he is clearly one of the leaders; in my view he is the modern Paul Samuelson. I know no other such talented person in the profession. I remember him being at a 1999 conference on contract economics, where there were some Chicago economists who giggled like 7-year-old children during Jean Tirole's talk about crowding out of intrinsic motivation. It was a term that was completely alien to economists at the time. It was only Bruno Frey who was arguing that it could be important for economists. All these contract theorists were suddenly surprised that their big hero was bringing psychology into economics. It was Jean Tirole who invited me to give the Schumpeter lecture (Fehr and Falk, 2002) and Matt Rabin to do the Marshall lecture at the annual meeting of the European Economic Association in 2001. It is remarkable how open-minded he is.

With the change in the value of the dollar, is it possible that European economics could actually become a serious competitor of US economics?
I hope so. We are trying hard to compete. While it is difficult to compete with the business schools, we can compete with the economics departments. Our state universities have a salary cap, which can be gotten around by joint appointments with research institutes.

Recently, you've become involved in neuroeconomics research, attempting to identify areas of the brain that provide pleasure. Does this mean that Bentham was right? Or is there a higher rationality? Or more generally, where do you see neuroeconomics going?
My interest in neuroeconomics stems from my interest to get at the biology of behavior. It is extremely exciting to see this possibility and to contribute actively to this endeavor. Social scientists probably never thought that this will be possible while neuroscientists never thought that one could measure concepts like trust, altruism or risk preferences in a clean way. By combining the skills and technologies of economics, neuroscience and psychology

it is possible to provide an understanding of the neurobiological basis of economic and social behavior. I am personally particularly interested in the biological forces behind the non-selfish motives. What we've found is that there is probably a hedonic component behind these non-selfish behaviors. On the neurobiological level, non-selfish choices involve the brain's reward system similar to the processing of pecuniary rewards (Fehr et al., 2005; Fehr and Camerer, 2007). This provides another argument that these behaviors are true preferences. At some basic biological level there is not much difference between consuming a chocolate and consuming charitable giving. At the moral level, we make a distinction, at the biological level both decisions involve the brain's reward areas. If people derive hedonic benefit from non-selfish choices we have to be clear what we mean by "selfish" and by "non-selfish". Non-selfish then means that we forgo material benefits for the sake of increasing or decreasing the material benefit of others. In this context it is, however, important to recognize that we don't yet know whether people behave non-selfishly because of the hedonic benefit or whether the hedonic benefit is a by-product of their non-selfish choice.

Where do you stand on the controversy between lab experiments and field experiments?
There is no doubt that both lab and field experiments are important tools for empirical enquiries and that they complement each other. Our recent paper (Fehr and Götte, 2007) reports results from a field experiment that we conducted in 2000 already. However, I also believe that recently there have been some unfair criticisms of laboratory experiments. Levitt and List's recent paper (2007) falls in that category; it is an ideological paper, because they don't give a balanced assessment of the evidence. Let me give you an example. The usual experiment in experimental economics is single anonymous. The subjects don't see each other and don't learn the identity of their interaction partners. But the experimenter often can establish a link between a subject's identity and the subject's behavior. At the very outset of social preference research there have been claims that the very fact that the experimenter observes their behavior makes the subjects more pro-social. That is a legitimate concern and can be an argument for field experiments if subjects in the field don't know that the experimenter observes their behavior. Levitt and List put forward the hypothesis that double anonymity leads to less pro-social behavior compared to single anonymous experiments. They discuss at length two studies (Hoffman et al., 1994, List et al., 2004) which find evidence for their hypothesis but relegate the contradictory evidence to a small footnote.

That is not the way one fairly treats the evidence. They should have been willing to lay out the evidence on both sides. The problem is much more subtle than they portrayed. There may be an experimenter demand effect in Hoffman et al. (2004) as well as in List et al. (2004). If you come to my experiment, and I tell you that I can't observe your behavior, what do you infer from that statement? It could be interpreted as a hint for the person to act more selfishly. So the real challenge is to conduct an experiment that does not say explicitly that the experimenter cannot establish a link between a subject's identity and its behavior, but nevertheless it is totally transparent to the subject that this is the case. It can be done. The technique used by Laury et al. (1995) when examining the role of double anonymity in public goods provision nicely shows this. The results in the Laury et al. (1995) paper show, by the way, that cooperation behavior under double anonymity does not differ from behavior under single anonymity.

I think that one problem with the Levitt–List paper is that the early versions of it were extremely biased and explicitly claimed that the lab systematically overstates the extent of social preferences relative to the field, which is unproven and, in my view, just wrong. The paper never lost this bias although in the final version, after a lot of criticism from the profession, the bias became smaller. There are plausible reasons why subjects could have more social preferences in the field than in the lab. Of course, in the field we have lots of repeated interactions and many economists tend to interpret pro-social behavior in the field as purely strategically motivated, because it may provide pecuniary benefits in the future. But it is equally plausible that this is not the whole truth. Often you start to like these people with whom you interact repeatedly, and sometimes you start disliking them. Thus, repeated interactions may be a generator of true social preferences towards the persons with whom one interacts repeatedly. Many economists automatically tend to attribute pro-sociality in repeated interactions to enlightened self-interest and by doing so they may overlook possible preference changes induced by repeated interactions.

Where do lab experiments have an edge, and where do field experiments have an edge?
The first best solution is a field experiment that offers the same level of control as lab experiments. But the first best is rarely in our choice set. Therefore, we have to face trade-offs. If I want to know how an incentive change affects effort behavior I rather would like to conduct the experiment in the field if I can control the environment reasonably well. However, the lab is typically better suited for the examination of institutional design questions and for rigorous tests of theories, for examining why theories

fail and why they work. The laboratory also offers better opportunities to examine the existence of social preferences because in the field it is rarely possible to limit reputation building and future interactions. Why are we talking about social preferences today? Twenty years ago the term wasn't even part of economists' terminology. This is a tremendous change; we now acknowledge three big classes of preferences – time, risk and social. Previously social was not on the agenda. It is only due to the lab experiments that it is now on the agenda. The same is true for loss aversion and non-linear probability weighing. That was first found in the lab, and then people went out into the field to check whether similar phenomena can be found there.

The field experiment is also not good at looking at second round effects and dynamic repercussions. The lab experiment is much better in this regard. In the field, you can basically make a one-shot experiment. It would be very difficult to observe the unraveling of cooperation in the field, but in the lab you can. Whenever there is dynamics involved, the lab is often superior. When you look at first round comparative statics, you can do it in both the lab and the field, but – *ceteris paribus* – the natural environment lends more credibility to the results.

Where do you see economics in general, and European economics in particular, going over the next 25 years?
I believe that economists will become more interested in the interaction between biological and social factors. There is some interesting work under way on the connection between genetics and economics; neuroeconomics is work in this direction. Most people equate neuroeconomics with neuro-imaging, but it is much more. I rather like to call it an enquiry into the biological determinants of individual and social behavior.

I think the movement toward applied empiricism will continue. There will also be huge gains to be made for theorists who are willing to interact with empirical economists. Pure theory will be less and less important, and theory that is closer to the facts will gain in value.

European economics will gain some ground; we will have better PhD programs; there will be many more good centers over in Europe. There will be an integration of the European job market for economists, at least in the long term. Europe will lose some of its diversity, and some of the severe forms of provincialism will be wiped out, but maybe we will also wipe out some creativity in the process.

Is the cost worth the gain?
Having been in Europe, and experienced a lot of provincialism, I think we need to make a move toward a more organized PhD program. It will be

far harder to abolish the chair structure that prevails in German-speaking countries; that will require a little revolution. Professors will not give up easily. It will take a very courageous politician to go in that direction. But it needs to be overthrown. There is so much waste of resources. In this sense the new evaluation pressures are good. While there is a downside to focusing on a publication metric, it does add accountability.

5. Cars Hommes

This interview took place on 16 May, 2008, in Harrisonburg, Virginia

Your major thesis advisor was Helena Nusse, who is a mathematician. Was your PhD actually in mathematics or economics?
I came out of mathematics. I did a master's degree in mathematics and after that I did alternative service in the Netherlands. Instead of going into the army I taught at the University of Groningen for a year and a half in their economics program. I taught mathematics to economics students. It was there that I met Helena Nusse. She needed a research assistant. This provided me with an opportunity to work with her on a PhD in chaotic dynamics applications in economics (Hommes, 1991). She was my main thesis advisor. Mathematician Floris Takens and the mathematical economist Ad Pikkemaat were my secondary advisors. But from the start I was mainly interested in economic applications and less so in developing mathematical theory.

You published several papers with her?
Yes, we did a variety of things that came out of my assistantship. Some of the papers came out of work she was already doing and some came out of issues I developed in my dissertation (Hommes and Nusse, 1989; 1990; 1991; Hommes et al., 1995). My research assistantship was in 1987. At that time a personal computer was not easily available to PhD students. In my department you had to make an appointment, like on

Wednesday afternoon, to use the department's computer for a few hours. So I remember using a programmable calculator for simulating a fairly complicated model. At the beginning, I would program it and put it on my desk. I would go and teach for two hours, and then come back to see if it converged to a fixed point, to a limit cycle or whether chaotic behavior would arise. In 1988 I had use of my own personal computer and I could get the same computation done within seconds! That helped a lot with my research.

What made you interested in non-linear dynamics and why did you think it is important? What economic issues does it relate to and what were you interested in?
My interest comes from my background in mathematics. In mathematics chaotic dynamics is just one of the generic possibilities of long-run dynamics, next to other possibilities such as a stable fix point or a limit cycle. When I started reading economics there were all these issues about global stability of the economy, and I couldn't believe that this was the only generic possibility relevant in economics. So it became very natural for me to look for other models that would show limit cycles or even chaotic behavior. But there's always some external shock to the system. Since my thesis, I always considered simulations of the non-linear models buffeted with (small) stochastic shocks.

Your dissertation work was about chaotic dynamics in various models, both microeconomic, such as cobweb models, and macroeconomic, such as the Hicks trade cycle model. How did you become interested in this? How much of your subsequent research has followed up on those themes?
I had been working initially on the Hicks trade cycle model (Hicks, 1950; Hommes, 1993; 1995). It was a traditional textbook non-linear business cycle model, so it was a natural model to work on. It was interesting and to my surprise I found some chaotic dynamics in the model. It is remarkable that in his book Hicks actually has a figure with a simulated time series, computed by hand, that shows the first part of what seems to be a chaotic time series. It is interesting to speculate about the consequences for economic science had Hicks had a computer on his desk and discovered chaos back in 1950.

Another nice model I worked on in my thesis was the cobweb model, originally developed to study the dynamics of agricultural markets when farmers make planting decisions in advance of harvesting without the benefit of hedging (Ezekiel, 1938). I finished my dissertation in 1991, but I started working on the cobweb model in 1990, when I was visiting Helena Nusse and Jim Yorke at the University of Maryland.

In the cobweb model you could generate chaos, but the examples in the literature were unrealistic in the sense that you needed very strong non-linearity, because you needed a backward bending supply curve, like in fisheries, to get complicated dynamics. It may be interesting as an example, but also unsatisfactory because you need extremely strong non-linearity, so the question becomes, is it realistic? What I found in my thesis is that even for monotonic demand and supply curves the cobweb with adaptive expectations can generate a chaotic behavior (Hommes, 1994).

I'm still using this model in my classes and a lot of my later work has been inspired by it. If demand and supply curves are monotonic and farmers have naive expectations, the cobweb with unstable prices converges to a two-cycle. But along this two-cycle, farmers make systematic mistakes. When they predict a high price the realization is low, and when they predict a low price the realization is high. So they are irrational. When all farmers are rational in this framework, the price will converge to the stable rational expectation equilibrium. What is interesting with adaptive expectation is that there is just a parameter that goes from 1, where farmers have naive expectations, to 0, where farmers have rational expectations. And in between you have behavior that is more complicated. Under naive expectations the price converges to a two-cycle with a large amplitude and farmers making large and systematic mistakes. Under adaptive expectations the amplitude of the price cycle becomes smaller and the fluctuations become chaotic. So, the errors of the farmer are much smaller and, because these errors are chaotic, any underlying structure is much harder to detect. So we have a much more bounded rationality equilibrium, and it is not so easy for farmers to improve upon their adaptive expectations rule. In a way, my research has continued within that theme of bounded rationality.

Some of your most influential work has been done as a co-author with William (Buz) Brock, such as your 1997 paper in Econometrica, *"A rational route to randomness". What were the main ideas of this paper, and how did you two follow this up in other research? Are you pleased with the influence of this paper more broadly in the complexity economics community?*

When I visited University of Wisconsin at Madison for the first time in the summer of 1994, Buz Brock had a bunch of wild ideas about non-linear models to work on. Many far too complicated for me. And then the last two weeks of my stay he was reading my thesis and we talked about the cobweb and then he brought in his general ideas on heterogeneity in expectations and we applied it to the cobweb framework. The last week we agreed that this was an interesting model to work on, for it was about the simplest model with heterogeneous expectations you could think of. The heterogeneity idea, with agents switching between different forecasting rules, was something new and since then it has become quite popular (Brock et al., 2005, 2009; Hommes, 2006).

Why did you go to Madison? Did you know Buz at that time?
I had met Buz at a conference in Vienna in 1990. After I finished my dissertation and published what I could from it, I wanted to start something new and wanted to spend some time in the United States. I wrote to some people and one was Buz. He responded quickly and in a very positive way and that is the reason why I decided to go to Madison. It turned out to be a very good decision. When I was there we talked every day. At the end, especially the last week, we started to work on a paper and by the time I went back to Amsterdam we had an 11-page draft. After long extensions and many revisions that paper was published in *Econometrica* (Brock and Hommes, 1997).

The nice thing about that paper is that the economic intuition of the model is very simple. You have two choices for market expectations: you accept rational expectations, but you have to pay for some information, gathering cost, or you accept naive expectations where the information is freely available. Then by intuition you know if your cobweb is unstable and you start with a situation close to a steady state, almost everyone picks the free naive expectations, since it gives almost the same forecast as the costly rational expectations forecast. But since the cobweb is unstable, eventually the errors of the naive forecast will accumulate, making it profitable to buy the information, and many agents switch to rational expectations, forcing the price back close to its steady state. We are then back to the original position and the story repeats itself. The suppliers switch back and forth between cheap naive and costly rational expectations, with prices switching between unstable and stable phases.

To work out that simple economic intuition required some difficult mathematics. Interestingly, the mathematics goes back to Poincaré (1880–1890), because the strategy switching is closely related to the existence of so-called homoclinic orbits, a key feature of chaotic systems. One can apply the strategy switching also to financial markets, where traders switch between fundamentalists' and chartists' investment strategies (Brock and Hommes, 1998; Hommes, 2002). This kind of switching of investor sentiment may explain temporary bubbles and crashes and other stylized facts of financial markets such as clustered volatility and fat tails.

How would you classify the relationship between non-linear dynamics and the mainstream?
I thought that after we got the paper published in *Econometrica* non-linear dynamics would become more accepted in the mainstream. But looking

back, we only won a battle, not the war. Our *Econometrica* paper has had some impact, more than we initially expected. So I believe non-linearity is more accepted than it was in the 1990s. Bounded rationality and heterogeneity are much more accepted now, and since they lead naturally to non-linearities, more economists are recognizing the relevance of complicated dynamics (Hommes, 2009). So there is more awareness, but it is still limited and, in my view, underestimated.

You have been involved with studying the evolution of expectations and how that interacts with dynamics, as in your paper in 1998 with Gerhard Sorger in Macroeconomic Dynamics, *"Consistent expectations equilibria". What are the key ideas in that paper, and how have you followed that up in subsequent research?*

The key concept here is a self-fulfilling mistake (Grandmont, 1998), picked up by Sorger (1998) and Hommes (1998), and worked out in more detail in my joint paper with Gerhard Sorger (Hommes and Sorger, 1998). The agents of the economy act on their belief in their own forecasting. The agents do not know the true non-linear law of motion of the economy, but instead use a simple linear rule and try to optimize that linear rule in a complex environment. We came up with a simple one-dimensional example in which the agents attempt to forecast a stochastic time series of prices driven by an underlying chaotic dynamic. We came up with a model where agents are trying to learn the parameters of a simple autoregressive process that they use for forecasting. In that framework the parameters of their linear forecasting rule converge and agents believe prices follow a simple stochastic process, while the actual dynamics of the economy follows a non-linear, chaotic process. We called this situation "learning to believe in chaos". Barkley and I later applied this model to the analysis of fishery dynamics (Hommes and Rosser, 2001).

If you were living and teaching in the United States do you think you would have been pursuing the same research interest?

I don't know, it's hard to say. After my PhD at Groningen in the Netherlands I could get an assistant professorship at Amsterdam in 1992 and I could get tenure with it. After two years if you show good teaching evaluations and publish in good international journals they give you tenure. This was a very comfortable situation. This gave me the opportunity to choose the topics that I really wanted to work on, without having to worry about publishing papers in the top five or six mainstream journals. Of course you have to publish papers in good international economics journals, but your scientific life does not depend on the top mainstream journals. This gives much more intellectual freedom. In the end, I got lucky and did publish the *Econometrica* paper in 1997. But if it was 1992, and if I was in the United States and had to publish in the top five mainstream journals, I'm not sure that I would have chosen non-linear dynamics and would have written that paper with Buz. Of course Buz could have written that paper alone for he already had tenure and did not have to worry about what to work on. But for a young fellow like me, if I would have worked at a United States university it would have been a very risky and not an optimal strategy.

You are the founder and first director of the Center for Nonlinear Dynamics in Economics and Finance (CeNDEF) at the University of Amsterdam. How did you come to establish this center and what have been its foci of research? Has its influence been pleasing to you?
I was very lucky to get a very big *Pionier* grant in 1998 from the *Netherlands Organization for Scientific Research* (NWO). It is given to a young researcher to set up a new research group by hiring a few post-doctoral students. After the five-year period of the grant, the department gives tenure to some of those post-doctoral students. Until 1997 I mainly had been doing theoretical work. A pioneering feature of the grant was to discipline the theoretical work of non-linear dynamics, bounded rationality and heterogeneous expectations by empirical work and laboratory experiments with human subjects. This is something that Buz always pushed. This discipline is very important for studying models of bounded rationality. And the Americans seem to be better at this than Europeans. If you go to a conference and you hear a paper from an American, they often start with a time series or some observation about the data and then start developing their model. The model can be very theoretical, but their main goal is often to explain some empirical phenomena.

Are Americans more pragmatists? Why do you think Americans are more this way than Europeans?
Very good question, but it is hard to answer. Maybe the freedom in Europe provides one with the opportunity to continue to do theoretical work. But it is more challenging and more difficult to discipline theory by empirical work. If you look at non-linear dynamics, I think there are more people in Europe working on it than in the United States. But, although this is changing now, I believe there have been too many simple theoretical models without much empirical calibration. There is a danger that people just keep coming up with examples of models with chaotic behavior without worrying about empirical regularities of the models.

Do you see these areas, more empirical and experimental work, a direction where the profession should be going?

Absolutely, non-linear dynamics and bounded rationality needs to be disciplined by empirical and experimental work. This is also the way to get it more accepted by the mainstream. And I believe that is where the profession is going (Hommes and Wagener, 2009).

There is a lot of debate about calibration. When one has calibrated, what has one actually done?
Well, what is calibration? What I'm trying to say is that when you write down a simple model, one should compare the properties of simulated time series that you get out of it to empirical and laboratory data. As a starting point one could estimate some simple statistics, such as the mean, variance, autocorrelation patterns, fat tails, etc. and see whether these match with empirical data. Ideally one would like to estimate models, but for agent-based models this is hard to do.

Do you find public policy institutes like central banks more open to these ideas like agent-based models in Europe than we find in the United States?
I believe most central banks in Europe still rely on Dynamic Stochastic General Equilibrium (DSGE) models for policy analysis. But some banks, such as the Bank of England, are interested in heterogeneous expectations models. At CeNDEF, together with five other European universities, we started a new EU project, POLHIA, on macro and monetary policy with heterogeneous expectations models. Together with the Dutch Central Bank we started a new research project on complexity to build an agent-based model of the financial crisis and to develop early warning systems to prevent future crises.

Let's go to a different but related question. Macroeconomics in Europe never really signed on to rational expectations in the way that we find in the United States. Why was that the case? What is your view on that?
I think partly it has to do with the fact that in Europe you have more freedom to do and explore different ideas and not feel the pressure for tenure to publish in the top five mainstream journals, which means following particular trends as you find in the United States. You are not constrained by rational expectations models and can explore alternatives. You have more diversity of views and approaches to macro in Europe than in the United States.

Do you think that regional differences also play a role, different countries with different historical and social factors? Do you see a distinct Dutch School tradition today? Or do you see that there is more an overall European tradition and that you might pay homage to your Dutch tradition?

Yes, absolutely, regional differences are important. In the Netherlands, of course, we have the empirical and econometrics tradition. This is one of the things that came from Jan Tinbergen, who shared the first Nobel Prize in economics with Norway's Ragnar Frisch. He was also the first director of the Netherlands Bureau for Economic Policy Analysis. In the tradition of Tinbergen, Dutch universities still have distinct bachelor and master programs in econometrics where students learn much more statistics and mathematics than in the economics program.

The size of a country is also important. Compared to other countries like Italy and France, the Netherlands is a small country, and we all learn English in high school. So the Dutch early on started to publish in English and fitted in with international journals quite early. Some time ago the Dutch journals switched to publishing all articles in English, so compared to the bigger countries, the Dutch moved earlier to the United States type system with its graduate program and publications. In Germany, France and Italy you had groups that continued for a long time to write and publish in their own languages, and some still do. That disappeared early in the Netherlands.

Have the Dutch universities moved away from a traditional Germanic style hierarchy of professors?
When I was in graduate school they had already moved away from that model. For example, we had a common room, where faculty and PhD students jointly had coffee; it was more open and easy to talk to your professors and not that formal. What did change about 10 years ago by law, was a shift from a more democratic Dutch university system to a system where the dean of the faculty has more power and can make important decisions. So in that sense it has become more administratively hierarchical, following the United States model.

Is this a good or bad thing?
Well, it depends on the dean (*laughter*). The purpose of the law was to make universities more efficient. Now it is more like running the university as a business. If you have a good dean then the department will benefit. For example, our dean set the goal of becoming a top department in Europe. He set a clear goal and our department has certainly benefited from it.

Our graduate program, run through the Tinbergen Institute, follows the United States model, with a two-year masters program with, especially in the first year, just mainstream courses like micro, macro and econometrics. Only in the second year there are more non-mainstream courses, for example on non-linear dynamics and bounded rationality. There is actually some disagreement within the faculty about our graduate program. Some have argued for more diversity in the first year of the program. In my view, the first year should already include some non-mainstream topics, such as some non-linear dynamics, complex systems and bounded rationality.

What does it mean to say that you are a top department in Europe? Forget the rankings. How would you decide what are the best schools?
Personally I find it important to have strong groups of researchers. For example, here in Amsterdam there is a very strong group in experimental economics, doing a lot of work on behavioral economics. There are also strong groups in, for example, econometrics and macroeconomics. Our own CeNDEF group is strong in complexity and bounded rationality. For me it is very stimulating to have a strong group at CeNDEF around me and, as a group, we benefit a lot from the experimental, econometric and macro groups. When the quality of all groups increases and each publishes a lot that has a high impact on those at the top in their field, you will automatically get a top department. Individual researchers are stimulated within their own group, and interactions between groups lead to further synergies. For example, CeNDEF has done quite a lot of experiments in cooperation with the CREED experimental group here.

How would you compare the United States groups with European groups?
Experimental economics is about equal. It is well established in the United States and also in Europe. In general Europe, in particular the Netherlands, has more a tendency to have research groups, while the United States seems more focused on individual quality than group quality. In complexity, for example, there are a number of groups in Europe. Six of them have cooperated in a European project called 'Complex Markets' led by Mark Salmon from Warwick University. There are regular workshops and visits – a very stimulating experience. There have been a number of different complexity projects in Europe, led overall by the physicist, Sorin Solomon. This is a nice transdisciplinary approach. I don't know if you have something like this in the United States. Maybe the Santa Fe Institute is like this. And then you have important and excellent individuals, like Buz Brock. But you do not see as many research groups working on common projects, especially not on topics out of the mainstream. In Europe you do have research groups working on non-mainstream topics. This might be due to the flexibility that we see in Europe where people are not forced to publish only in the top five or six journals to get tenured.

Let's go back to your work. You have been very much involved with experimental economics. Where do you see this going and what are you doing in this area?

We talked about my work with Gerhard Sorger and up to that point I had been doing theoretical work. What was interesting when I presented this work with Sorger at, say, a conference, the audience would be split over consistent expectation equilibrium. Half of the audience would say the agents in our model are really stupid because they are trying to optimize a simple linear model in an unknown, complex non-linear world. The other half would say your agents are really smart, because in reality who can find the best linear model? I wasn't quite sure who was right and so there was a motivation to find out. And then we started thinking about running experiments. An advantage of experiments is that you can find out what subjects are doing at the individual level, what are the consequences for aggregate behavior, and you have full control over the economic environment.

So we did a lot of what we call "learning to forecast experiments" on expectation formation (Sonnemans et al., 2004; Hommes et al., 2005; 2007; 2008). You can measure expectations in the laboratory by looking at individuals' forecasting ability. All subjects have to make individual forecasts. The better they forecast, the more they are paid. All other factors like equilibrium, rational utility, and profit maximizing are taken care of by the computer. Therefore the experiment may be viewed as a clean test on the expectations hypothesis.

For example, we ask six subjects in a market experiment to forecast, and then the computer uses this information to calculate a competitive equilibrium derived from maximization principles, and the computer-derived equilibrium price then is given back to the subjects. The subjects again make another forecast with this information. The information that the agents are provided beforehand is qualitative market information. For example, in an experiment the subjects are advisers to a pension fund that invests in the stock market. In the lab you do this for fifty periods, and you can see what comes out. You can see in the experiment whether there is a convergence to a rational expectations equilibrium point or whether aggregate prices converge to a cycle or keep fluctuating without converging.

What is the most common outcome? How well do people learn to forecast?
The aggregate outcome depends on the market environment. We have done two types of experiments, one with cobweb markets and the other in an asset pricing framework. And the stylized facts of those two types of experiments are different. With the cobweb, the average price is always very close to the rational expectations models. If you look at the volatility in the cobweb experiments it depends on the demand and supply curves.

In fact, if the cobweb is stable under naive expectations, then the experiment converges very quickly to rational expectations. Here you have an example where there is very little knowledge about the market and yet there is rapid convergence to rational expectations. However, if the cobweb is unstable with naive expectations, then one gets high price volatility in the experiments. With the asset pricing model the aggregate behavior is very different and you get persistent price behavior. The market price may deviate persistently from the rational expectations benchmark.

Why do you think that is happening?
The nature of expectational feedback is different in these different market settings. It is negative in the cobweb model and positive with the asset pricing model. We have a recent paper (Heemeijer et al., 2009) where we do the experiments in opposite situations, with the only difference being a positive or negative sign in the expectational feedback equation underlying the experiment. With the asset pricing setting with positive feedback, a high forecast leads to a high demand for the asset and therefore a high market equilibrium price. In contrast in the cobweb framework, a high forecast leads to higher supply and therefore a lower realized market price. This difference in expectational feedback leads to different individual behavior and aggregate outcomes. In the cobweb markets individual forecasts and aggregate prices quickly converge to the rational expectations benchmark. In the asset markets, however, individuals may for example coordinate on simple trend-following forecasting rules leading to oscillatory price movements persistently deviating from the rational expectations benchmark.

Now we are trying to come up with a model that will explain individual and aggregate behavior in the experiments. The types of models that we are trying to develop here are an extension of the type of models I have been working on in the past, for example with Buz Brock, of a kind of evolutionary selection, simple heuristic forecasting models (Gaunersdorfer et al., 2008; Anufriev and Hommes, 2009). So we have evolutionary updating models that fit the experiments quite well. The primary difference between the cobweb and the asset pricing model is that, if one of the heuristics is a trend following forecasting rule – taking as its prediction the last price plus last price change – that rule does pretty well because of positive feedback with the asset pricing, but that rule does pretty badly with the cobweb because of the negative feedback. So in the asset pricing, setting that rule gets more and more followers until it dominates the market and thus explains coordination on trend-following rules and persistent fluctuations in asset prices (Hommes, 2010).

How do you see current economic research in the Netherlands fitting in with broader trends in Europe and the world?
In general I would say that the quality of economic research in the Netherlands is quite high. On the one hand, there is a tendency to copy

graduate programs from the United States, for example in Tilburg and through the Tinbergen Institute (jointly by Erasmus University Rotterdam, the Free University Amsterdam and the University of Amsterdam). On the other hand, there is a lot of variety in research groups including a number of different heterodox groups. I already mentioned the experimental economics group in Amsterdam, but there are also strong groups in Tilburg and Maastricht. The Free University is strong in spatial economics, evolutionary economics and environmental and ecological economics. We have a particularly strong tradition in econometrics, with research programs at all Dutch economics departments. And then complexity work is taking off, with groups such as CeNDEF. The Netherlands Organization for Scientific Research (NWO) will be funding a multi-disciplinary complexity research program in the Netherlands, following European developments.

Where do you see economics going in Europe during the next twenty-five years and then where do you see economics going globally?
Well I think in the end it is going for bounded rationality and agent-based modeling. I think this is where the future is heading. Europe is strong here and more open to bounded rationality and agent-based modeling than the United States. In Europe the acceptance of large deviations from rationality is greater than in the United States, though there are some signs that more journals and research institutions are becoming more open to this. I think the future for European economics is to find a new equilibrium, if possible, where it keeps its diversity and supports academic freedom for individuals and groups to explore a variety of different approaches, some that will be different from the mainstream, but also to recognize some of the benefits of the United States system and its structure of graduate studies.

6. Mauro Gallegati and Laura Gardini

This interview took place on 18 May, 2008, in Harrisonburg, Virginia

Why don't both of you tell us how you got into economics? Mauro, let's start with you.

Mauro: I graduated from a small university in Italy, Macerata. I wrote a thesis in history of economic thought, which focused on neo-Ricardian economics. Then I went to Torino and Cambridge University. I finally did a *dottorato* (PhD) at Ancona. I spent the second year of the *dottorato* with Hyman Minsky in St Louis, and then at MIT with Lance Taylor. I also did some work with Moses Abramowitz at Stanford, where I met Joe Stiglitz and since then we have done some work together (Gallegati and Stiglitz, 1992). I received an assistant professorship in Urbino in 1988, and that is where I met Laura, who was interested in chaos theory. Actually, my thesis was on business cycles with ceilings and floors. I became an associate professor, then a full professor in 1995. I moved to Ancona in 2001.

You have followed an unusual path for an economist. You were initially interested in history of economic thought, publishing work on the influence of Alfred Marshall in Italy (Gallegati, 1990; Dardi and Gallegati, 1992). But then you moved on to be a more mathematically oriented economist. Why did you leave history of thought?

Mauro: I became more and more interested in real economics. In Italy there is a tradition of theoretical economics. Empirical economics in Italy is mainly due to Giorgio Fuà, the founder of the "school of Ancona". There was an international committee that was responsible for doing GDP estimates of several Western countries like Japan, United States and the United Kingdom among others. The leader of this committee was Simon Kuznets. Giorgio Fuà was in charge of coming up with the Italian GDP estimates. Empirical work in Italy started with him and I had an opportunity to work with him (Fuà and Gallegati, 1996). It was instructive and fun. But the mainstream box of tools I found very inadequate and I tried to do some work to improve those tools.

Laura, how did you get into economics?
Laura: I started in 1989. Before then I was teaching mathematics. I got interested in economic applications because I was looking for interesting questions. Economics seemed to me to provide some interesting questions. After I started doing research in economics, I realized that most of the models were discrete time models, while my previous interest was in continuous time models. I was searching for a way to study them and found a book by Christian Mira, who is Tunisian, on chaotic dynamics. The book seemed important, and it opened up a door to a marvelous new world for me (Gumowski and Mira, 1980). So I went to Toulouse to study with him, but that meant I had to learn and master French.

How was your experience in Toulouse different from your experience in Italy?
Laura: The systems differ markedly. France was directed toward theory, so people interested in applied models such as Mira had a lot of problems. His work has never been appreciated in France. When he retired, he never was given the title of emeritus professor, even though he was world-renowned. So he refused to have any contact with his university. We continue to work together (Bischi et al., 2006, Mira and Gardini, 2009). The French school was totally closed to his innovative ideas; without his work discrete models would have taken a lot longer to develop. Indeed, it still isn't all understood. Recently I read a paper by Banerjee, where Mira had already covered those ideas in his 1987 book. He also pointed out that some Russian researchers had covered those ideas before him. I believe that there is a lot of research in France and Russia that is entirely unknown. I have also worked with Ukrainian mathematicians, especially Irina Sushko (Gardini et al., 2008) who now works on economics models with us.

Both of you have become leaders of strong research groups. You founded the workshop on agent-based heterogeneous agents, Mauro. When did you make the move to this approach?

Mauro: Domenico Delli Gatti of the Catholic University of Milan and I started it in 1990 when we were at Stanford, where we were working on asymmetric information in a financially fragile Minsky-type model. But then, it became clear to us that you couldn't solve these models analytically by using the framework of the representative agent. That led to some papers on financial dynamics and chaos (Delli Gatti and Gallegati, 1996).

Laura: I think that for most economists they look at dynamical systems theory as not being very useful for economics. Chaos is of secondary importance. Often it is more important to find the basin of attraction. When there is a very small basin of attraction, the models become more "dangerous". Stabilization requires an understanding of dynamical systems. You need to understand the dynamics of a system to understand the stability of the model. The basin of a fixed point can be very small, intermingled with the basin of a different attractor. Then one can have a small change leading to a large (may be catastrophic) effect. Recognizing that that can happen is very important for policy. When we showed our models to researchers at the European Central Bank, they were quite interested.

You've built up quite a group in dynamical systems there at Urbino. Was it easy to create a group there?
Laura: It actually was very easy. When I became an associate professor I had more flexibility and I asked Gian-Italo Bischi what he was interested in. He told me that he was interested in biological models and dynamics. I suggested we work together, and from there he established his career at Urbino (Bischi et al., 2000). I was promoted to full professor in Parma, and I met Roberto Dieci, who is now at Bologna. I asked him what he was interested in. And we also decided to work together. We worked with Carl Chiarella from Australia and Anna Agliari here in Italy (Agliari et al., 2002; Agliari et al., 2006; Chiarella et al., 2002). I had way too much on my agenda for one person, so I was happy to share the work.

How did you get to know Carl Chiarella, and Tönu Puu and others in the non-linear network?
Laura: Carl Chiarella wrote to me because he was interested in one of my papers related to non-invertible maps, and we started corresponding. The group in Florence working in dynamical systems also invited him to Italy. Then later I invited him to Urbino. It's the same with Tönu. I met Tönu at a conference in Vienna, and he was invited to Urbino (Agliari et al., 2000).

Can you give us a general summary of your views of the Italian university system? Both of you have used it to your advantage – and you succeeded in creating groups with focus, direction and specialization. Is that something that happens throughout Italian economics? What are the strengths and weaknesses of the Italian academic structure?

Laura: The weakness is that research is not sufficiently appreciated. There aren't enough incentives to do it. It needs more support. I did my research often without support. That also happened in France with Mira. We never got support from the European Community. We were considered too applied for mathematics and too abstract and theoretical for economics.

Mauro: My group in Ancona has about 10 people, including post-doctoral students, as well as professors and graduate students (Delli Gatti et al., 2003; Delli Gatti et al., 2007; Delli Gatti et al., 2008). We have a lot of research grants so we don't have a problem with financing. In large part this is because we regularly publish in journals in a wide range of areas. One of the major weaknesses is that we have a lot of turnover. Roughly one fifth of the group moves outside of Italy each year. They get spread all over.

How is hiring handled in Italy?

Mauro: It is problematic. There is very little competition. Universities tend to hire people who have "contacts", rather than if the person is a good scholar. You do not need a connection, but it helps quite a lot. They have been trying to introduce reforms, but they haven't been successful. It matters little where you get your degree; there is no difference in Italy. So why should you go to a difficult top university if it isn't going to make a difference in the job you get?

Laura: The situation has gotten worse year by year. The new reforms involved mainly teaching, not research; research is completely forgotten. They also tried to change the selection of professors – introducing competition, but in practice it didn't improve the situation.

So what should be done?

Laura: Research must be supported.

Mauro: Up until 1970 the public debt was roughly 60 percent of GDP, but that jumped to 120 percent of GDP more recently. When money is short, they cut from the university system without any reference to the scientific productivity. I don't see that changing any time soon.

It seems like complexity economics and agent-based modeling gets support – at least Italy is very strong in these areas? How has this happened with the financial cutbacks in research?
Mauro: Agent-based modeling is done in Pisa (Dosi et al., 2005), in Milan, and in Ancona. That's all. Maybe there is a bit done elsewhere but those are the main groups working directly on it. So we have been lucky or good enough to get some grants. Basically, finance for research is unpredictable and we "lost" some very good researchers. There are changes going on in Italy. A lot of Italians now go to foreign universities. If they come back they teach mainstream economics, so in a way there is a shift that is taking place – toward mainstream economics. I'm not sure this is displacing the Italian tradition because there is not an Italian tradition. But Italy is divided into local areas, and it is that autonomy that allows something like agent-based modeling to flourish.

Laura: In part it is because dynamic model research doesn't require as much money as you expect. One only needs some support for researchers to travel and go to conferences. We pay for these conferences with local grants from universities. Now with the internet people can work from all over, which means even less support is needed. But conferences are still important.

Bocconi University has established a name for itself. What's your view of Bocconi, and how does it compare with the other universities in Italy?
Mauro: Bocconi is private; it has an excellent reputation, at least as a mainstream school.

Is it the best because it is more Americanized? Would the other universities be better if they too were Americanized?
Mauro: Bocconi has very good connections with mainstream and top ranked American universities.

We're hearing a contradiction. You're telling us that the models they work on are not especially useful, but that the school is the best.
Laura: I mean good because of their teaching; the professors and students work hard – they have courses that cannot be found in other universities – this is just for teaching, not for research. The research is separate.

Mauro: I mean good in the sense that their teaching is quite good from a technical point of view.

So it is their connections that make them good?
Mauro: It is not the entire story of course, but it helps.

Many outside observers see academic relationships in Italy as resembling the Roman Catholic Church, with Popes and Cardinals, and Bishops.
Mauro: In Italy there are a lot of local and hierarchical schools, and connections are very important. The school has a leading professor at the top. In Italian we call them *baroni* (barons); these are usually old full professors who have younger professors working under them. It is more outside observers who make this comparison with the church hierarchy, but being mostly local, there is no Pope.

Do you see the future of Italian universities as being more integrated with the European Union?
Laura: I think that integration will be difficult.

Mauro: I see it as almost inevitable. The Italian university system is at a critical state in its history. The Japanese phrase for crises is danger + opportunity. Hopefully, we'll use the opportunity side of the coin.

Laura: Each country still maintains its own methods; they are completely different from each other. In Germany, they had no fixed positions for a long time. They had to move. A student who gets a PhD with a professor at a particular university cannot get a position at that university. He or she is forced to move. It is difficult to create a permanent staff. At least, this isn't the case in Italy.

Is there a lot of ingrown activity in Italy, and is it a problem?
Mauro: Yes, and sometimes it is a problem and sometimes it isn't. I've worked at Urbino, Pescara, Teramo and finally Ancona.

Laura: And I've worked at Urbino, Macerata, Brescia, Parma and Urbino again. We have both had to move a lot. It seems that Italy has the two extremes. Either you can't move or you are obliged to move.

An issue we are interested in is national tradition in various countries and how they are surviving. After the war and the fascist period, how did Italian economics change?
Mauro: Schumpeter describes Italian economics at the turn of the century as second to none, with theory lead by Vilfredo Pareto and others, and there was important work being done, especially in public finance, such as by Maffeo Pantaleoni. Then Mussolini came and the corporativist economy. Only after the war was the Keynesian message accepted. Then Sraffa published his book in 1960, and since then Italy became a sort of a "temple for the Sraffian religion". There were, here and there, some small

but flourishing experimental islands of research, doing mostly applied research. It seemed that we were at the eve of the mainstream supremacy, but the empirical evidence now shows we are not.

Is there much focus on teaching in Italy? How do they divide up their time between research, teaching and service?
Mauro: The main problem is that once a full professor is appointed in Italy, it is forever. It is sort of like a life annuity. If I don't write one single line after I am full professor, no one can do anything.

*So does that mean that they do a really great job of teaching? (*Laughter*)*
Mauro: It means that they have free time. You are going to be required to teach 120 hours every year.

Laura: Things are going to change; it is supposed to go up to 120 hours, and there is going to be more pressure on people to publish in English. If you want to get your ideas out there, you have to publish in English. If I wrote in Italian, there would be about two people who would read it.

It seems in Italy, there are still a lot of economics journals that are in Italian.
Laura: In mathematics, that isn't the case.

Mauro: And in economics it is changing fast. They are all now at least bilingual.

Is there pressure in Italy to adopt lists to rank economists?
Mauro: Refereed journals in English are best; chapters in English in edited books come second, and Italian publications come third. There is an ongoing debate among Italian economists about a recruiting strategy. They want to give points for various journals. But in the end, this system isn't applied.

Laura: Things will likely change, but it will take time.

Mauro, tell us about your recent work with Joe Stiglitz.
Mauro: Joe has contributed significantly to several important topics in economics. But I regard his work on asymmetric information as his best and most disquieting to the mainstream paradigm. In my opinion, if information is not complete and asymmetrically distributed, agents have to be heterogeneous and interacting. Moreover time and debt become important, bankruptcy is crucial and agents self-organize in an uncertain world. Moreover, asymmetric information requires the use of public intervention to offset the market failures that result from asymmetric information. We're

working on some policy issues where we believe interacting agent models with networks can shed some light on these issues (Battiston et al., 2007).

When did you start working on agent-based models?
Mauro: In the 1990s. We held three workshops on agent-based models starting in 1996, in Ancona (Gallegati and Kirman, 1999; Delli Gatti et al., 2000; Gallegati et al., 2003), which began the series of the WEHIA conferences.

You've been active in econophysics. This is another area in which Italy is quite strong. Is there some reason why Italy is strong here as well?
Mauro: The strong autonomy that local professors have allows such focus, so you can do your own research. Our friend, Rosario Mantegna, is one of the best econophysicists in the world. He has a group in Palermo that is very successful in their work.

Laura, you've entered into other fields such as natural resources and economic growth. Can you tell us a bit about that work?
Laura: I am primarily interested in modeling, not only in economics, but in a lot of areas such as biology, electrical engineering, and physics. Other fields of research are starting to follow economics and use models also. The school of Mira in Toulouse was in electronic engineering, and after Mira, they told me that I was considered the successor of his school. People write me when they are exploring this work and when they have problems. I get questions from all over.

How would you summarize your view of how an economist should best react to your models?
Laura: When a model isn't acting as expected, you are motivated to understand why, and to modify it.

But if you change the model to give you the results you want, what is the model adding?
Laura: If you want to show your idea, you have to find the right instrument to show your idea. It is not the model that *tells you* about the real world; it is the model that *is informed* by the real world.

But then it would mean bringing the model to the data. But these models are extraordinarily hard to bring to the data. What check do you have that the models are actually adding to our understanding?
Mauro: I have been more involved with doing some empirical work on chaotic and non-linear models. Unfortunately, there is no real test on

non-linearity. There is the BDS (Brock et al., 1996) test. Over time, I've been more and more convinced you can't offer testable explanations for the real world. That's one of the reasons why I moved to agent-based models. Suppose you have interaction among agents, or non-linear models, then the three principles of mechanical physics (determinism, causality and reductionism) are disrupted. There are a lot of different individual behaviors that could lead to an emergent macro behavior.

Let's return to agent-based modeling. Is it the future to how one does macroeconomics?
Mauro: Which day is it? (*laughter*) Seriously though, I think that it is quite important and a must if one wants to carry out seriously a microfoundation project.

Agent-based models could give very important hints. Think of the sub prime crises. If you have an agent-based model, you don't look at the average behavior. You can look at the behavior of a bank in a "bad" situation (because of its own financial condition or the network it belongs to). That allows calculating the possibility of the spreading of the contagion. That's only because one can look at how heterogeneous agents interact and modify their behavior. Agent-based models allow you to get insight into how you can prevent the dominoes effect – the spread of a crisis.

How do you answer those critics who say, yes, you can reproduce any result with these agent-based models, so what are they telling you? By modifying the agents you can calibrate a model to any set of data.
Mauro: We do not calibrate, we validate, eventually. I would argue that we develop a model, and if there is empirical support and their short-term predictions are good, we work on it. Otherwise we modify it since the model can be falsified because our methodology is not axiomatic.

What do you mean by empirical support?
Mauro: The agent-based model is a new tool for theoretical and empirical research. For me, doing "scientific" research is trying to understand and explain empirical evidence. In order to understand an observed macroscopic regularity on a timescale of interest, one should show how a population of heterogeneous interacting agents could generate the investigated evidence. If it does, then there is empirical support for the model.

In DSGE modeling and calibration, people often complain that they are twisting the parameters to fit the data. It seems that you are doing the calibration in modeling the pieces.

Mauro: Again, agent-based modelers cannot calibrate millions of agents. They endogenously evolve toward a statistically stable distribution (stable for some periods).

If somebody says yes – you can calibrate these models to the data. But they also believe that there are an infinite number of other agent-based models that could also be calibrated to the data. How do you know that the agent-based model that you've developed is the right model?
Mauro: I don't think there is one model of the economy. There is nothing like a natural model to be calibrated to fit the data. I recognize one has to be very smart and talented to get plausible numbers from implausible models, like those using representative agents, no interaction and so on. The only "calibration" we use is the survival condition. For example, in the model of *Emergent Macroeconomics* there is a price under which the firms go bankrupt. We do validation, not calibration. The validation of our agent-based model is twofold: (1) output validation to match computer generated output real data; and (2) predictive output validation matching computationally generated output against the forecast of the model itself at a different scale of aggregation.

How does one choose between a DSGE model and an agent-based model?
Mauro: One can do, of course, encompassing tests between models. With an agent-based model you can validate that model with the real data at each level of aggregation – micro and macro.

In your new book, Emergent Macroeconomics *(Delli Gatti et al., 2008), you said that the one area where your group had problems was in labor markets. Why was that particularly hard?*
Mauro: In the new book, we analyze the labor market as a search process with limited information. The main problem we face is that there is a strongly pro-cyclical behavior of the real wage, the correlation with the cycle is greater than 0.6. Whereas in the real data there is a pro-cyclical, correlation greater than 0.2 but less than 0.6.

If the agent-based models of finance that you are dealing with generate the fat tails and kurtosis, does this mean that they are converging on the econophysics models (Mantegna and Stanley, 2000)?
Mauro: They are separate because econophysicists still use the physics tools, as if there are natural laws. The main difference is that physics looks to the natural laws approach. In complexity, to which the agent-based models belong, you may have a natural law. But it can lead to a behavior that results from the learning and the interaction of agents, which can be

different in different institutional settings. It is not necessarily a natural law per se. Let me try to clarify this point. If a physicist discovers how to predict earthquakes, the behavior of the plates will not change. But if an economist understands how to forecast the stock market dynamics, agents' behavior will change accordingly.

You, Steve Keen, Thomas Lux and Paul Omerod (2006) wrote this paper "Worrying trends in econophysics". What led you to write that, and how serious do you think those problems are?
Mauro: Some of the problems are still there and some have improved, and there are some econophysicists who don't talk to me any more. For example, one of our complaints was that they didn't take as close a look as necessary at the statistical tests. They are now taking seriously the need to detect a power law from a log normal distribution. Some always did it well. But before, there were a lot of claims that some distribution was a Pareto law that in fact wasn't. I guess this is partly due to the difficulties emerging from the mix of different disciplines.

Could that be a difference in the nature of publishing in physics and in economics? In physics one publishes more quickly, and leaves it to the group to find what is right. In economics there is a larger push to get it right before it is published.
Mauro: That's true, and in a way, I think it is much better the way physics does it. We know that in economics there have been a lot of papers rejected just because they have no microfoundations. But is a macro model with microfoundations with the representative agent more "scientific" than a macro model without them?

Where do you see economics in general going, and where do you see European economics going over the next 25 or 50 years?
Mauro: Look at the ratio between students in business schools and economics in the last 20 years in Europe and it is skyrocketing. I expect a rejection of the mainstream approach. It is a hope rather than a theorem, nevertheless ... . As I said before, you cannot apply the neoclassical approach to the real world. We should take seriously what Lucas said about microfoundations. True microfoundations must take agent interaction into account, and I think the future of economics involves doing that. Also as Marshall said, the "Mecca of economics is biology", and I see the complexity approach as a good framework for economics.

How will that rejection come about, when both of you earlier, when asked which is the best department in Italy, chose a straight American-influenced mainstream. How do you reconcile the two? Is Bocconi going to change, or will it be overthrown. What are the dynamics that lead you to the new equilibrium?

Mauro: Bocconi's reputation is high in Italy. There are a lot of serious economists there. But I think that the future of economics is much more in programs like the agent-based models and complexity. After all, economics should explain the real world, not the "best of the possible worlds".

7. Tönu Puu

*This interview took place on 18
May, 2008, in Harrisonburg,
Virginia*

How did you get into economics?
I got interested in economics in high school. I happened to borrow a book
by Gustav Cassel (1918) called *The Theory of Social Economy*, which is an
elegant general equilibrium textbook. The book also discusses intertem-
poral equilibria, and that fascinated me. The grades I got in high school
were not very good, so I was limited in what I could study at the university.
When I went to the University of Uppsala, I got into a program called
'politices magister', which had three compulsory disciplines – political
science, statistics and economics. My entire education was at Uppsala. I
also received an assistant professorship there. Having no open chair positions, I had to go somewhere else.

There were only 15 chairs in economics in all of Sweden. Whenever
a position opened there was some competition from people outside of
Sweden, but generally they had only Swedish applicants. I got a job
at the Umeå University, where later I founded CERUM, the Center
for Regional Science. I stayed there until I retired in 2001. At that
time, people did not stay at the same university where they got their
degrees because there was seldom an opening at one's school. Things
have changed. Today, a committee of experts from other universities is
appointed to select the chair holder. The first step is to find if anyone is
appropriate for the chair. The second step is to select a person among

the top applicants. In the end, the university and the government sign the appointment letter.

How were the candidates chosen for chairs in Sweden?
When I first got my chair, it was a very elaborate procedure for deciding who gets a chair. Three experts were selected from other universities, and they got three months off just to read everything that the applicants had written. Of course they looked at quantity, but mostly the evaluations were based on the quality of the research. There were no special criteria. Each of the experts wrote their evaluation individually. They had one meeting to discuss things, but they were supposed to make an individual judgment. They considered all forms of publications. In fact, unlike now, monographs were regarded as having somewhat higher weight than journal articles. Today nobody writes monographs, in part because they don't get any credit for doing so.

When they were searching for a replacement for me when I retired, I was prohibited from being on the committee. But as I remember, the procedure was the same, although they didn't get three months off. That disappeared long ago. Today, all people get is a moderate honorarium. And the procedure has changed. People could split the reading, so everyone no longer had to read everything. Several times it was noticed that no weight was placed on teaching. So they made new rules, that said pedagogical and research qualifications should have equal weight. Finally, later, they added service. However, there were no criteria for judging quality of teaching. So the experts generally said that he has been teaching for 10 years and no one has complained, so we will make the judgment only on scientific output. There was no argument about where things were published. People made the qualitative judgments about the research.

Did you serve on such advancement committees?
Yes, I've done it ten times in Sweden. I did it mainly in my younger years, when we always had a Nordic pool of experts. That's changed; now the pool is more fully international.

You've published a lot. Did you feel a lot of pressure to publish?
Internal and personal forces always drove me. One of the reasons I changed areas so many times is that I didn't want to get bored. I never wanted to become an expert in a particular topic. A well-known economist once claimed you can use the same principles for all kinds of economic problems. I think that is right. I've found that you can easily move from one area to another, and you don't need to learn specific information.

Also I received some excellent advice from my supervisor. He said, never read anything about a new problem you want to investigate before you have a clear idea of how you want to treat it yourself. Reading what others have written directs your thought along certain lines, and you cannot do anything new. Over the years I have followed his approach. That has kept me from getting bored, but it also means that you invent a lot of stupid models. I once had a discussion with Martin Beckmann in which we disagreed about the number of models one has to scratch – whether it was 80 percent or 95 percent. But it was high in any case. But I never felt the pressure to publish – I always did it for fun. When some people said – look – you have only done theoretical research; if you want to be promoted, you must do some empirical research. Then I felt aggressive and a little obstinate, and decided that I didn't want to do any empirical research. The work that I do is for fun and because I think it is important.

Let's look at your work. Some of your early writing was on complementarity of factors. Did you know at that time the link between your work and the Cambridge Capital controversies? How was this work received?
I worked strongly in the Nordic tradition. And I was following the work of my supervisor, Tord Palander, who was mainly following the work done by Ragnar Frisch at the University of Oslo. So I would say my sources of inspiration were from Frisch's theory of production and also from Sir John Hicks's (1939) *Value and Capital*. I was not aware of the Cambridge controversies at the time.

The work was received rather well. I was recently contacted by a young professor in the United States who is working on a biography about Ferguson, who wrote about the same topic – the decomposition of the demand function for production factors into an income effect and a substitution effect, which had not been properly analyzed either by Hicks or Paul Samuelson (1947) in his *Foundations of Economic Analysis*. I published the first part of this work in France in *Critique de Économie Politique* (Puu, 1966) and the second was published in Belgium in a book (Puu, 1968).

Your work was a lot more mathematical than most of the work at that time in a Nordic tradition. How did that fit into the tradition?
Actually, I interacted very little with other Swedish economists. The mathematical tradition was not strong in Sweden. But I learned from my supervisor the need to show mathematical relationships and not just to specify a qualitative relationship. Instead, I developed models with explicit functional relationships. This was outside the tradition of the time. For instance, if you wanted a cost function that looked like a cubic function, you made a cubic function and made actual calculations based on that function.

You've also done work in macroeconomics. What's your sense of the Wicksell tradition in Sweden that developed many Keynesian ideas independently? Does that school still exist?

I think people still consider what Knut Wicksell (1898) called the cumulative process as a step toward the *General Theory* by Keynes (1936), but I would say that the Stockholm school of economics has withered. Both the Stockholm school and the Keynesian school lacked dynamic analysis. My mentor, Palander (1953), wrote an extensive critique of the Stockholm school making this point. According to him, aggregate equilibrium analysis was incomplete because of this. This was the only work by Palander that was translated into English. Later, when I did work in philosophy of science (Puu, 1969), I classified equilibrium analysis with a teleological explanation to be contrasted with dynamical analysis, describing exactly how an equilibrium price is reached, or how equilibrium of savings and investment is reached.

Bertil Ohlin, who was Palander's cousin, represented another side of the Stockholm school (Sweden is a small society). He corresponded a lot with Keynes, and he had some influence. I don't see the Stockholm school as monolithic.

Did your interest in regional economics also follow from Palander's interest?

No. Palander had written about the topic in 1935 long before I became associated with him. It was only around 1980 that I became interested in spatial and regional topics. Palander and I worked together in the mid-1960s, and his interest at the time was inflation theory and monetary issues; he was an advocate for indexed bonds. The first time I worked with him I tried to estimate future expected interest rates from the term structure of interest rates. After I had worked on this for a couple weeks, we decided Lutz's (1940) formula was wrong. This later became one small chapter in my thesis (Puu, 1964), which was on portfolio selection theory. When I wrote this, Markowitz's theory was relatively new, so I think I produced the first application of Markowitz's (1952) theory that actually derived demand functions for bonds. But the thesis was in Swedish so it never became known; it was never cited.

How many different languages have you published in and how do you decide which language to publish in? When did English become the required language of economics in Sweden?

Today, I don't think that anyone writes economics articles in Swedish. When I wrote my thesis in 1964 no one told me to write it in English. It was quite technical, and only 27 copies were sold. A few people from outside

Sweden read it, but there were not many. Starting a couple of years later, people started writing in English.

Was writing in English the end of the distinctive Swedish school?
Yes, I think so. Earlier, Swedish economists had a strong German influence, and the major works by Swedish economists before the 1960s were all published in German. But around 1965 English became the standard language. I should add that the reason I published my production theory papers in French is that I was invited to write in the journal, and the French government required all scientific journals to be published in French if they wanted government subsidies.

You've been the economics editor of Chaos, Solitons & Fractals, *which is a highly multidisciplinary journal, for a long time. How do you see economics fitting in with other disciplines?*
That's a difficult question. My path to non-linear dynamics was through regional science. When I really became interested in this area, I started collaborating with Martin Beckmann from Brown University. We did some joint work – a couple of books (Beckmann and Puu, 1985; 1990) and articles. My main interest was in answering the question of how spatial patterns arise. What we found was that even if the geography is all the same, spatial patterns can emerge. Then I found this elegant theory by Beckmann that was as general as Arrow and Debreu's general equilibrium theory. I put some structure to the theory, and I added some work on differential equations (Puu, 1979). This led me to consider questions of structural stability. Using these results, I could apply structural stability analysis to general models of price and trade equilibria, to find what situations are stable and which are not. Then I came across catastrophe theory and found that there were two different topological structures that were stable, and I could use the elliptic-umbilic catastrophe, one of those classified by René Thom, to describe the switches between the two structures (Puu, 1981). Then I got stuck.

I was invited to a conference in Washington DC at the National Academy of Sciences, and I tried to advocate the use of partial differential equations as modeling instruments to find out about the emergence of spatial temporal patterns. But there was an American mathematician who argued that everyone moves in the opposite direction – I guess he had Lorenz in mind and the Navier–Stokes equations, and that everyone is going from partial differential equations, like the Navier–Stokes equations, to ordinary differential equations and from that to maps. He argued that there was no new research going on in partial differential equations. I took the point and moved more and more away from spatial issues to general dynamics models (Puu, 1989; 2003).

Where did the non-linearity occur in the regional models?
Beckmann's model for interregional models has a non-linearity in the shape of the partial differential equations directing trade. The non-linearity comes in the limited roads that limit transportation and vary from point to point. The model becomes non-linear because the Euclidian norm of the price is equal to transportation costs.

Which of your work have shown you can generate chaotic dynamics?
We did so in oligopoly theory by making the reaction functions come in several pieces (Puu, 1991; 1995; Sushko et al., 2002), following a suggestion of Joan Robinson (1933). Also, in macroeconomics (Gallegati et al., 2003; Puu et al., 2005; Puu, 2007), following suggestions by Hicks that there could be some highly irregular outcomes from the business cycle model, which you can see in the appendix to his *Trade Cycle* book (Hicks, 1950).

In terms of spatial structures, what do you think of the Santa Fe approach using computer simulations and the "nearest neighbor" model, derived from the Schelling model, to study it?
I think that is a very useful approach.

How do you see your models being empirically applied?
That's a problem, and I always have difficulty answering that question. But I would say that even in science there is an advantage of specialization. Some people may specialize in empirical research, others on theoretical work. So that is a problem of the empiricist. Of course, I am always driven by choosing reasonable assumptions for the model – that they make sense in terms of how the economy functions. I very much dislike combinations of models that are put together that don't match any intuition one has of how the economy functions.

The older I get, the more I want very simple models based on a few simple principles that are easy to accept. Some theoretical results are very difficult to implement in any reasonable way. But I see science as an idealized model of real life, and in this respect we are quite like physicists. For in acoustics, they discuss the vibration of a string, which is just a line without any thickness. Then they deduce the wave equation; they see that under certain circumstances, you get certain results. You can explain why an oboe sounds different from a flute. There are lots of things we imagine we can understand through the idealized models, but as soon as you are approaching reality, things become extremely complicated (Puu, 1990).

In some of my research on sound engineering, I once read an article that extended in two parts to over 40 pages each with gigantically long formulas. The authors wanted to approach reality assuming there was a cylindrical sound hole in the middle of the cylindrical flute with soft edges so there would be no turbulence. They wrote on and on, but they could not reach any conclusions. Sometimes physicists say that physics is so simple, but the economy is complex with conscious interacting agents. My point is that physicists do exactly the same thing that we do. They oversimplify and think they understand something. And often they do. I would say the same is true about economies. Even in a stylized model, say the simple multiplier-accelerator model, you have a model that gives you a sense of how a bounded cycle might work.

Since 1969 Sweden has hosted the committee that decides who receives the Bank of Sweden prize in Economic Science in Memory of Alfred Nobel. Has this affected the economic development of economics in Sweden, and if so how?
I'm not quite sure. In the beginning there were a few European prize winners, but then after a couple of years, it switched to almost exclusively selecting American prizewinners. I believe that this made the connection between Sweden and the United States stronger and also gave young Swedish economists the impression that in order to work at the highest level they would have to take inspiration from the United States economists.

Even though Americans dominated the Nobel Prizes, some of them were not really Americans, but were immigrants. I'm also thinking about your co-author, Martin Beckmann. He was at Brown University, but he moved there from Germany. What is your feeling about this movement of people from Europe to the United States? How has it affected the interaction of United States and European economics?
It definitely strengthened American economics. (*laughter*)
    There was such an enormous movement of economists because of the Nazis. Almost all intellectuals left Europe. Only a few remained. It decimated German science, including economics. For example, one who stayed, August Lösch (1940), was not given a permit to teach because he refused to sign a loyalty oath to Hitler. In some ways he survived as a private scholar. On the other hand von Stackelberg (1934) remained; he was a great theorist – not only because of his oligopoly model, but his other work as well. But for some reason that I could never understand, he became a Nazi. These are only two examples – one who was against the regime, another who approved of it. Almost all the other good economists left. The same thing happened to countries invaded by Germany. They went to the United Kingdom and the United States. Of course, this was not only the case in economics. It happened in most other fields as

well. The supremacy of United States science is, to a large part, due to Hitler.

Are there any areas of economics in Sweden or in the other Nordic countries that you see as particularly innovative now?
I don't think there is anything that is particular to Sweden or to Nordic countries right now. Sweden followed the United States first; Norway followed it later, because they had this strong tradition from Frisch and Trygve Haavelamo at Oslo and were very self-conscious. The third person there was Leif Johansen. They did very original work. Unfortunately, Johansen died young.

Did they publish in English or Norwegian?
They published in both. Once English became the general language of science, it gave English speakers a large advantage. Non-English speakers are hesitant to say as much as they would in their own language.

When we interviewed graduate students in continental Europe, most reported that they did not feel at an enormous disadvantage, because they had learned it from the beginning.
I think that there is more to it than that. With English as the general language, the terminology develops in English, and new terms are defined in English. This creates a difficulty for non-native speakers of English, because every time they come to conferences, and there is a debate, non-native speakers cannot contribute with the same eloquence as native speakers can.

In our introductory essay to this book, we quoted your book on arts and economics (Puu, 2006), where you suggested that earlier economists published when they had something to say, whereas now people publish just to publish. Can you expand on that?
Yes, those are my views. However, I'm not sure what the reasons for the change are. I don't think it is only the American influence. Universities have developed into something very different from what they were. On the one hand, I feel that it is good to have some pressure to publish. There are some lazy Swedish professors, so to put some pressure on them to publish is understandable. You cannot just let everyone hang around. Once a university research community has grown significantly, it is a rather costly business not to have people publish. When universities were much smaller, it wasn't so costly. I think one of the reasons for the structural changes in requirements is the growth of the institution. With growth comes the need for more control.

Are they using actual journal rankings to evaluate research?
I have seen such lists, but I doubt that they are used. Since I have retired, I've been apart from such issues.

Where do you picture economics going in the next few decades – both economics in general and European economics in particular?
That is hard to say. I am not in a position to say where economics is actually going, so let me concentrate on what I hope will happen. I hope that the current mainstream would get less weight and we will see more development in dynamic analysis. Also I hope that its influence will spread and its importance is recognized. I hope that regional science, or what they are now calling economic geography, will be reintegrated into economics, and that equilibrium analysis loses a little of its weight.

I also hope that economics also returns to the issues that were dealt with from 1920 to 1950 that is captured in the work of Harold Hotelling (1929) and Joan Robinson, which I find is the most exciting period in economics. In that period they were more focused on imperfect competition and non-linearities which in that period was the norm. Linear presentations were just textbook simplifications. Think, for instance of Joan Robinson's book on imperfect competition (1933). There she draws this picture of a kinked demand curve, with a marginal revenue that jumps up and down. It was one of the first multiple equilibria models. These models can reduce the focus on unique equilibria and welfare economics that I think has given economics a bad reputation among the general public. This I believe is where the action is and where current cutting edge work is doing exciting work and the mainstream needs to go.

8. Søren Johansen and Katarina Juselius

This interview took place at Copenhagen University in October, 2005

How did you get into statistics and economics? Søren, let's start with you.
Søren: That is a long story. Both my parents were trained actuaries. When I finished high school in 1958, I knew that the actuarial study would be split into statistics and actuarial science. I decided to do statistics, which started with courses in mathematics, and later statistics. I became one of the first graduates of the program in 1964. So I guess it was basically the background of my family that made me aware of statistics and want to study it.

Katarina: My background was just the opposite; I was the first one to get a university degree in my family, they were farmers. As a child I was a 'reading horse'; at the age of 12 I had already read all the books in our local library, many of them two or three times. I just loved literature and after high school started studying literature and humanities. But I quickly realized it wasn't really for me; you had to read huge volumes on the history of literature and learn it by heart. I wasn't very good at memorizing and decided to study something more analytical, which was economics. One of the more influential professors in business administration had a strong influence on me and he encouraged me to continue my studies after my BSc and MSc exams.

I chose to specialize in econometrics because it had a logical structure that appealed to me. By understanding the logic, I didn't need to memorize the details; that was crucial to me. I visited London School of Economics (LSE) as a research student in the spring of 1979. This was clearly an eye opener for me. I realized there was a whole world outside the narrow circles of my own university, and that scientific criteria were completely different from those I was used to. I was fascinated by this. In Helsinki I had studied statistics without any guidance and I could easily have stopped after my Licentiate degree without getting a PhD. I was not sufficiently focused, but London School of Economics provided me with the focus that I needed.

Who was there at that time?
Katarina: David Hendry had been there and left, but his spirit was still there. I read many of his papers and was excited about them. Andrew Harvey and Jim Durbin were there, and Rob Engle visited the LSE for a year. There was a lot of theoretical time series work going on, but I guess I felt most positive towards David Hendry's ideas, partly because they seemed to represent a more novel approach to do time series econometrics. It also appealed to me that his paper conveyed an urge to go behind the theoretical model and understand the mechanisms that had generated the data.

Let's go back to you, Søren.
Søren: As I said before, from 1958 to 1964, I developed a strong background in mathematics, probability and statistics.

You did very technical proofs, right?
Søren: Yes, you are quite right; I was very much a mathematician. Around that time, the Professor of Statistics was Anders Hald, who introduced R.A. Fisher's ideas of statistics in Denmark. The idea of creating a statistics curriculum in the 1960s was a new idea. It involved trying to combine the British interest in applied statistics with the formal mathematical training that we had. So throughout our studies, we had this combination of a genuine interest in applications with a genuine interest in model formulation and analysis of the model. I did a lot of work in mathematics. In 1965, after my studies, I went to Berkeley for a year. I remember I took a course with Loeve who was a professor of probability, and I was presenting some complicated work in Choquet theory. So I spent a lot of time doing mathematics. My primary interest was, however, in statistics and the analysis of statistical models. I pursued my interest in probability theory for ten years, and then started collaborating with medical doctors on modeling the liver and analyzing their data.

What led to that collaboration? That is quite a shift from statistical and probability theory work.

Søren: We were always taking in applied work throughout my education and subsequent teaching. We would contact people in biology and medicine and talk to them about the problems they were analyzing. We would then introduce the data and their statistical analysis in our teaching. Our ambition was that no practical exercise was ever based on simulated data; it was all real data. Sometimes data were chosen to fit what we were teaching in the course, but basically the data analysis we taught was always inspired by problems from the natural sciences.

One of the contacts was the medical doctor Susanne Keiding, and that turned into a long and very interesting collaboration. The medical doctors were doing research on the liver because they wanted to prepare for the day when Danish hospitals could transplant a liver. So they set up this system of experiments on pigs in order to see if they could make quantitative measurements of the function of the liver. I found that very interesting. Apart from the medical collaboration, I kept my interest in pure mathematics, so I was still publishing a lot in statistical and mathematical journals.

That takes me up through 1982 when I gave a lecture at the Nordic Statistics Meeting entitled "Some topics in regression". I used the medical data as an illustration. Katarina was there and she introduced me to statistical work done in economics; in particular she showed me Clive Granger's discussion paper (1983) on the duality between error correction and cointegration which contained the first analysis of the so-called Granger representation theorem. Katarina asked me to explain the mathematical and statistical problems surrounding Granger's work and it became clear to me that one could probably build a beautiful statistical theory on these ideas. I took it as a challenge and began working on the topic. This has continued now for 25 years. In the beginning, most of the work was about understanding the mathematics of the structures that Granger had suggested, not the statistics. That led to a completely incomprehensible paper that I wrote in 1985, entitled "On the mathematical structure of cointegration models", which was published some years later. More importantly, it led to the paper, "Statistical analysis of cointegration vectors" in the *Journal of Economic Dynamics and Control* (1988b).

Is that the paper you did for the Econometrics Society in Copenhagen that you submitted late and it was almost not accepted?

Søren: That's right; the Econometrics Society Meeting was in Copenhagen in 1987. In 1985, I had done the mathematical structure, and I had started thinking about how to do the statistics. I was, of course, used to working with analysis of variance and regression, but I'd never worked with time series before. However, it was pretty obvious that the mathematics of this reduced rank formulation was similar to an additive decomposition in the analysis of variance. I'd seen papers in *Biometrika* on multiplicative decompositions, which lead to eigenvalue solutions. So the whole idea of working with the multiplicative formulation of reduced rank was very natural. I was also familiar with multivariate analysis, and the multivariate normal distribution. But even though I knew a lot of what Ted Anderson had written, I did not know what is now called reduced rank regression. In fact that was pointed out to me by Helmut Lütkepohl at the meeting in Copenhagen.

Nonetheless, I managed to produce the formula for the maximum likelihood estimator and the asymptotic distribution of the rank test, just after the deadline for submitting papers to the meetings. But Timo Teräsvirta on the program committee was kind enough to accept it.

At the meeting, the introductory lecture on co-integration was given by Rob Engle, and he kindly included some of my results in his survey. So there was a lot of interest in the results, already from the very beginning. Many people found it exciting to work on inference for co-integration. Of course it happened at roughly the same time as Peter Phillips was working on his triangular system representation for estimating co-integration, and Ahn and Reinsel were actually working on exactly the same model. So many people at different places in the world came up with similar ideas at the same time. It often happens. So that takes us to about 1987.

The two of you met in 1982? Did you start collaborating immediately?
Søren: No, I think that we started collaborating in 1983–1984. It must have been around 1982 or 83 when Katarina asked me to present a paper on Clive's ideas. I wish I had that first copy of Clive's discussion paper because it was never published. But, one of the papers that really led me to understand the formulation of the problem was a paper by Mark Salmon. He has not worked on co-integration since then, but he had some mathematical ideas that were very useful for thinking about such systems, for instance, how you reduce the order of integration by differencing. It was a very nice paper.

Katarina: At the same time as Søren was developing the statistical theory, I decided to apply the co-integrated VAR to the Danish money demand relation. Because it turned out to be incredibly stable over time (probably one of the most stable relations ever seen in macroeconomics), it was an excellent data set for the illustrative purpose at hand. I can think of many, many other applications which would have driven me to despair, and probably never would have led to anything. To develop ideas and questions from a data set where things actually work is much easier than to work with some of these terrible data sets.

So, Katarina, were you teaching in Helsinki at that time?
Katarina: Yes, until 1985 when I moved to Copenhagen and started teaching there.

And Søren, by 1986 you had left your work on medicine and moved to economics?
Søren: Actually, that happened a couple of years before. Susanne Keiding moved to Aarhus and got a job where research was not her main responsibility, so our collaboration died out after a while. Her move coincided with my interests changing from one type of application to another.

What's the difference between the two applications?
Søren: Well the economic application involves time series analysis, which, initially, I really didn't know anything about. I had to learn it by myself. The medical application was basically (non-linear) regression of the velocity of the metabolism of sugar or alcohol as a function of concentration. The regressor was extremely accurately measured. The measurements were gathered under experimental conditions. The biological models for these metabolisms were only partly understood, and I actually ended up writing a paper on a mathematical extension of a theoretical biological model. Otherwise the group produced many papers, where I was the last author, and only did the statistical appendix.

It was very interesting to work with medical people. First of all, they are extremely competent people and they really appreciated the collaboration. They were not afraid of asking questions or exposing their need for statistical help. They accepted that I was an expert, but at something else. That was a very positive attitude.

You have not found that as much in economics?
Søren: I found that my work with Katarina was immediately accepted by many econometricians, and I have had many interested and competent collaborators in the econometrics profession. I have not collaborated so much with theoretical economists, probably because my background is too different and their interest in analyzing data is not so pronounced.

You went to San Diego in 1985 and then to Baltimore. Who was there, and what role did those visits play in your thinking about co-integration?
Søren: In San Diego there were Clive Granger, Rob Engle and Hal White. They were the main people we interacted with. It was a wonderful place,

and I went back for three months in 1989. It was at that time I wrote the two papers mentioned above. After San Diego Katarina and I wrote three additional papers together – one on the basic model where we worked out the rank tests for different deterministic terms as an extension of the statistical modeling paper, the next one on hypothesis testing for the co-integrating vectors and the third one on the identification of the long-run structure. This was a fruitful collaboration because the theory was developed in close contact with the applications. It is the reason why the results are being used a lot.

Katarina: A good illustration of how empirical analysis can guide the theoretical work is an early work on purchasing power parity, and uncovered interest rate parity. It was based on two price levels, exchange rates and two interest rates for Germany and Denmark. The results were very puzzling. The test suggested a rank of three, implying three stationary co-integration relationships. But the graphs of these relations clearly indicated they were highly non-stationary. However, the graphs of the cointegration relations when the short-run effects had been concentrated out were completely stationary. This suggested that the nominal variables were I(2), that co-integration in such a model is from I(2) to I(1), and finally that stationarity can be achieved by combining the I(1) co-integration relations with a linear combination of the differences. It also suggested a straightforward way of analyzing I(2) models using the two-step procedure. Later on the two-step procedure was replaced by the ML procedure. But, the whole I(2) approach was initiated by first looking at the empirical results, and then discussing why they looked so peculiar.

The approach you're following is used more in Europe than in the United States. Would you agree? And if so, why?
Katarina: I think it is correct in the sense that the number of people who press the J button when applying the co-integration method is much larger in the United States than in Europe. Having said this, there are generally too many papers applying our approach without really understanding the methodology and they also come from Europe.

Søren: That's a good question. There was a time some five, ten years ago where any decent econometric conference would have six or seven sessions on co-integration. That has died out. The novelty is gone.

Katarina: I believe this is a natural progression. In the beginning papers were accepted just because they had applied the novel co-integration approach. Now a paper is not accepted just because it is a co-integration analysis, it has to be something more.

Søren: I think there was a time when all the theoretical econometricians were working on topics related to this methodology and many were applying it. Now many econometricians work on other topics – panel data, financial econometrics, factor models, analysis of large data sets, and so on. But the people who make a living on analyzing the usual monthly or quarterly data sets – they routinely apply co-integration methods, and that is possible because the programs are there.

Katarina: Unfortunately, this is not a method that can be applied routinely using standard co-integration software; it requires interaction between the analyst and the data; it is a powerful tool for an expert to use, not a tool for someone who doesn't understand the methodology.

What do you mean, it is not a method that can be used routinely?
Katarina: A good co-integration analysis is when you structure the information in the data, so that the complexity of the empirical reality can be grasped and better understood. I strongly doubt that one will ever get a program that does such an analysis for you. Serious data analysis is a long process that requires a very systematic study; continually working with the data, trying different specifications until reaching the point where one can say: now I understand the basic features of the data (statistically as well as economically). To achieve a baseline model that it makes sense to continue working with, you have to carefully check for misspecifications – whether the sample period is correctly chosen, whether there have been intuitional changes that need to be corrected for, and so on. These steps are enormously important. If you sidestep them, believing that you just need to press the button and out come some useful results, you will get nonsense. Always!

Søren: In other words, the reason it is a useful tool is that it is based on the analysis of the model. Before you use the results from this particular model you have to check the assumptions behind it. This is not understood in the econometric literature. So there is now something called the Johansen Procedure, and it is completely misleading to believe it can be applied to data that are fractionally integrated or heteroskedastic, or whatever. The Johansen procedure consists of checking the assumptions and then once you know the model is reasonably OK, you go and apply it. It is not just pressing the J button – that is certainly completely inappropriate – but this is unfortunately how it has often been used. It may look like you are doing sophisticated econometric work, but what you are doing is probably close to worthless. My contribution to co-integration analysis was simply to analyze the maximum likelihood estimator and the likelihood ratio test in the Gaussian model. But before you use maximum likelihood, you have to be sure that you have the right model, otherwise the estimator and test do not have the optimal properties you think they have.

Most econometrics is still taught as methods – almost like a cookbook where you have recipes for method 1, method 2, and method 3. That's not the way Katarina and I approach the data. We first choose the method that fits the circumstances. It needs a lot more careful thinking than is usually associated with writing an applied paper in econometrics. Of course, this has nothing to do with co-integration, but it has everything to do with carefully applying statistical methods to data. With modern computers, it is getting easier to do, but it is also getting easier to do it wrong.

Now let us move to 1994 – 1995. Søren, that's the time you moved from Copenhagen to Florence.
Søren: In 1996, I took a position at the European University Institute in Florence.

How was that different?
Søren: It was like night and day. I was suddenly there representing mathematics and statistics. The students I got there – and I had many PhD students – were completely different from the students I had in Copenhagen, which were from a much smaller and more homogeneous group. The Copenhagen students had five years of hard training in mathematics and statistics, and after that they would continue for three years as PhD students, often going to United States for a year. They would choose a new direction in which to go, and then follow it. Their dissertation was directed toward producing new theory. Of course, they may not have done everything in three years, but after having defended their thesis, they would continue to develop theory. Many of the statisticians I trained in Denmark have been very successful.

In Florence the idea was completely different. Students came to Florence with an interest in some economic phenomenon, and picked up whatever they needed to do a PhD. It sometimes looks as if a student could start a PhD in economics if he or she has a good background in philosophy, mathematics or physics. I often felt that there was very little background knowledge I could rely on the students having. On the other hand, they were extremely engaged students – but supervision was quite different from what I was used to. It was, however, an interesting experience. I ended up being chairman of the economics department, which is something I'm very proud of.

Do you see yourself as an economist?
Søren: No. I'm not an economist; I don't really understand economics.

What do you mean you don't understand it?
Søren: Because I don't understand the economic motivation for acting in real life and I do not understand how economists think when they model an economic problem. I have no tools to discuss whether something is good or bad economics. It is in that sense I am not an economist. I hope I have never given any other impression. I have, of course, been a co-author on papers which have economic content.

Katarina, do you see yourself as an economist or a statistician?
Katarina: There have been periods when I preferred not to be called an economist. I think it was because there was an enormous gap between the issues I thought were important and the ones my colleagues were discussing. What I found in the data by structuring them in short-run and long-run components was often quite different from what one finds in standard economic text books and totally different from what I saw in the most influential research papers. I became increasingly concerned about that, in particular as I found that many theoretical economists did not seem to care. I am quite convinced that if the economic reality had been more in accordance with standard theory models, the co-integrated VAR model would probably have been embraced with much enthusiasm by theorists as well. As the economic reality *is* very different from the empirical results we find in many high-ranking journals, I cannot help suspecting that these might have been obtained by torturing the data until they confessed. I believe this is what the present incentive system does to economics: it encourages scholars to maximize A and B journal publications, rather than to search for "the truth". The reluctance among economists to take the empirical reality seriously has convinced me that economics is too important to be left to the theorists alone.

What are the central results that differ from your statistical analysis from those in economics?
Katarina: I would first of all say that most theoretical models seem to make sense in a stationary world, but not necessarily in a non-stationary world. This is a very important point as most time-series data can be shown to be non-stationary. Another point is the *ceteris paribus* assumption which allows you to keep certain variables fixed in a theory model. In an empirical model you have to bring these *ceteris paribus* variables into the analysis by conditioning. If these *ceteris paribus* variables are stationary, the conclusions are more likely to remain robust, but if they are non-stationary,

the conclusions often change completely. The third point concerns expectations. From the early outset it became obvious that structuring the data using our approach would never provide anything that even vaguely resembled model-consistent rational expectations behavior, not even as an equilibrium condition. So I think these three elements are the central points of difference. Since most theory models contain all three elements, I often felt I had no ground to stand on. How can you go on doing anything when the most fundamental building bricks are not there? It was a difficult period until I gradually began to see how one should re-organize the information in the data so that they started to make economic sense again. Still, many economists would not accept that it makes sense, because it does not necessarily do so in a stationary world. However, I believe it does make sense in a non-stationary world.

But, admittedly, I would never have expected the empirical results to deviate so significantly from standard theory. In the beginning I thought our procedure would provide an efficient way of getting parameter estimates which had previously been difficult to estimate properly. I never expected that the results and the conclusions would be so different. Discovering that the empirical results often suggested that some very fundamental relationships, based on which most theory was relying, were lacking support in the data was a real shock. For a long time I simply didn't know what to do about it.

How would you say that the approach that you follow differs from that of Chris Sims, for example?
Katarina: Chris Sims, because he is a Bayesian, would not, for example, use likelihood inference on the orders of integration and co-integration of the data as a structuring device. We argue, for example, that the order of integration of a variable is extremely useful because one can tell from the outset that a non-stationary variable cannot be related to a stationary variable. In this case you need the non-stationary variables to be co-integrated before you can associate them with a stationary variable. I don't think Chris would accept that by exploiting the information in the data given by the integration/co-integration properties of the variables he could improve the specification of his economic model. Perhaps, one difference is that with the Bayesian analysis it is not easy to know when you are wrong, whereas with our approach the whole idea is to find out when, where and why you are wrong.

Could you expand on your criticism of the Bayesian approach?
Søren: Some people use Bayesian analysis in order to reach a compromise between a VAR model that is a good statistical description of the data,

and the theory model which is a bad description of the data. So they put a prior on the parameters of the VAR model which emphasizes the theory model. This is a compromise between theory and reality, which is very strange to me. One way of expressing my concern is that such an analysis can not tell if the theoretical model needs modifications. There are lots of situations where Bayesian analysis is the reasonable thing to do, such as monitoring of patients in medicine, analyzing pedigrees, or constructing optimal sampling inspection plans. But when you use it as a cover-up for a discrepancy between model and data, then I can't go along.

What is a model?

Søren: You'd have to say what type of a model, for example, probability model, statistical model or economic model. I think the model is an important tool for formulating your understanding of the phenomenon you are talking about. There is a quotation by Mark Katz that I put in my book, which states that although models have to be used for forecasting, the real function of a model is that it allows you to pose sharp questions. But precise questions are not enough. You still need criteria for rejecting models. In the natural sciences the criteria for rejecting models are more clear-cut. You do experiments to bring the model to the empirical evidence.

What I'm missing in some of the macro work is the idea of using empirical evidence to find out if there is a need to modify the theory. That idea does not seem to be around a lot. The reason why, I suspect, is that it is extremely difficult to model economic phenomena.

So does your new book build economic models?

Katarina: No, it does not. I'm just trying to present a framework in which economists would be able to go back to their theory model and properly test their assumptions – bringing those assumptions to the data. If the outcome of the empirical testing is that a particular assumption isn't in the data and that the economic conclusions using that assumption are not robust, it is an important signal to the decision maker. Using this framework allows one to do sensitivity analyses – seeing how the answer might change if one modifies the economic model in an empirically more relevant direction.

One important example is that most theory models are based either explicitly or implicitly on the *ceteris paribus* assumption – real exchange rates, real interest rates, and interest rate spreads are all stationary. For example, such stationarity assumptions are consistent with essentially all Rational Expectations (RE) models. When you relax these assumptions, allowing for non-stationarity you get into a world of imperfect knowledge economics (IKE), where agents are behaving rationally but the outcome is very different from a world of model consistent RE economics. Based on numerous applications (small, large, open, closed economies) I have found that the stationarity of the parity assumptions does not hold – the persistent movements away from the parities are simply inconsistent with the RE assumption. The policy implication this has for our economies is serious and requires a complete rethinking of our policy models.

What is one of your robust findings?
Katarina: One of the most robust and interesting findings is that the deviations from some of the basic parities – the Fisher parity, the term spread, the purchasing power parity, the uncovered interest rate parity – exhibited a persistence that is empirically close to unit root behavior and clearly untenable with standard rational expectations' theories. Instead, we have found that the domestic–foreign long-term interest rate spread is co-integrated with the PPP (the real exchange rate). This finding is extremely robust; I have found it everywhere. It turned out that exactly this empirical regularity was one of the predictions from the IKE theory developed by Frydman and Goldberg. It led us to start working together and the results look extremely promising. Another robust finding is that inflation and the short-long interest rate spread – both approximately I(1) – are often co-integrated. If the latter is considered a measure of inflationary expectations then it says that inflation and inflationary expectations move together (which is not so surprising). A very robust finding is, however, that it is inflation that adjusts upward (though with a tiny coefficient) when the short-term interest rate increases more than the long-term (presumably as a result of a monetary policy reaction). This of course is not the intended effect and suggests that CPI inflation has primarily been influenced by aggregate supply (cost push pressure) rather than by aggregate demand (demand pull pressure).

What implication for policy do these findings have?
Katarina: The fact that equilibrium in the goods market is not necessarily associated with purchasing power parity but with a relation between PPP and the interest rate spread, in which both can be non-stationary, implies that the real exchange rate can persistently appreciate, say, as long as the domestic interest rate increases more than the corresponding foreign rate. These persistent movements are essentially due to speculative behavior in the market for foreign exchange – when agents' forecasts are based on imperfect knowledge, that is not knowing the right model, nor the right variables – and hence, are basically outside domestic control. So, one implication is that by deregulating capital markets politicians have to a large extent deposited the power to influence the domestic economy into the hands of the financial market.

Today's monetary policy is mostly based on the assumption that central banks can control CPI inflation by controlling the short-term interest rate. To efficiently do so would among others require that the above parities hold as stationary conditions. When they do not, an important part of the standard transmission mechanism is missing. I have seen little evidence that the short-term interest rate is an efficient instrument for CPI inflation control, even though the inflation rate, admittedly, has been low in the period of inflation targeting. However, my claim (backed up by numerous empirical results) is that that it has been so for other reasons, primarily global competition, and would have been so independently of monetary policy interest rate changes. When this is said Central Bank interest rate control is definitely extremely important for real growth and employment in the domestic economy. One recent and still preliminary result is that the low interest rates we have seen over the last decades have increased excess liquidity, and this seems to have caused the recent increase in house price inflation and stock price inflation, while not CPI inflation.

What is the future of co-integrated VAR models over the next ten years?
Søren: The model has found its way into many textbooks, and it will stay as a useful methodology. You can then say that as long as these four, five or six macro variables need to be analyzed, it needs to be there. But there are lots of extensions now. One is to combine with volatility models; another is to combine with non-linear models, but the data requirements of these extensions are larger than in the usual macro models. I think that co-integration will be around as long as we are analyzing non-stationary time series.

Katarina: Though I agree with Søren, I have a somewhat different view of the future of co-integration. I believe that the future will see more applications of larger and more realistic VAR models at the expense of these very small, partial models which seldom can say something interesting about the economy. By gradually increasing the information analyzed by the VAR model it should be possible to obtain a more realistic picture of the sensitivity of the *ceteris paribus* assumptions for empirical conclusions. In the end I believe this is a powerful way of obtaining an empirically relevant understanding of our complicated economic reality. I also believe the VAR model will be further developed towards an expert system. These extensions are necessary for the models to become really useful.

Would these expanded models replace standard macro econometric models?
Katarina: To start with let's consider the big Cowles Commission type of macro models everyone likes to hate. They consist of a set of behavioral

relations, assuming endogeneity and exogeneity, tied together into a big structure. One could take these blocks of behavioral relationships and do a co-integrated VAR analysis of each of them. Based on such an analysis one can get Maximum Likelihood estimates of the parameters of the behavioral relations, possibly identifying new relations, but more importantly, one can also learn about the dynamics in this part of the economy – what are the pushing forces and what are the pulling forces. In the end, you can combine these partial dynamical models into a much bigger model resembling something that may come close to a more general long-run equilibrium model.

What are some of the challenges that you faced along the way of developing your approach?
Katrina: The first challenge came when realizing that most economic series were in fact non-stationary but the statistical theory available for analyzing them was developed for stationary processes. The question was whether it implied that all results based on stationary processes were more or less useless. Luckily, it turned out that the only non-standard distribution that had to be found was the one for the trace test which was needed to determine the co-integration rank. But after the rank was found, it was straightforward to transform your non-stationary data using differencing and co-integration and you were back in a stationary world again. It was a great relief to realize that standard statistical theory could be used again – that is one could test hypotheses using Student's t-tests, chi-squared tests, and F-tests.

Then the second challenge occurred when I started to analyze economic data more seriously. Nothing seemed to fit with what I had expected. Then it was the same type of doubt knocking on the door; what to do with the theory models after I had empirically rejected many underlying assumptions. This phase took much longer. I felt I was in no man's land. It is only in the last ten years that I have found a way to bring the old theories back. Now I can see that they are useful, provided they can be reformulated to fit the features I've learned from the data analysis. For example, the non-stationarity of the data implies that the model can contain a static long-run relationship, but it has to be combined with a dynamic adjustment relationship. But the most crucial thing was to get to know the theory behind Imperfect Knowledge Economics. I am convinced that this theory will eventually bring empirical evidence and theory together in a relevant framework.

Let's now talk a bit about the changes going on in the European economics profession. What is your view of these changes?

Katarina: I have been quite critical of the ongoing attempts to make European Economics a "carbon copy" (if I may use your illustrative analogy) of American Economics. In my view it has had the (unintended?) effect of streamlining the way we think, make research, and make policy, which I find extremely unfortunate. In many ways I believe many things have gone in the wrong direction over the last decades. We have all these fantastic electronic tools, fast computers, sophisticated software, the internet, etc. that should help us improve our research productivity. But it often seems to me that we are pressing the buttons and producing results at an ever increasing speed, without allowing for the fact that novel, genuine thinking is a painfully slow process for most of us. While previously European research was allowed to take time (admittedly this also led to waste) it has nowadays been replaced by the "publish or perish" culture with "quality" weighted publication counts adopted from the United States system. With this incentive system there is however an inherent risk that young PhD students, in particular, will choose quick and safe research topics, while more complex topics, of possibly high relevance for our society, might be considered too risky. With regard to my own students, I have to tell them from the outset that I am willing to guide them through an exciting, interesting, frustrating research process, that their empirical results are likely to challenge the standard view on macro and may suggest how to improve policy, but that the results will hardly be publishable in the top United States journals. Just to give an illustration: to help young scholars into a US top journal publication, I have suggested how to rewrite their paper to maximize the chance of getting past the "gate keepers" of the journal. This involves among others: not mentioning in the abstract, introduction and the conclusions any critical results that demonstrate flaws in previously published work of the journal; emphasizing any result that might be interpreted as evidence for the views held by the editors. This, in my view, is one of the unfortunate (and probably unintended) effects of the change in the European incentive system to mimic the US system.

Another less desirable effect is the streamlining of research. Some 10–15 years ago I found it exciting to participate in the Econometric Society Meetings because of the lively debates and the exchange of ideas. Nowadays I tend to find it almost a waste of time: you present your paper to a small audience of people who most likely agree with your ideas (otherwise they would not be there); you might go to one or two of the main invited lectures and that's it. But the debate and the excitement seem somehow to be gone. On the other hand, why should one get excited about yet another twist of a DSGE model when it is quite obvious that its basic assumptions would not pass any serious econometric tests, or about a new

epsilon change in a representative agent, infinite horizon rational expectations model, or about yet another twist of an econometric test developed
for a very special situation with little generality outside its narrow context?
But many of these papers are likely to find their way to good journals.

Søren: I have certainly also seen the changes going on in Europe in the
academic world, but I do not have enough knowledge about economics to
discuss the consequences for the economics profession.

How could the changes be made so that they work more positively?
Katarina: Before suggesting possible changes it is important to discuss
why there have been all these recent changes in the incentive structures
of European economics. Few politicians would deny the importance of
today's information society and, hence, of the university that provides
the information. This, of course, explains why there is this strong political interest in how we manage our universities: whether we do enough
research; whether the research is of sufficiently high quality and of relevance to the society. As an illustration, our Danish research minister uses
the slogan "from innovation to invoice" to stress that our research should
produce jobs! He is also the one who introduced quality weighted publications as a basis for university funding. As the A journals mostly consist of
United States top journals, European economists, to be promoted or to
get a job in the first case, are more or less forced to direct their research
toward these journals. Since United States journals are not necessarily
interested in specific European conditions, our economists have instead
to engage in the United States economics discussion, which may not be
highly relevant for Europe. The numerous objections by the profession
that such criteria by themselves are likely to lead to distortions over time,
and that there are infinitely many irrelevant ways of measuring quality
research and probably no relevant ones, have no visible effect. So we seem
to be stuck with these rules.

Finally, a large part of research funding is now tied to strategic research
projects chosen by the government. Furthermore, previously autonomous
government research agencies have now been incorporated with our universities. Even though the Danish experience might be somewhat excep-
tional, I believe similar developments have taken place in other European
countries. This in my view is a serious threat to European research diversity, at least in economics, but probably also in other sciences.

You've read our introductory essay; any comments on it? What did we miss?
Katarina: You speak a lot about the diversity of ideas in Europe, but there
is another aspect that is important: the strong sense of competition typical

of the United States system is not at all as pronounced here in Europe. I do not think it is any coincidence that the journal, university, and scholar rankings were invented in the United States. You have a long tradition for asking "who is the best, who has the most original idea, etc". In Europe we did not have this strong feeling of competition: university life was much more about debating, arguing, and working together.

There used to be a lot of generosity among scholars, a willingness to share new ideas rather than hiding them until publication. When the theory of co-integration was worked out over the last decades it was the immense pleasure of working together as a group that made the whole thing worthwhile. That Søren was the top brain in all this was never disputed and therefore not anything we felt we had to compete with. This kind of collective desire to understand more by developing the procedure was an extremely appealing feature of our work that no pay increase or top journal publication ranking could have compensated for. I believe many research oriented professors have chosen to work at the university because they love the intellectual challenge, the stimulating discussions, the exciting ideas, not because of the pay they get. Over the last decade, the Danish government has introduced differentiated salaries for professors as a means to promote research efforts. It has not turned out to be very effective as few professors seem to care about negotiating for higher salaries.

Any final comments?
Katarina: I would like to thank all of you for putting all this effort into providing us with these insightful discussions on European economics, lining up our strengths, and weaknesses, and suggesting how to maximize the former while minimizing the latter. It has given me food for thought which I hope to be able to use in the ongoing public discussion about how to organize our universities.

9. Geoffrey Hodgson

This interview took place on 12 July, 2007, at Le Moulinage Ouest, Privas, Ardèche, France

How did you come to move from being a computer programmer in Essex in the mid-1960s and a mathematics teacher in Manchester to becoming an economist in the 1970s?

When I was between school and university, I used my mathematical knowledge as a computer programmer at a research institute in Essex in the 1960s. Computers were then slow and scarce. In 1963 Harold Wilson famously declared that a new Britain would be "forged in the white heat" of a scientific and technological revolution. Computers and technology were seen as instruments of a new rational order that would displace the ossified institutions of the past. In 1964 a socialist government was elected after 13 years of Conservatism in Great Britain, with Wilson as Prime Minister.

I studied for my first degree in mathematics and philosophy at the University of Manchester in 1965–68. I was affected by political movements like the campaign against the war in Vietnam and I got drawn into left-wing politics. I got interested in economics while I was doing my first degree in Manchester. I was attracted by a subject with greater social relevance. After four years as a school teacher in mathematics, I returned in 1972 to the University of Manchester to study for a master's degree in economics. I then got a job as a lecturer in economics. I have been in academia ever since.

*Your early work in Manchester seems related to that of Ian Steedman, with
an early paper on the Marxian Transformation problem (1974), on worker
participation (1982–83), your later book* After Marx and Sraffa *(1991),
and later papers and chapters in books on the Cambridge capital theory
controversies (1997). What are your views on that today, and how did you
move from that to your interest in evolutionary and institutionalist economics ("Post Keynesianism and Institutionalism", 1989)?*

In the 1970s I described myself as a Marxist – both politically and aca-
demically. But taking an analytical approach, I looked at the core of
Marxism, and over time I became a critic. After examining many of the
theoretical foundations of traditional Marxism, like the labor theory of
value, I became dissatisfied with Marxian theory.

When I studied economics at Manchester, Ian Steedman was my masters
advisor and I got involved with Sraffian critiques of Marxist theory. But
like Steedman I remained sympathetic towards aspects of Marxism. My
After Marx and Sraffa book was published in 1991, after I had moved on
and developed institutionalist ideas.

Regarding the Cambridge capital theory controversies, I think that the
Sraffa-based critique still remains a powerful internal attack on aggregate
capital theory. It successfully shows that aggregate production functions,
like the Cobb–Douglas, are based on very strict assumptions, which if
relaxed lead to outcomes quite different from those typically invoked by
mainstream economists. But I would make two qualifications. As Frank
Hahn pointed out in the *Cambridge Journal of Economics* (1982), you can
start from a disaggregated general equilibrium framework and reach the
same critical conclusion. I agree largely with this article. Work by Gerard
Debreu (1974), Rolf Mantel (1974) and Hugo Sonnenschein (1972) also
showed that obtaining aggregate regularities is a problem from a general
equilibrium perspective.

Not so much in United States, but in places like Great Britain and Italy,
Sraffian approaches enjoyed a phase of popularity in the 1970s. Some
post-Keynesians and others saw his work as not just an internal criticism
of neoclassical economics, but a foundation for a new system of economic
theory. Sraffian economics was seen less as an internal critical tool, but
more as the basis of a new heterodox theoretical construction that would
sustain Keynesian and other ideas. Advocates of this "constructivist"
approach included John Eatwell in Cambridge and Pierangelo Garegnani
in Italy.

*How did this approach relate to that of the post-Keynesian view in America of
Davidson and others and to the split within the post-Keynesian camp? Where
did this lead to, especially in conjunction with the debates over Marxism?*

I was never fully persuaded by the constructivist approach. I flirted with it as a possibility in my 1982 book, where I tried to marry Paul Davidson-type post-Keynesian economics with a Sraffian analysis. But in trying this I realized all the problems and limitations, particularly with the introduction of money, dynamics and uncertainty. For me this was the beginning of the end. They were different approaches that could not be reconciled. This realization, with my earlier criticism of Marxism, led me to search for an alternative approach.

I wanted to address a problem that I saw in heterodox critiques of neoclassical economics. It is particularly striking that in both Marxism and Sraffian economics there is little sense of what the individual is and what the individual is going to do. Even in neoclassical economics there is an individual preference function. When it comes to the nature of the individual, the economics of Marx and Sraffa are even more impoverished. Most heterodox approaches then focused on macroeconomics and lacked an adequate alternative microeconomic theory.

My search for an alternative theory of the individual, which would be informed in particular by psychology, led me to Thorstein Veblen and the early institutionalists. I was also influenced by economists such as George Shackle and Herbert Simon, who emphasized the profound uncertainty of the human condition and the limited computational capacity of the human brain.

While I was visiting Bennington College in 1980–81 I came to the conclusion that unless there was some alternative to the neoclassical view of human agency then the heterodox game had to be given up. At the time, Marxists like John Roemer had bought into neoclassical microeconomics and were applying to Marxist issues such as class. "Analytical Marxism" was in vogue, but it was little more than neoclassical economics dressed up in Marxist language. As Joseph Stiglitz stated in 1993, there is little difference between standard neoclassical theory and this version of Marxism.

At this fundamental level, either you need to accept the neoclassical view or find an alternative. This drew me to the original institutionalism. I searched for a serious critique of individual rational choice theory, for an alternative to traditional neoclassical preference functions, and for foundations for an alternative microeconomics.

How did this relate to your political views and activities through this period?
Margaret Thatcher's election in 1979 affected me deeply. Although her policies led Britain into a very deep recession, behind her there were people with intellectual credibility who were waging an intellectual debate. I did not like many of their arguments, but I felt that the British Left and others had failed to understand or come to terms with them. Friedrich

Hayek in particular stressed problems of uncertainty and tacit knowledge and the limits of rational design. My own ideas had moved on since the early 1970s. I was already convinced of the importance of these Hayekian themes.

I read up on the socialist calculation debate. After wrestling with the detailed arguments of Hayek, von Mises and others, I concluded that many left-wing thinkers had an inadequate understanding of the importance of the market. I was already convinced that some significant use of market mechanisms was unavoidable in any complex developed economy. But I did not follow the Thatcherite intellectuals in their view of the market as a universal panacea.

At this time there was a strong current in the British Labour Party that would minimize the power of the market. Tony Benn and others favored democratic planning and lambasted "market forces". But they evaded the practical details of their alternative society. I came to the conclusion that socialism was in deep trouble unless it was able to reconcile itself at some level with market mechanisms. This was an Achilles heel within socialist thought. Complete overall planning – whether bureaucratic or democratic – of a modern complex economy was impossible. The problems of complexity and localized knowledge ruled out such an option.

However, the Hayek extreme of a fully marketized system is just as inconceivable as a fully planned economy. No society can or does surrender everything to the market. Neither the traditional Left nor the market fundamentalists had an adequate explanation of the mixed nature of all advanced economies. Addressing more mixed and variegated solutions, I abandoned Marxism and became a social democrat. (In the United States context I would be described as a liberal.)

A central focus of your work on evolutionary and institutional economics is Thorstein Veblen. Is he the most influential economist for your current view on where economics should be going?
For me, Veblen in many ways is one of the most influential of economists. But his impact on me was not immediate. Reading him is difficult because his prose is dense and idiosyncratic. He is a deep but not a systematic thinker. His prose is very measured – every word counts. But sometimes he fails to structure his discourse in a logical way.

One reason why Veblen is important is because he takes on board the psychological insights of William James and others. This pragmatist psychology has strong connections with Darwinian theory. This leads to a rethink of human agency, where features such as consciousness and deliberation have to be placed in an evolutionary context. Instincts and habits become important as underpinnings of reasons and beliefs. This evolutionary approach supplants a mind-first perspective where mental capacities are simply assumed.

Much theory in economics and other social sciences starts from an agent having a set of beliefs who then deliberates about what to do. These views are belief-first or mind-first. To some degree they make sense, since you can't explain everything at once. But any such assumptions need to be consistent with an understanding of where our minds come from, and with an evolutionary view of how we developed an ability to make reasoned choices. Veblen and James adopted an evolutionary perspective on the development of mind and thought. The essential move behind evolutionary thinking in this area is to regard deliberate rationalization as after the event. Before their decisions, individuals have feelings or dispositions that are biologically inherited or culturally acquired. These drives and emotions lie behind our choices.

Even in the process of abstract thought we are using intuitions. Studies of the process of scientific discovery also confirm their role. Mathematicians use their intuitions to begin to solve problems. Behind our rationalizations there are intuitions, feelings and emotions. This is an inversion of the mind-first theory, which Veblen takes on board with his emphasis on habits and instincts.

Compare this with the Marxian view, which relates the dispositions of individuals to the position in the social structure in which they are located. For Marx, the structure of the capitalist system bestows the capitalists with greedy dispositions and impels the workers to struggle for better wages. Marxism thus subsumes the individual into the social structure.

For Veblen, one cannot understand the texture of reality without focusing in part on individuals. For Marx, conditions for the socialist revolution are prepared by the development of capitalist social structures. Veblen is more detailed and specific, asking how workers develop a socialist outlook. Veblen criticizes Marx for losing sight of the individual. As well as relations between workers and capitalists, there are legal, social, historical and cultural differences that characterize different types of capitalist system. Classical Marxism misses this. There are different types of capitalism that traditional Marxism has difficulty explaining in adequate detail.

What was Veblen's role in evolutionary and institutional economics?
An important point about Veblen is his Darwinism; Veblen was the first economist to bring Darwinian ideas fully into the discipline. He saw that Darwin is too important to be left to the biologists. What Darwin gave us was a set of abstract principles to deal with a broad category of a complex evolving system. He developed a trinity of concepts: variation, selection

and inheritance. These concepts can be used to help to explain other complex systems, in addition to those in the biological sphere. Veblen understood this.

Veblen also understood the difference between Herbert Spencer and Darwin. By contrast, Spencer took as axiomatic a teleological view of evolution. Veblen followed Darwin more than Spencer, despite Spencer's enormous popularity at that time.

Using Darwinian theory in the social sphere does not mean biological reductionism. As Veblen stressed, culture and institutions remain as important explanatory factors, as well as biological characteristics. The processes of replication in social systems are very different from those in the biological sphere. Darwinian theory has generality, but it is not sufficient in itself to explain all the relevant mechanisms.

For Veblen, units of Darwinian selection in the social sphere include habits and institutions. He also considers their replication and durability, as well as the sources of variation and novelty.

Despite all this, Veblen's Darwinism was long ignored or downplayed, even by his institutionalist disciples. Even today there is no general consensus on this view of Veblen and his adoption of Darwinian theory. There is still a debate going on.

Historically this Darwinian agenda, promoted by Veblen and a few others, was abandoned by American institutionalism in the inter-war period. It did not return to the social sciences until Donald T. Campbell revisited it in 1965. Even after the rebirth of evolutionary economics in the 1980s, with the work of Kenneth Boulding, Richard Nelson and Sidney Winter, Darwinism remained off the agenda. It did not become more prominent for evolutionary economists until after 2000.

Is it true that Clarence Ayres was both Veblen's strongest advocate and his worst enemy, as you appear to have argued (2004)?
In some respects the role of Clarence Ayres is ironic for American institutionalism. He completely rejects Darwinian theory in his book on *Huxley* in 1932. He sees Darwin as out-of-date, throws out the Veblenian evolutionary research agenda, and regards Veblen's Darwinism as an awkward appendix instead of being a major core theme. When Ayres uses the term "evolution", it is not in reference to Darwin, but to express his notion of progress involving technological development and institutions. A technological imperative lies at the heart of Ayres's view of transformational economic growth; for him, institutions are negative impairments. Hence he argued that institutionalists should drop the term "institutional economics" and use "evolutionary economics". But the latter term did not refer to Darwinism but to his notion of technological advancement. Ayres

became very influential after the 1940s, but his radical break from Veblen was inadequately appreciated.

Ayres transformed institutional economics to fit the views of the time. During the inter-war period, behaviorist psychology had supplanted the psychology of James. Biologically grounded concepts such as instinct became deeply unpopular in the social sciences. In profound contrast to Veblen, Ayres was a behaviorist in psychology and he rejected the concept of instinct. Another characteristic of Ayres is his reliance on social entities to explain individual behavior. He wrote that there is no such thing as the individual. He took a similar line to the Marxists: the individual is explained by the social slot that they find themselves in. The adoption of Ayres's views meant a huge change within institutionalism, making it very different from Veblen but compatible with sociological views at the time. Significantly, Ayres taught Talcott Parsons, who was extremely influential on post-war sociology. Although he later rebelled against institutionalism, partly to maintain his credibility among orthodox economists, there is evidence that Parsons was influenced by Ayres's socially-determined view of the individual.

Ironically, the Association of Evolutionary Economics was thus named in the 1960s because Ayres and his followers did not like the term "institutionalism" and saw institutions as universal barriers to progress, but their embrace of the "evolutionary term" had nothing to do with Darwin. In fact they were uncomfortable with the Veblenian notion that Darwinian principles could be applied to economic or social evolution.

Do Veblen's views on evolutionary institutionalism have any link to complexity economics and the concept of emergence? Does this relate to your own more recent work with Thorbjørn Knudsen (2004, 2006)?

Veblen's evolutionary economics has strong actual or potential connections with the work of Simon and other behavioralists, agent-based modeling, computational economics, and much work on complexity that is going on today.

I once corresponded with Herb Simon. He said he was influenced by institutionalists, particularly John R. Commons. I showed Simon an article by the institutionalist J.M. Clark (1918), which contains a notion of bounded rationality. He had no recollection of reading this, but these ideas were in the air in the early decades of the twentieth century. Clark supervised Frank Knight, whose PhD dissertation also has a notion of bounded rationality. William James and the influential sociologist Charles Cooley had previously acknowledged limits to the human ability for rational computation.

Global and all-purpose rationality is challenged by these approaches. We function not through some type of maximizing or optimization process, but instead we are obliged to follow what Simon calls rules of thumb or heuristics. Veblen describes them as habits of thought.

As well as limited brain capacity, we also have the classic problem of dealing with other individuals and trying to estimate their intentions. Do we model other agents with very strong informational and rational assumptions, as in some versions of game theory? Or do we assume that agents do not have complete knowledge of other agents' intentions or choices?

The latter approach would move us into the area of heuristics solutions and algorithmic behavior, where there is limited common knowledge of rationality. Instead of a rigorous and complete analysis of the assumed rationality of others, we act according to heuristics or rough-and-ready rules, and assume that others are doing likewise. This is again redolent of Veblen and takes us into a radically new direction today.

One of your more famous papers would seem to be your 1993 Economic Journal *article on "The mecca of Alfred Marshall" (1993a). You noted his ambivalence towards evolutionary theory.*

In this 1993 paper I discuss the relationship between Marshall and Spencer, and more broadly Marshall's relationship with biology. I argue that in favoring Spencer over Darwin, Marshall backed the wrong horse. In many ways this was understandable because at the time that Marshall was writing his *Principles*, Spencer was at the height of his influence both in the UK and in the United States. Spencer overshadowed Darwin, partly because his work seemed to cover a broader area. Spencer had written volumes on psychology and sociology as well as biology. But by backing the wrong horse, Marshall's project was impaired. Spencer's teleological thinking later opened the door to an equilibrium-oriented interpretation of Marshallian theory. By contrast, in Darwinism any equilibrium is always temporary and accompanied by variety. We can only speculate what would have happened if Marshall had taken more of the Darwinian view.

More recently in my book *How Economics Forgot History* (2001), I revisit Marshall and discuss his relationship with the German historical school. Robert Skidelsky and other historians of thought have argued that Marshall was critical of this school, that he promoted this criticism in Cambridge, and that he downgraded economic history in favor of economic theory.

I think this account is wrong. Marshall studied with Karl Knies in Germany, who was a member of the historical school. In his *Principles*, his correspondence, and his inaugural lecture Marshall shows an immense respect for these German writers. This is not to underplay Marshall's important role in developing neoclassical economics. However, Marshall makes it clear that besides borrowing from other neoclassical thinkers, he was also influenced by the German historical school, including in matters of economic theory. Marshall did not believe he was in opposition to the German historical school, rather he was refining and developing their views.

It is also widely upheld that Marshall was engaged in a battle against the so-called English historical school. (In fact, most were Irish or Scottish, so let's call this school British.) In fact, Marshall was not against this school as such, but against certain members of it, William Cunningham in particular. Another prominent member was Herbert Foxwell, significantly a close friend of Marshall until 1906. Marshall and Foxwell fell out over Marshall's support for Arthur Pigou as his successor to the Cambridge chair in economics.

Marshall and Foxwell were not at odds with one another over matters of economic theory. But Marshall stood for international free trade, with Foxwell, Cunningham and others in favor of protectionism. If one makes the mistake of defining a theoretical school in terms of its policy output, then one exaggerates the divide between Marshall and Foxwell.

If there was one significant theoretical dispute between Marshall and the British historical school, it was the altercation between Marshall and Cunningham. Methodologically, Cunningham was very much a Comtean, saying that all we can do is look at history and facts, and we must not presuppose any methodological or theoretical view. From history some theory may emerge, but we cannot presuppose it.

Marshall criticized Cunningham for being atheoretical. In a much more sustainable argument, Marshall upheld that we need some preconceptions to order the information we receive about the world. On this point he was not attacking the British historical school as a whole; he was attacking Cunningham who represented an extreme and empiricist wing. Such crude empiricist thinking had become outmoded within the German historical school by the 1890s. Its leaders such as Gustav Schmoller had ruled out this extreme empiricist position and were more favorable toward theory. In his *Principles*, Marshall favorably quoted Schmoller and his view that theory and evidence are both required, as we need two legs for walking.

But did not Marshall play a crucial role in establishing neoclassical orthodoxy?

Sure enough, Marshall's role in establishing and synthesizing neoclassical partial equilibrium analysis was very important. But some have further argued that Marshall suppressed the heterodox and applied economists in Cambridge. As well as the Cunningham episode, they point to the backing of Marshall for the appointment of Pigou as his successor.

In fact, Marshall's support of Pigou is quite defensible. In terms of the quantity and quality of publications, Pigou was far ahead of all other candidates. Probably the closest rival was Foxwell, who had published much less. Pigou was a brilliant thinker and he became the sole chair in economics at Cambridge. But he was then very young. This meant a huge generational shift, and the historical school was forgotten because Pigou was not really familiar with it.

The isolationist mentality in Cambridge exacerbated the problem. There is a joke that Geoff Harcourt repeats about Cambridge: time is a device that stops everything from happening at once, space is a device to stop everything from happening at Cambridge. This joke captures a Cambridge attitude that downplays contributions from elsewhere.

The economics department at Cambridge was small. Pigou became a major architect of neoclassical welfare economics. He dominated Cambridge economics because there was only one chair in the economics department until the 1920s. When a second chair was established it was in economic history, and John Clapham was appointed. This belies the idea that Marshall or Pigou drove out history in favor of theory. They both recognized the need to balance theory with history.

In several papers (1993b; 1998) and books (2001, 2004), you have discussed the relationship between the "old" and "new" institutional economics. More recently you have founded and now edit the Journal of Institutional Economics. *How do you see these relating and can they be reconciled?*
In the 1993 article and in some later pieces I draw a line between much representative work in old institutionalism and the new. This line is whether or not it is deemed legitimate within economic theory to assume or accept endogenous preferences. The difference between the new and the old institutionalism is over whether the individual is taken as given or not.

But there are some problems with this line of division. Other economists such as Marshall, Marx, Schumpeter and Keynes also accepted that it is legitimate to accept endogenous preferences within economics. Yet they are not normally described as institutionalists. This means that this criterion is insufficient to define the old institutionalism. We also have to take into account that the original American institutional economics was a specific movement in a specific milieu.

There are further complications; there is massive heterogeneity within the old institutionalism, including between leading figures such as Veblen, Mitchell, Commons and Ayres. Their philosophical and psychological outlooks differ significantly and there was a substantial diversity in policy terms.

Similarly, there is immense heterogeneity within the new institutionalism.

For example, there are big differences between the new institutionalism of Masahiko Aoki and Oliver Williamson regarding their views of the firm. Compare also Williamson and Douglass North. North accepts the possible suboptimality of institutional evolution and emphasizes path dependence, but Williamson upholds some more-or-less efficient competitive selection process that reduces transaction costs. Williamson also has his differences with Ronald Coase over the nature of human agents and the concept of asset specificity. There is also a range of policy views within the new institutionalism, from advocates of free markets to critics such as Andrew Schotter. So there is enormous heterogeneity on both sides.

Also since 1990 there has been some acceptance of preference endogeneity by new institutionalists, particularly by North. Hence there is blurring of boundaries between these two major groups, and the former distinctions are less meaningful.

The Journal of Institutional Economics was founded in part to facilitate conversation between the old and new institutionalism. An important stage of development is occurring where differences are becoming less sharp. Instead of defining institutionalism by some methodological underpinnings, the journal looks at the role, nature, function, and mechanics of institutions in an economic context. Anyone – from any discipline – who believes that institutions are important will hopefully be attracted to this journal.

In your 1999 Economic Journal *paper with Harry Rothman, you criticized the "Diamond list" of 30 top journals that was being used for evaluating British economists in the Research Assessment Exercise (RAE), and posed an alternative ranking of journals that could be said to favor more heterodox journals. How was that alternative received?*
To correct you slightly, the purpose of this article was not to criticize the Diamond list, although anyone who looks closely at the historical derivation of that list will acknowledge that it is crudely and arbitrarily constructed and long out-of-date. Our purpose was also not to provide an alternative list.

Instead, the paper by Harry Rothman and me used a citation impact ranking to obtain a list of the "top 30" journals. This was not meant as an alternative list. Citation impact is a simple and least controversial means of selecting the most prominent journals by an objective (but admittedly imperfect) criterion. We noted the editors of these journals and the authors that get published within them. We found that the major part of both groups come globally from very few academic institutions, mainly in the United States. This was less a critique of the Diamond list and more about a globally oligopolistic peer evaluation and publication process that is concentrated in just a few institutions.

We argued that this institutional concentration was a potential threat to the processes of scientific creativity. We focused on the issue of scientific innovation and suggested that we should consider alternative methods and networks of peer evaluation that allow for a wider range of views.

The United States now dominates economics to an unprecedented extent. Former rival centers of excellence such as Britain have declined in relative and absolute terms. If you consider Great Britain 30 years ago there were several internationally well known British economists like Nicholas Kaldor, Joan Robinson, Piero Sraffa, George Shackle, Edith Penrose and others. Sadly, with this generation dying off they have not been replaced with so many globally familiar names. British economics is much less prominent today.

Why did this happen in Britain?

The global prestige of British economics has gone down, and at the same time it has become narrower and more homogeneous. Much of this transition occurred in the 1980s and 1990s. There are several reasons, but two come to mind. First, the government of Margaret Thatcher severely constrained university growth by holding down their budgets. Second, economics became a less popular subject and a number of students shifted into the business schools. Economics became regarded as highly technical and esoteric, and the fashion among students was for more vocational and business-oriented courses. Consequently, economics departments found themselves even more squeezed financially than the universities as a whole. There were limited opportunities for new hiring, and for people with innovative ideas.

Consequently there are research areas that developed in the United States during the 1980s and 1990s that were not developed in the United Kingdom. One example would be Williamson-type transaction cost economics. Despite its global prestige and popularity, there are still relatively few people working in this area in the United Kingdom. In another relatively new area, there are some experimental economists, such as at the University of Nottingham. But despite some important work, overall this is not a strong area for British economics. The costs of experimental work are significant in this case. Consequently, many new recruits in economics departments are in standard areas of inquiry like game theory and econometrics. Economics departments have become more like highly specialized departments of applied mathematics.

How has the Research Assessment Exercise (RAE) affected British economics?

I am not in principle against research assessment. It is necessary because of the vast expansion of the university system in recent decades. Larger university systems take up large amounts of public expenditure and there is some kind of responsibility to the public to account for the money that is spent. Also an objective of this evaluation in Britain was to stimulate research, where some academics – even in prestigious universities – were not doing a lot.

The impact of the Research Assessment Exercise was different in different disciplines and depended on specific assessment processes and mechanisms. In economics the responsibility for the assessment was devolved to the Royal Economic Society, which is dominated by orthodox economists. This created a dynamic which further constrained and narrowed the development of economics in Britain. Despite a widespread belief to the contrary, this group did not announce an official list of suitable journals. But there is a second order process where departments second-guess what the privileged list may be in the minds of the assessors. These departments then hired people who had published, or they believed would publish, in such a presumed top list of journals. This second-guessing led to more narrowing in the range of types of economists being hired.

Hence the lack of an official list had even more insidious effects. The whole process just fed on itself, making the second-guessing more and more narrow in its scope. With over twenty years of this system, a whole generation has gone through the process with significant side-effects. For example, a number of refugees (including myself) moved from economics departments to business schools, where they are not exclusively assessed by economists, but by a business panel with broader guidelines in terms of the type of research and journals being admitted.

Isn't modern United States economics also narrow in its scope?
There has been a narrowing process in the United States as well, but because of the scale and diversity of American universities it has not been as severe. Compare the (British) Royal Economic Society [RES] annual meeting with that of the American Economic Association [AEA]. The AEA meeting is under the larger umbrella of the ASSA [Allied Social Sciences Association], which includes heterodox groups.

Consequently the whole ASSA meeting is by far the broader in the diversity of topics and approaches. The RES has considered this umbrella idea, but turned it down. It does not want its delegates distracted by alternative perspectives. Furthermore, even within the AEA, there are sessions there that are broader in terms of the topics and issues being discussed. The European Economic Association [EEA] is also narrower than the AEA. The British are the most homogeneous and narrow, the Americans the least, with the EEA in between.

How does what has been done in Britain compare with such processes in other European countries?

It is interesting to compare with other European countries. For example in the Netherlands, where there is a state-run university system, in 1992 they came up with a list of over 1000 journals for research in the social sciences. My view is that it is better to have a list and even better a long list, than to have no list at all. The existence of a list, notwithstanding its defects and limitations, reduces the second-guessing phenomenon that I mentioned before. Furthermore, the defects of any list can be openly challenged. In Britain, since you do not have an official list, then you cannot have such an argument.

As part of its research assessment, the national research council in France has developed a relatively long list of several hundred journals in economics and management. It has some defects but it is much broader than the Diamond list. It has some redeeming features and it allows some space for heterodoxy and new journals. This is particularly important since there are battles going on in France about the direction economics is taking.

The anglophone world has suffered from Robbins's definition of economics as the "science of choice" – where the individual is taken as given. On Continental Europe, Robbins was accepted only partially. In practice, the boundaries of economics are defined differently in Great Britain. The standard way to deal with heterodox economists in Britain is to say: "That is not economics!". End of story. Only recently is this Robbins definition being implicitly undermined by the work of mainstream economics.

Notably, some countries such as France have resisted the use of English as the universal language in economics. Notably the French *Régulation* School has published most of its work in French and not in English. But that is now changing, where even French economists accept that they have to publish in English. The positive effect of this is that it makes it much easier for economists to communicate with one another. But it also makes it easier for those in power to impose the research standards of English-speaking countries as the only possible model. For this reason, research in European economics is at a crossroads today.

In 2003 you wrote a chapter for a book on post-austistic economics edited by Fulbrook, entitled "How did economics get into such a state?" How did economics get into such a state and has the post-autistic movement helped deal with the problem?

Mine was a brief contribution but hopefully it raised some important questions. It was not written to provide answers. I enquired as to the forces behind the development of economics today that have led to the dominance of technique over substance and an impoverished narrowness of scope. I argued that the increasing specialization of scientific research was a factor that ought to be taken into account.

There are different schools of thought on the problems with orthodox economics today. Many people are worried about the prominence of mathematical techniques. But note that the French students who started the "post-autistic" movement are not concerned about modeling per se – they are from the top French universities and good at mathematics. The concern is not with formal models as such, but the way in which formal techniques dominate issues of relevance, policy and substance. Like many, they are interested in economics as a means to deal with real world problems. Instead they found an agenda that was dominated by mathematical techniques, and they complained against this imbalance in the curriculum. Consequently, the French President set up a committee led by Jean-Paul Fitoussi to look into the matter. Other students in other countries followed with similar protests, including at the University of Cambridge. But its economics faculty rejected the idea of making any official response to such concerns.

Tony Lawson argues that the very use of mathematical techniques characterizes mainstream economics. He points out that all models, of any kind, assume a closed system. He argues that because these models are closed, they are appropriate only if the object of analysis is also closed, or closure is approximated. At most such closure is "very rare" in reality, to use his words. For him, formal models are a mismatch with the openness of the world that we are trying to understand.

But many so-called heterodox economists also use models, including post-Keynesians and Sraffians. Many self-declared heterodox economists would also use econometrics to try to understand aspects of open systems. So Tony broadens the boundaries of what is conventionally described as orthodox or mainstream economics, to include some of these formerly described heterodox studies.

Overall, I think his argument is wrong. He highlights the mismatch between the ontology of the model. But matching reality is a very restrictive view of the role of models. If you believe that models are simply there to map reality, then you can see the problem. But models often have other uses, such as heuristics. Heuristics try to come to grips with a limited key process found in the real world. By modeling an abstract version of that process, they can reveal results that might not be obvious. Thomas Schelling's (1969) discrimination model is a good example. He shows that very slight discriminatory preferences can have big overall effects. Many models are of this heuristic character.

Now that doesn't mean I don't see any problems with the use of formalism in economics today. The problem, as I have mentioned, is that technique dominates substance. The solution is not to get rid of technique but to put it in its proper place.

Where do you see economics going in the world during the next twenty years?
I cannot look into a crystal ball and give you a detailed view, but one can identify some important forces impinging on the discipline. To understand where economics is going, one has to appreciate institutional pressures as well as doctrinal developments. On the positive side, there is ongoing progress in some areas. Many economists now recognize the role of institutions. Evolutionary ideas are having some impact on the mainstream. It is possible to publish articles in leading economic journals on institutional and evolutionary themes. In many ways economics is more exciting than it was twenty years ago.

Another important issue coming on the agenda is the question of boundaries with other disciplines. It is likely that the Robbins view of the nature of economics will be further questioned and sidelined. This will encourage useful discussion and debate about the nature of economic inquiry. Other disciplines, notably sociology, have similar problems in defining their boundaries. Hopefully all this may lead to a reconstruction of the architecture of the social sciences, where economics learns more from other disciplines. We may even approach the goal of a unified social science.

But on the pessimistic side, as long as technique dominates substance, the isolation and narrowing of economics will continue. If their gaze is fixed on technique, then economists will not learn much from elsewhere, except from mathematics.

There is also the growing commercialization of universities. This encourages researchers to chase grant money, from public and private institutions. Much grant money is for research with immediate practical uses. This discourages long-term research of uncertain benefit. Academics become money-chasers rather than guardians of truth and values.

A negative outcome of some research assessment exercises is that they encourage people to publish in quantity in narrow outlets. They create incentives to publish articles in the right places instead of being a scholar in pursuit of truth for the general benefit of society. The further commercialization of universities and inappropriate auditing of research may create a dynamic that erodes the spirit of enquiry and innovation, to the extent that creative thinking in economics and elsewhere becomes even more difficult. My hope is that the spirit of rigorous and creative enquiry will nevertheless prevail.

10. Joan Martínez Alier

The interview was conducted at the Hotel Majestic in Barcelona, Spain, 10 July, 2007

After being at the University of Barcelona, you spent a long time in the 1960s and 1970s at Oxford University before you returned to finish your PhD in Barcelona. What did you study at Oxford, and how did it influence your work?

I went there because I got a scholarship. During the time that I was there I had an opportunity to write two books. The first book was on laborers and landowners in southern Spain (1971). It was about conflicts in Andalusia and problems of land tenure and land reform. It looked at unemployment and the theory of sharecropping, and the relationship between the land tenure system and the productivity of labor. I pictured sharecropping as a type of piecework system. I am still quite proud of my work on sharecropping. This was in the mid- and late 1960s, and there was still a lot of political tension then. Half the book deals with issues of fear and repression in Andalusia under Franco, although people were leaving the countryside because of economic growth. I learned a lot about the history of Spain when I was doing fieldwork in Andalusia. I remember at the age of 21 staying up all night reading Hugh Thomas's book on the Spanish Civil War (1961). Before then I knew nothing about it.

The second book (1977a) was on sugar cane plantations in Cuba, and on shepherds in large haciendas in the highlands of Peru. This is a book on peasant studies; it related land tenure to social aspects. I was a research fellow at St Antony's College in Oxford, and from 1968 to 1971 I traveled to Latin America. It was during this time that the *Journal of Peasant Studies* was started. I went to Cuba for one year. I wrote about the agrarian structure of Cuba before the Revolution and land reform after the Revolution. After my year in Cuba, I went back to Great Britain. I decided to go to Peru to work on the archives with others related to Peruvian land reform. So, I became a specialist on agrarian reform. In Peru, the situation was very different from what I had seen before. It was indigenous peasants against the big haciendas. The peasants did not want to modernize. The Indians didn't want to move from their land; they had been there before the haciendas. The haciendas wanted to expel the shepherds and their livestock, and import good quality sheep from New Zealand or the United States. This type of anti-modernism was very prevalent in Ecuador, Bolivia and Peru at that time. They were not socialists, but peasants who were concerned about communal land (like Narodniki or agrarian populists).

It was in Peru when I first encountered ecological anthropology. I met some anthropologists who were discussing what they called the "vertical economy", looking at how the people in the mountains would exchange goods with people at lower levels. The exchanges were often by barter. R. Brooke Thomas (1976) was counting the calories (maize, potatoes) going up the mountains and calories (meat, wool) coming down the mountains. I found this framework very interesting; I already knew about the economics of food consumption. This was about 1973. Another influence to this work was a book by Roy Rappaport (1967), which is about the ecological anthropology in New Guinea.

I remember reading an article on agricultural energetics in *Science* by David Pimentel et al. (1973). This article showed that modern corn production had lower energy efficiency than traditional corn production. This was puzzling from the point of view of productivity – the economic productivity increased, but the energy productivity decreased. So it helped me to become more interested in this area, and it is fair to say that my work on ecology was a natural evolution of my reading and thinking of energy and agriculture (Martinez Alier and Naredo, 1979).

When did you come back to Barcelona?
I came back in 1975, when I was offered my current position at the newly established Autonomous University of Barcelona.

You are one of the developers of the term "ecological economics" in your influential 1987 book. How did you come to think of this term?
The inspiration was Nicholas Georgescu-Roegen, although he was using the term "bio-economics" rather than "ecological economics." But his

book on the entropy law and economic process (1971) was really the inspiration. I already knew about him because of his famous article on the peasant economy, which had been published in 1960.

In 1971 he was arguing that when you look at the economy from a physical point of view you get a very different perspective of the economy. It is what we now call non-equivalent descriptions. You can look at the economy as a circular system of prices and quantities, or you can look at it from a thermodynamic point of view in terms of energy flows. You get a quite different view depending on how you look at it. So for me the inspiration was Georgescu-Roegen, and not from the other two originators, Herman Daly (1968) and Kenneth Boulding (1966).

I invited Georgescu-Roegen over here to the Autonomous University in Barcelona in 1980, so I got to know him. He was a European figure, even in his American exile. He wrote me that he had always felt that he was in exile from a poor underdeveloped country (Romania), so he could sympathize with my work – somebody from Europe studying peasants. So we got along well.

I should probably also point out that ecological economics, even that part that started in the United States, has a European base. Ken Boulding was born in Europe, as was Georgescu-Roegen. The only one of the founders who was not was Herman Daly, and he is half Brazilian.

When did you discover Podolinsky? Did you discover him when you were in Berlin?

I discovered him in a collection of letters between Marx and Engels (1975) about natural sciences. Engels wrote two letters on Podolinsky's work in 1882. I read the original article by Podolinsky (1880) who was quoting Clausius on thermodynamics and other scientists of the mid-nineteenth century whom I then read. Podolinsky looked at agriculture in terms of flows of energy. That led to the question of why Marx or later Marxists were not doing a type of ecological economics history. Marx could have done it because he was using the word "metabolism" as a relationship between nature and society. But he did not do the energy accounts. Later, Podolinsky was highly praised by the ecologist Vernadsky (1924), who wrote that Podolinsky studied the energetics of life as an open system and he applied this knowledge to the study of the economy, which is a good description of the social metabolic part of ecological economics. The question is why this criticism of economics from a physical and biological perspective was not taken up by anybody else for so long, except for Patrick Geddes, Frederick Soddy, and a few others (Martinez Alier, 1987), although they were not economists.

In your 1987 book you use the term "neo-Narodnik". How do you see Podolinsky fitting in with Marx, Georgescu-Roegen, and your views?
The word should probably fall in the category of an anti-American word. There are no peasants in the United States, which makes it very alien to American traditions and brings us back to the question of European traditions. The agrarian tradition is very much a European tradition, although it has relevance for India, China, Mexico (the uprisings led by Emiliano Zapata), Peru (Mariátegui, 1996), and other countries. It has political implications of a populist nature. Podolinsky was a Ukrainian Narodnik and a medical doctor. Georgescu-Roegen was pro-peasant.

Is the homogenization or globalization of economics undermining some of the national traditions in Europe?
The two most famous Catalan economists are Andreu Mas-Colell and Xavier Sala-i-Martin, and they are typical of the new globalized economics (and Catalonia has the most prominent economics departments in Spain). Mas-Colell is my age; he is a brilliant microeconomist. He very briefly joined the Communist Party because of the anti-Franco resistance and had to leave the university, so he moved to the United States. He first went to Minnesota, then Berkeley and ultimately ended up at Harvard as a professor. He is a very civilized person who has been a Catalan Minister for Science. He did very well; people are very happy with what he did by getting contracts for scientists from outside of Spain. He is at Pompeu Fabra University here in Barcelona. He was once a candidate to be Rector of Pompeu Fabra, but lost the elections because he was a bit too elitist. I like him being elitist because he insists on higher standards.

But he is the typical abstract mathematical microeconomist (Mas-Colell, 1985); he is a very metaphysical economist. One time someone asked him about the environment and he responded that one could be a very good economist but not know the second law of thermodynamics, which is quite true.

The second most famous Catalan economist is Xavier Sala-i-Martin, who is a fanatical developer of metaphysical theories of economic growth (Barro and Sala-i-Martin, 1995), but very competent in his own way. He is much younger. He was a student of mine; when he came to university he was already twice as good as the next best student. When he finished here, he went straight to Harvard and then he became a professor at Columbia; he is also part-time at Pompeu Fabra. He has become very much a public intellectual. He has not been a strong supporter of ecological economics; in fact he strongly denied climate change very openly until three months ago. Now he is more careful.

Both of these are examples of the new European globalized economists;

they have been trained in the United States, but they still consider themselves European. Perhaps they show the reemergence of European continental traditions that were lost 50 to 75 years ago, in large part because of the European wars, the European civil wars one could say. You see, even the Chicago School has roots in Hayek, from Austria. The true European tradition is the acceptance of several European traditions in economics, all are respectable intellectually. Many were transplanted to America but with unequal success.

You have written a number of papers dealing with the Spanish economy, calling it "neo-Corporatist" (1977b). Did Franco destroy the Spanish tradition of economics, which left it open to American influence?
These are different questions. Yes, I agree; Franco destroyed the universities. But it is important to also say that economics did not exist as a separate field before the war. At that time economics was inside the law faculties. Because of the Franco experience many Spanish economists moved to the United States. A number of students went to the University of Minnesota, which had an institutional connection with Spanish economics.

On "neo-corporatism", this was an attempt to make sense of the pacts between unions and employers, and between the Communist Party and the Right, at the time of the political transition after Franco. Not my best work, really.

Let us get back to the question of the beginning of ecological economics.
It started in 1986. There is a book by Herman Daly (1972) and a work by Costanza (1980) that interested me. In 1986 I visited Richard Norgaard (1984) who had an important paper and Charles Hall (Hall et al., 1986) whose book on ecology and energy in the United States economy I found fascinating.

Back in 1982, there was a meeting of ecologists and economists in Sweden organized by AnnMari Jansson. This led to a book (Jansson, 1984) integrating economy and ecology. The ideas were there but not the name. Many of the originators were at that meeting. In 1987 we had a conference here in Barcelona sponsored by UNESCO and a group of us decided to create a society of ecological economics.

There was a debate about what we should call the organization. Some favored "environment and economics", but then the term "ecological economics" came up and everyone decided that was the best. The downside with the name is that some people think it is a branch of economics, which it is not; it is a transdisciplinary field. In 1989 the association came out with its journal *Ecological Economics*. This was Bob Costanza's work. He has enormous energy, and a good sense of how science works. The older professors who didn't have to worry about advancement were far less concerned about the journal; we were thinking more about writing books. But younger professors thought that professional advancement requires journal publication.

There seems to be a debate about what to call work that includes multiple disciplines. Some people prefer "multidisciplinary", some favor "interdisciplinary", but ecological economists seem to favor "transdisciplinary". What is your view about those terms?
I'm not so worried about the terms, but I think it's important to include multiple disciplines in one's study. There is a conflict between the economy and the environment and so it's important to use many disciplines. Consider the conflict about bauxite mining in Orissa in India, which I am currently following closely (Martinez Alier, 2001; Martinez Alier and Temper, 2007). You have to ask questions about geology, hydrology, the metallurgy of aluminum, and electricity sources. You have to know anthropology, because these are tribal people who are being displaced, you have to know about economics in terms of prices, and you also have to know about the Indian political system. It is difficult for someone to know all these different areas, but problems do not follow specific disciplines. This makes it difficult for a student to do a PhD thesis, but that's what they should do if they want to be ecological economists.

What is your major critique of mainstream economics, and what is being taught here in Europe?
I recently read an article about the economics that is being taught in Pompeu Fabra, which is one of the leading global economics programs in Europe. Ecological economics did not figure in what was being taught. The environment wasn't there. Students there aren't taught anything at all about climate change.

My view is that the mainstream economics being taught is a very metaphysical type of discipline. Some parts of it, such as game theory, whether theory of institutions or doing some parts of policy, connect very much with some parts of ecological economics, since we don't use different tools than mainstream economists use.

But the big picture of how the economy works is very different. For mainstream economics the economy is a closed, circular system; for ecological economics the economy is an open system. We would like to bring the externalities into the price system but we know this cannot be achieved. The way resources and social externalities are considered is very different. In ecological economics we're careful to specify the economy is embedded in the social system and the social system is embedded in the physical system. This is standard in all ecological economics textbooks, but you'd never find it in a mainstream textbook.

How do you see your work influencing mainstream economics?
It is not my work; it's the work of all ecological economists. It's unclear how much we can change mainstream economics. There are different ways in which we are influencing the mainstream. Some people associated with ecological economics are becoming important in certain policy areas. This is because what they are studying, like energy flows, are more relevant to policy makers. But the influence is on society, not on economics. It is now important to do the energy balance to accompany the economic balance. We try to introduce statistics on material flows (in order to disprove the hypothesis that the economy is "dematerializing") and also statistics on the HANPP – the human appropriation of net primary production of biomass. The higher the HANPP, the less biomass is available for other species. I am a member of the Scientific Committee of the European Environmental Agency, and we have discussions about such issues. So these issues are working their way into statistical offices, such as Eurostat, and into policy.

But we have not had much influence on mainstream economics. The predominance of a highly formal neoclassical economics that has occurred over the past half century has meant economic history has lost a lot of importance. Today economic history is taught only to show the relevance of neoclassical economic theory. The much broader economic history, which was a European tradition – linking with the old German historical tradition – is disappearing. If economic history links up with this study of social metabolism then it could recover some importance, such as with the work led by John R. McNeill (McNeill, 2000; Hornborg et al., 2007). There is room for these types of studies within universities, although not generally in departments of economics.

What are the major environmental challenges we are facing today?
One challenge is population growth; the other is coming from use of energy and materials. You can see it in climate change, but also in land use. If the population actually does rise to 9 billion, as it is likely to do, that means about 3 billion more people will exist. By adding only one ton of carbon per person will increase significantly the ecological imprint we make on the environment. Because of peak-oil and later peak-gas use, the first part of the twenty-first century will be the century of coal, which will impose enormous environmental challenges. Coal use increased seven times in the twentieth century, and that use will continue in the first part of the twenty-first century.

How would you respond to the standard mainstream argument that if we have free markets, the price system will solve the problem. What's wrong with this answer?

Prices are very myopic. So the neoclassical answer is that some backstop technology will appear; and that backstop technology appears to be coal, which is not new, and which has significantly negative effects on the environment. But who can blame the people who use coal – that's what they have.

What about the time problem? In your 1987 book you spend a lot of effort critiquing conventional views of allocation over time? How central of an issue is that in ecological economics?

I think it is a very central issue. The proper discount rate should be the rate at which the economy grows sustainably (Howarth and Norgaard, 1992). Unfortunately, there seems to be too much optimism about the growth of the economy; we have to be careful. As long as we assume that future generations are going to be richer, we are making myopic political decisions today because we heavily discount their needs. We ecological economists call this the optimist's paradox, because it allows us to pollute more now than we otherwise would, because we assume that future generations are going to be so much richer than we are. We then apply a higher discount rate because we assume they will be much richer than we are, with lower marginal utility. They will have four or five cars per family. That is what we assume. It is a self-defeating assumption, it allows us to use more resources now and produce more carbon dioxide, undermining the future standard of living. In my view the economy currently is growing at more than a sustainable rate. It is a mixture of growth because of technological innovations, and the overuse of the environment. So the discount rate should be lower.

So you prefer Stern's (2007) lower discount rate compared to Nordhaus's (2007) higher discount rate for evaluating global climate policies?

Yes; it doesn't have to be zero, but it should be low. But there is no final answer because of the uncertainty. How to apply the Precautionary Principle? Do we require economic accounts for this?

The inventor of the term "ecology" was the late nineteenth-century German scientist, Ernst Haeckel (1866). You identify him with Social Darwinism, and we know that there were links between some of Haeckel's followers and Hitler. While we tend to think of political ecology or Green movements as progressive, is there a strain in it that can be associated with fascism, with this perhaps manifesting itself in some countries even now, such as with nationalists in Russia?

You have two different issues here. It is true that there is a whole branch of the environmental movement which is concerned about nature and not at all about humans. The second is the interpretation of the right-wing or Nazi movements in Germany as being ecological. There is a book about this by Anna Bramwell (1989) that makes this argument. I have a joke about this – the only joke I have invented in German. It goes as follows: Hitler talked a lot about Blut und Boden (blood and the soil) but in fact, the memory that he left was Blut und Autobahnen (blood and highways). The older people in Germany thought that Hitler was very bad, but at least he gave them the autobahn. But more seriously, Hitler was very much pro industry; he was not an ecologist. He was a friend of industry; he pushed the Volkswagen and aviation.

Some people believe that there is a division between the European and United States movements in ecological economics. Do you think that this split exists, and if so why?
I think there is a much larger emphasis in Europe on institutions, and looking at the economy through a lens of social inequality and linking this together with ecological issues. I think the real leader of this approach was K. William Kapp, who was born in 1906 in Königsberg and died in 1976. He was an institutional economist; he discussed many of the issues in ecological economics long before others (1963). He was a friend of Karl Polanyi, who was another typical European exile who did much of his work in New York.

What's important about Kapp is that in his view, ecological externalities were not market failures, but were cost-shifting successes. We are shifting costs to future generations, to other species, and to poor people, especially to people outside the richer developed countries.

I'm not sure how much that differs between the United States and Europe. In the United States there is a strong environmental justice movement. But they have not connected enough with the ecological economists, although Robert Bullard (2000) came to one of our conferences, and said that people are being polluted not because they are poor, but because they are Hispanic or Black. That shifts the language – he is not asking to compensate externalities in money terms. When you talk about pollution, you are talking about infringing human rights. This is a type of tactical move, since you can go to the courts with arguments against "environmental racism". In fact, to move away from economic measurement, this is one of the main themes in European ecological economics. We emphasize incommensurable values. It goes back to Otto Neurath's debate in the 1920s with von Mises and Hayek. You can measure everything in money terms if you wish, but there are other relevant non-monetary values. Who has the right or the power to simplify complexity and impose only the economic language of evaluation? (Martinez Alier, 2002). If in Ecuador or Thailand, mangroves are destroyed by shrimp farming, I could argue in terms of monetary compensation for the environmental services lost. Perhaps more powerfully I could argue in terms of territorial rights of a local community which has been using the mangroves for subsistence since time immemorial. I do agree that in Europe more attention is paid to such distributional issues and therefore to different languages of evaluation than in the United States. In the US there is an Environmental Justice Movement for minorities, but the environmental mainstream has more regard for issues like wilderness than in Europe and also more respect for economic valuation. In the culture of the United States, the bottom line is the bottom line in the profit-and-losses account, isn't it?

Tell us a bit about your views of the interrelationship between ecological and economic distribution.
Economic distribution has been studied for a long time, and it is an important social and political issue, but mainstream economics focuses on allocation, with distributional issues put in as an afterthought. In some other economics traditions, such as the Sraffian or Marxian, economic distribution is very much at the center of the study. But neither in Marxian nor in mainstream economics has there been a discussion of environmental or ecological distribution. It is now entering into the social picture because there are so many environmental and ecological conflicts. Who are the de facto owners of the oceans and the atmosphere as sinks or deposits for carbon dioxide? In ecological economics we make the point that the way in which such rights are distributed influences prices, and can change prices. Thus, the study of distribution is prior to the study of allocation, which is what mainstream economics focuses on. That's why we call them ecological distributional conflicts.

As I stated above, externalities are not market failures, but cost-shifting successes. That success depends on the social situation. Poor people are cheap; you can pollute them and you don't have to pay very much. This was what Lawrence Summers wrote in 1992 in his famous internal memorandum in the World Bank. He wrote that from a strictly economic point of view, it was a good idea to pollute where there were no people or where people were poor. He was right from a strictly economic viewpoint. In the market, the poor have little to say. But they can complain outside the market, and they do. So that's why ecological economics links up with *political ecology*, the focus of work by Martin O'Connor and me (Martinez Alier and O'Connor, 1996). In environmental conflicts, people use non-economic languages of evaluation. They say that it is not a question of paying for externalities, although, of course, they will not turn down the money, they say it is a question of human rights and territorial rights or sacredness or human livelihood. All this cannot be translated into money terms.

Central to all this is power. Power is important at two levels. First, there is the power to impose a decision, and then there is the power to set the rules about how decisions should be taken.

In terms of language, about half your books were written in English, and half in Spanish. Is there a separate Spanish language tradition in economics, and should this be preserved?

My first book on ecological economics was written in Catalan in 1984, but there aren't many who speak it. I then rewrote it in English, and it is better because I had a chance to rewrite it. Then there were Spanish, Japanese, Italian translations. It just doesn't make sense to write a scientific book in any other language than English today. For younger people, English is a matter of academic survival. Languages change over time. In the fifteenth century European books were in Latin. In the nineteenth century science was often written in German.

There are some victims of this convention. For example, René Passet, a French writer and economist, in 1979 wrote a great book on the economics of life. He made the point that economics was within the society and the environment. But because the book has not been translated into English, he is not known as well as he should be.

You're from Catalonia, which is becoming more independent from Spain. Is this related to Spain joining the European Union?

It may be playing a role. The existence of a central European government and parliament will allow Europe to divide up more into regions that transcend current state boundaries. This I feel will be good for Europe; although I don't know whether Europe is good for the world. I am very strongly pro-European, probably because of my age and my Catalan heritage.

Under Franco it was forbidden to give Catalan names to children. I was originally given a Spanish name, Juan, under which I published my first books. I now use its Catalan equivalent, Joan. At my university today, some undergraduate courses are taught in Catalan while others are taught in Spanish, and many graduate courses are taught in English.

Is the world heading into an ecological crisis, and if so, what can be done to avoid it?

Yes, I think we are entering into a crisis because of climate change and also because of the loss of biodiversity. For example, in India the number of tigers has fallen in one hundred years to one tenth of what it was. The reason is population growth. In Europe there is a debate starting about the need for sustainable de-growth. That means to have an economy that does not grow in physical terms. On the contrary, it must shrink in terms of production of carbon dioxide, in terms of use of biomass. This shrinking economy must be socially sustainable. Because if we don't have growth, it is not clear that our society can manage it. Unemployment would increase, debts would not be paid. So, we must de-link employment and remuneration much more than now. We should take seriously the Easterlin paradox, that after a certain level of income more income does not make us happier or increase welfare (Easterlin, 1995). Behavioral and experimental economics is helping to reinforce this view. Sustainable de-growth (in French it sounds better, *la décroissance soutenable*) implies new institutions that affect distribution, like basic income. I think it would be politically easier to accomplish this in Europe than in the United States. I would be in favor of it, in order to give room for China and India to grow more. I believe that this should be linked to a strong position on population growth.

For example, there is a push now for more population growth so that we have young people to pay the pensions of old people. Say, two young people for one old person. But then in one generation we will need four young people to pay for the pensions of the two old people. There are better ways to handle it, such as to reduce the pensions, or to increase the retirement age.

Does complexity enter into ecological theory?
Complexity theory sees the need for multiple perspectives, as does ecological theory, and also emphasizes uncertainties, which is much linked to the post-normal science terminology of ecological economics, along with the emphasis on seeing the ecosystems and the economy as open systems and the focus on emergence of new properties. I see a parallel there, with non-linearities bringing about surprises that are the basis of uncertainty (Giampietro et al., 2000).

In our previous book, we characterized orthodoxy as an intellectual category, mainstream as a sociological category, with heterodoxy having aspects from both. Where do you see ecological economics fitting into that heterodox/ mainstream/ orthodox divide?
The orthodoxy of neoclassical economics is disappearing not because of outside critics, but because of inside discussions – work in psychology. This has led to good relations between critical mainstream economics and ecological economics with regard to consumption theory. On production

theory and growth economics, the mainstream is still rather metaphysical. They think we can live without natural resources because of substitution.

However, mainstream today is much broader than just a narrow neo-classical orthodoxy. It could also be defined as what appears in the news-papers as economics. There are many more economists than ecologists, so I don't think ecological economics is going to defeat mainstream econom-ics. But it will influence it. I don't see ecological economics as significantly challenging the mainstream, but I do see the environmental issues as growing in importance, and being integrated into the mainstream. The mainstream says, "we can have growth, but it should be sustainable". This is the social democratic, European Keynesian approach, as represented by the Brundtland Commission Report for the UN on sustainable develop-ment (1987).

As the same time, there is the radical environmental critique of ecologi-cal economics as developed by Georgescu-Roegen, later by Herman Daly and some others. This occurred simultaneously with the growth of market fundamentalism, which had almost disappeared in the Keynesian era. Yes, during that time the picture of the Walrasian invisible hand was taught to economists, but nobody believed in the automatic workings of the market after the 1930s. That only occurred again in the late 1970s. Market fundamentalism and ecological economics have never really clashed as they should clash. We know and read them, they ignore us so far. Some market fundamentalists are trying to integrate environment into econom-ics by property rights and so on, such as the Coase theorem, which Coase never proclaimed. It is ridiculous to think that you can solve the ecological problems through more markets, but some people think so. It is ridiculous because unborn people, poor people and other species do not come to markets.

Do you think the globalization of economics and the standardization of evaluation systems that seems to be taking place in Europe today is making it harder to teach students ecological economics, or for younger colleagues to work in this area?

In Europe there has been a Post-Autistic movement, so these things are being discussed. My view is that some of the changes are an improve-ment, since the old system of promotion here was based on patronage. It was not publish or perish; it was "parish or perish", and this happened in many places. Who your professor was played a significant role. The system before made the political party you belonged to extremely important; that's not a good system for academia. At the end of the Franco regime, Opus Dei controlled the universities in Spain. Of course, advancement based only on publishing has its own problems. What's important is that there are many journals. The journal *Ecological Economics* has been good for some of my students. They advanced because of publications in that journal, and other journals sympathetic to ecological economics.

The top schools in Europe – those that see themselves as part of global economics – have professors who have been trained in the United States, and who are happy with that. So they are creating rigorous programs that reflect that US tradition. At other schools, there is much more flexibility; the standards are lower. It is not that these other schools are more heterodox; it is that the level, in general, is lower. So the new schools are a mixture of high level, which I approve of, and indoctrination in orthodox economics and exclusion of ecological economics, which is more problematic.

I think it is good that Spanish and European professors think that they should publish in international journals, and they do, because research money now depends on it. Overall, the reliance on international standards, while it has its problems, is an improvement over uncontrolled patronage.

Do you see other alternative schools besides ecological economics to orthodox economics?
There are people coming from analytical philosophy like John O'Neill (2007), who is a professor of Political Economy at Manchester University, who are doing interesting work on the foundations of markets. I would like to see economic history develop more, and ecological-economic history, but it isn't happening to the extent that I would like; history is very much on the defensive. Social economic history, which was very important in France and Britain, is losing out, and that is sad.

What about the Régulation *School in France?*
They are losing, in part because they did not go early enough into the ecological issues.

How do you see ideas of ecological economics integrating themselves into mainstream economics?
Consumption theory is starting to change through the work of economists such as Amartya Sen and the social psychologists. Georgescu-Roegen talked about the division of goods into needs and wants. Needs must be explained physically and socially. Preferences should be scrutinized.

Evolutionary economics is sometimes used in mainstream economics, but the real evolutionary economics, which ties evolution back to physical reality, has not yet happened. It is not only to discuss the evolution of the economy looking at market structure and oligopoly and technical innovation as Schumpeter did; it is to simultaneously consider how much energy we are using, where the waste is going, and the whole embeddedness of the economy within the environment. This would be the real evolutionary economics, the sort of thing that Jeroen van den Bergh (1999) is attempting to do. Sometimes, I describe myself as a vulgar materialist, which is a joke because Marx described some of his enemies as vulgar materialists; he saw himself as a sophisticated materialist.

Where is cutting edge work in ecological economics being done in Europe?
One place where there is a strong tradition is the Netherlands. In the Netherlands, they developed multi-criteria evaluation in land use conflicts, because they had this tradition of physical planning. This is work by Peter Nijkamp (Nunes et al., 2003), and many others like Giuseppe Munda (1995). Participatory multi-criteria evaluation is a regular feature of ecological economics conferences. Instead of cost–benefit analysis in money terms, we do multi-criteria evaluation that respects the incommensurability of values. In Germany and Austria there is now a strong tradition of the study of social metabolism; they do research on flows of materials and energy, find out regularities in socio-ecological transitions. They do ecological economics but I am not sure they are economists – never mind. In Sweden there is a theory called physical resource theory, developed by some physicists who do ecological economics. There are also some ecologists in Sweden such as Carl Folke (Hanna et al., 1996) working on adaptive environmental systems and local institutions that enhance resilience, close to Elinor Ostrom's work.

Where do you see the economics profession going in the next twenty years in Europe?
In Europe, economists are expected to be more active in the public sphere – serving as public intellectuals, and to give advice to the politicians. This also happens in the United States, but it happens more in Europe. There have been more professors in Europe who did very little scholarly research but who played important roles as advisors. I don't know whether economists in Europe are going to continue this role, or if that role will be in economics. For example, Mas-Colell became a good Minister of Science in Catalonia, not a minister related to the economy.

In terms of economics, it is hard to say about the future. The secret agenda, which is not so secret, is that ecological economics is out to destroy orthodox economics. Some people in ecological economics, like Dick Norgaard and Clive Spash, are publicly passionate about this, and I understand their passion. But it is not clear to me this is the best approach. What should happen is that if you are right, you should win the argument, but we have all read Thomas Kuhn (1962), and we know that that is not how science progresses. As economics becomes more empirical it will help push us in that direction. But as long as economics stays mostly meta-physical we will still have many of these problems.

11. Robert Boyer

*This interview took place at 48
Boulevard Jourdan in Paris on
18 July, 2007*

Tell us a bit about your education and how you came to be an economist.
It was by accident. I started at Ecole Polytechnique where I was studying physics and math back in 1962. I planned to become a researcher
in physics, but when I had to decide about my career, I realized how
obsolete were the teachings of my professors, and simultaneously, how
difficult it was to enter research given the small size of the public budget
devoted to physics. By chance during that time I had a talented teacher
in economics, Jacques Dumontier, an administrator of the national statistical institute (INSEE). For me, but not my fellow students, he was a
wonderful teacher. First he would define the concepts. Then he would try
to measure them. Then, he would use a deductive method to derive some
predictions or consequences. And fourth, he would test this against the
data. It was a very scientific way of analyzing (Dumontier, 1970; 1971).
For me, it was wonderful; it was like physics, and the opposite of math.
Had I been taught general equilibrium theory at that time, I would have
never gone into economics. General equilibrium theory is purely axiomatic. It does not relate to reality. It was a fairy tale for children. The
focus of the economics I learned was on macro; you don't need economists to tell you how to run a firm; you just need talented people. You
need economists for macro.

   After two years studying civil engineering at Ecole Nationale des Ponts et Chausées (ENPC), I started my career in 1967 as an economist in charge of coordinating applied research on the formation of housing prices in various French cities. Two years later, I shifted to the Commissariat Général du Plan (CGP) where they had created a center for income and cost analysis, Centre d'Etudes des Revenus et des Coûts (CERC). It was supposed to be the think tank for income policy. There, I became interested in total factor productivity measurement and income distribution in France. This was in the early 1970s. Then I went to the Ministry of Finance. There, I was part of a small team in charge of developing a macro econometric model to be used for forecasting and studying the impact of economic policy. Instead of building a typical Keynesian model, we were inspired by Kalecki's work, in that it was a dynamical model of capital accumulation. It was named STAR, meaning "Schema Théorique d'Accumulation et de Répartition" and actually it was highly sophisticated with respect to the standards of that time. For instance, the model exhibited strong non-linearities, possibly multiple equilibria and required new econometric methods to be estimated. More basically, we designed one of the first investment functions with rates of return as well as financial fragility indexes. We were strongly attacked by many in the profession as being moved by leftist ideology in place of scientific rigor. Now, most of the standard econometric studies of investment do follow cash flow and financial stability. It was not surprising that STAR had no success at all, but there was another reason for this: when used to study the impact of the first oil shock it turned out to simply reproduce previous cycles. But we were rapidly convinced that the French economy was entering a totally new period. This is one of the remote origins of *régulation* theory.

When did you get your PhD in economics?
I never actually finished a PhD devoted to health economics of French hospitals over a century. I did lots of study, particularly of mathematical economics at the Paris 6 and then in economics in Paris I Sorbonne, but a PhD wasn't needed then to do research.

It seems that the 1968 student revolts played an important role for academics in France during that time. Where were you professionally then?
At that time quite all the intellectuals were from the Left. I was at the Ministry of Construction. My interest in economics was closely linked to how one might change the world. Most of the scholars of my generation were very naive and idealistic. For us politics was central. Our research reflected that. From the Ministry in 1974, I entered the Centre d'Etudes Prospectives d'Economie Mathématique Appliquées à la Planification (CEPREMAP) as a researcher, and then in 1978 I was admitted to Centre

National de la Recherche Scientifique (CNRS), and since then I have been working there full-time. At that time CEPREMAP was a research unit financed partially by the CGP. The idea was to have good academic economic research with some implications for planning. I was then part of another group that studied the long-run transformation of French capitalism, in order to understand the novelty of stagflation in the 70s. It was from this study that the *régulation* school evolved.

Tell us a bit more about the development of the Régulation *School.*
As I discussed in my *Regulation School: A Critical Introduction* (1990) the school developed in the 1970s. It emerged from the PhD dissertation of Michel Aglietta (1974; 1976) on the post-war development of the US economy, and he was (critically) inspired by the work of Destanne de Bernis (1975) and his colleagues in Grenoble. The team gathered in CEPREMAP intended to replicate for French capitalism Michel Aglietta's research; I was more of a coordinator than anything else. I did not invent *régulation*, but I coordinated the efforts of many different talented people (1975). There were essentially eight people each developing different parts of it, with Alain Lipietz (1977; 1986; 1993) playing an important role, who is now a Green representative in the European parliament. Jacques Mistral was part of the adventure, along with two Chilean economists, among them Carlos Ominami, who became afterwards minister of the economy in Chile after the transition to democracy. Another important participant was Jean-Pascal Bénassy (Bénassy et al., 1979), who would later be a prominent neo-Keynesian. We took the Fordism idea from Antonio Gramsci (1996), and we sought to model dynamic macro regimes.

We had some success; but for the wrong reasons. We analyzed the American model of the post-war period as Fordist by redesigning Gramsci's concept in rigorous economic terms, but it was a mistake to think that it was a general result of the theory. Since then, we have produced many different models for different countries. But many people liked the simple idea of Fordism that was supposed to capture all of the *Régulation* School. If Fordism was in structural crisis, then the theory was over, as pointed out for example by Bob Jessop, in spite of his extensive knowledge of the *régulation* literature. Too many observers have confused the regulationist methodology with the theory of Fordism.

What is the Marxist influence on the Régulation *School?*
There was a clear Marxist influence, but it is a complex legacy, significantly transformed. There are different interpretations of Marxism. The dominant interpretation in France in the 1970s was that of the economists linked to the French Communist Party, i.e. the state monopoly capitalism

theory. It held that the state was the key institution governing accumulation in contemporary economies. It taxed in order to subsidize capital. We rebelled against this idea. We saw the state as a political entity and an actor in the Fordist compromise between capital and labor. The state was not only the expression of capital interest.

Our second argument was against the strict structuralist interpretation of Marxism associated with Althusser (1971). He was a philosopher and a strange as well as fascinating person. We rebelled against him for his benign neglect of history, since we wanted to understand the transformation of economic structures, social alliances and the political process through which France moved into the post-colonial order. Another influence on the *Régulation* School was heterodox economic modeling and theorizing, such as the work of Kalecki and Joan Robinson. We wanted to formalize the dynamic process of accumulation. We also sought to understand economic history, following the Annales school approach of Fernand Braudel (1973a). When you mix all the influences, you get the *Régulation* School. This immersion of economics into related social sciences still is one of the main features of the regulationist approach to economic phenomena.

Marx was innovative and his followers are entitled to innovate too and update his analysis given the transformations of capitalism and the enlargement and sophistication of the tools of contemporary research. What remains? It seems to me, the sense of history, a bit of dialectic, the concern for the process of accumulation and a continuous refinement of the concept of crisis.

What is the relation of the Régulation *School to Post Keynesian theory?*
It is related, but Keynes worked out a very static model so he could tie his insights to neoclassical thought, and contrast against it. If you want to understand capitalism, Kalecki is much better since he considered the dynamic process of accumulation. Therefore the *régulation* approach is more post-Kaleckian than Post Keynesian. Some of the Post Keynesians are too faithful to Keynes, like the old Marxists. In my view Keynes's theory was highly time-specific to the post-World War I period. It fit the institutions of the time. Let me mention that Kaldor had a better view of long-run transformation and was a source of inspiration for some macro modeling of growth regimes.

Your Marxist colleagues at CEPREMAP, Gérard Duménil and Dominique Lévy, in 1988 raised questions about the Régulation *School. How do you see their views relating to yours?*
I learned many things from them since we share a common objective: how to formalize the long-run evolution of capitalism in order to

understand contemporary transformations in the light of the renewed Marxist approach. They tend to stress the permanence of typical capitalism mechanisms with few parameter changes, such as the speed of adjustments of disequilibria on the product market, profit allocation across sectors and technical change. The regulationists are more sensitive to the possibility of novelty in capitalist basic social relations, and the new patterns of capital accumulation thus generated. We stress the changing hierarchy of institutional forms, for instance the dominant role of the wage–labor nexus under Fordism, but the resurgence of competition as the leading forces since the massive deregulation of the 1980s.

How about the Régulation School's relation to radicals in the United States?
The parallel to the *Régulation* School was the Social Structures of Accumulation School (Bowles et al., 1983; Boyer, 2002). This proximity is easy to explain: we shared similar objectives and tools and we used to have frequent interactions in the 1980s (Bowles and Boyer, 1988). But with the death of David Gordon, who was the main macroeconomist formalizing their ideas, this parallelism has somehow vanished. Sam Bowles went in other directions: in order to understand the evolution of social norms that shape economic activity he developed evolutionary models and more recently experimental economics concerning the emergence of cooperation, but no more radical macroeconomics. Actually, few students and researchers continue building typical regulationist macro-models. Frédéric Lordon contributed to quite innovative dynamic modeling with multiple equilibria, but afterwards he went another way in the direction of Spinoza's philosophy in order to search for new foundations of individual actions. So, on both sides of the Atlantic, radicals have stopped working on formalization of macroeconomic dynamics. It is a pity, since there are few alternatives to the domination of the new classical macroeconomics

What do you think of Sam Bowles and Herb Gintis's new work?
It is interesting work. They are showing that the conventional theory of rationality does not fit with the facts, and they propose a quite stimulating alternative. Understanding how social norms shape out economic regularities is also interesting. Thus, it allows an interaction with the mainstream, and thus Sam Bowles and Herb Gintis have some influence upon the whole economics profession. Conversely, if you are totally insulated, you simply preach to the converted. The regulationists have tried to follow their own intellectual strategy but the institutional pressure towards the mainstream approach is quite strong for students and the new generation of researchers.

What is the connection of the Régulation *School with the Conventions School of Olivier Favereau (1993)?*
Intellectually, they are closely related. The Convention School emerged after the *Régulation* School, as a critique and possible complement. The economists belonging to the two schools created fifteen years ago a joint PhD program: "The Economics of Institutions", now transformed into a master's given the general reform of European universities. Furthermore, authors like André Orléan belong to both research agendas. Nevertheless, they differ on two issues. Conventionalists study basically alternative coordination mechanisms at the micro level, the certification of product quality and work at a very ambitious political philosophy project; regulationists are more interested in the transformations of accumulation regimes at the macro level and they have a strong interest in economic history.

They differ also concerning the conception of institutions: the Conventionalist School stresses the role of value judgments and legitimization whereas the Regulationist School is privileging the primacy of political alliances in the emergence of new institutional forms.

Do they deny that unjust institutions can survive?
They consider that they are the exception and not the rule. For us, the political economy of institutions should be largely independent from moral philosophy (Amable and Palombarini, 2005). Another source of disappointment is that the conventionalists have not yet produced any strong new empirical result, equivalent to the analysis of the Fordist growth regime. But this is not necessarily a surprise since conventionalists aim at an overarching theory in social sciences. In this respect, their achievement is quite clever and impressive.

In the introduction to your book on Régulation *(2002), you identified two related reasons why the* Régulation *School has not achieved significant influence within the English language tradition. One is that few of the French language texts have been translated or read and another involves an apparent mistranslation of "regulation". In French, "régulation" is a much broader term than the English term "regulation", that corresponds to "réglementation" in French, which involves a narrower and more trivial perspective (with "règles" meaning "rules"). Can you expand on that?*
The vocabulary issue plays a significant role in the misunderstanding of *régulation* theory in English-speaking communities. Basically for us, the term belongs to cybernetics and systems theory: how do various components of economic configuration achieve a form of structural stability. What are the dynamic processes according to which an economy could

keep going when it faces various shocks or endogenous transformations? It involves the equivalent of a meta-stable equilibrium of a cell in biology. That meaning was totally lost in the translation into English. Usually, "regulation" relates to the methods of public authorities in order to monitor the functioning of some specific markets that would translate back into French by "*réglementation*". Two other sources of misunderstanding have to be pointed out. First, the reference to system analysis might suggest that the State would be the equivalent of the engineer in charge of governing and fully controlling the economy. Quite on the contrary, the regulationist research agenda has shown that many other collective actors are playing a key role in such a complex process, recurrently destabilized by the very unfolding of the accumulation process. Second, the monitoring of product, labor and credit markets is part of the agenda of State, but the mechanisms involved in *régulation* are much more diverse: collective agreements, laws, conventions, routines. We desperately oppose the confusion between "*régulation*" and regulation, but the center of gravity of the interpretation of our research systematically bends towards the English meaning of this term.

To what degree does the spread of English as the lingua franca of global economics threaten the existence of European heterodox schools? Will they all have to move to speaking and publishing in English to survive?
This is an interesting question, and the answer is not that simple. Of course, if I were speaking in French now, you would think me much cleverer than I seem to appear in English. As pointed out by Claude Lévy Strauss: "Speaking in French I mean what I say; when I speak a foreign language I say what I can."

We apologize that this very question is a demonstration of the problem.
A simple but basic statement: the language is the matrix for concept formation. Therefore, even for economic analysis, the nationality of the researcher matters. . .even when he is working and publishing in the international language, i.e. English. Just an anecdote: I edited a book with an American friend of mine. Conceptually we had totally different matrices. In French, we are used to forming new concepts by borrowing terms, coming from Greek and Latin. In American and English the approach is much more pragmatic. Therefore, my American colleague was surprised to learn dozens of new terms, of Greek and Latin origin, he did not know. But we can even invent quite new concepts: Frédéric Lordon coined the concept of "endo-metabolism", to express the process according to which the very functioning of a system is altering its configuration, via purely endogenous mechanisms.

At a more practical level, the problem of using any language but English is the size of the market for economic ideas. The Anglo-Saxon market is leading in terms of publication. That makes it hard to write in any other language. Another argument is the large funding that United States universities are receiving and the higher efficiency of their university organization compared to French ones. In France, students have increased by a factor of five, and funding by a factor of two. We cannot attract widely recognized economists from the English-speaking world.

Back in the 1960s some scholars were coming to and even staying in France, and students were coming here for high quality education at the university level, such as the North-Americans. Now, with the exception of the Grandes Ecoles (such as the Ecole Polytechnique), which still continues to attract top French students, the most talented students want to go to the United States, the United Kingdom, or even Spain now, to study economics. In the new Europe, the French academics are suffering because the elite do not believe in the university, since they were trained in the Grandes Ecoles.

Lastly, public authorities want to have objective methods for measuring the performance of our economists. The journals that are used to measure the best output are published in English. It is more and more necessary to publish in them if you want to get into the academic system. So publishing in English did not play so much a role in my career, but it plays a central role for young students. Before, France had a quite specific style for the PhD: it could take 10 years to get a PhD! Now the PhD is composed of three papers that can be published in an international journal. Almost all the universities are copying the US model.

People are so anxious, that they want to go directly to publishing their papers, with a loss of self-reflection about the relevant concepts, methods and issues. So the danger is not the language, the danger is the fact that if your work is too new or too different, it will not be published. Thus, there are strong incentives to just amend ideas at the margin. When CEPREMAP was founded, people dared to advance original ideas. For example, Jean-Pascal Bénassy (1975) invented disequilibrium theory, Roger Guesnerie contributed to second-best theories and we contributed to the launching of *régulation* theory. So, French academics dared to launch new research agenda; now they are eager to follow international trends.

We should have the right to use any concept and tool that is relevant for the issue under review. Unfortunately, the trend is to use already existing theories and models and to test them in new territories. Therefore, for a majority of neoclassical economists, the problem for France is that its economic organization is not similar to the United States. So they argue that we have to shift the French institutions to the United States institutions.

Quite impressive indeed, when international comparisons show the exceptionalism of North America. The regulationist strategy is different: Let us look at the French trajectory in order to detect the factors inhibiting growth and job creation and eventually propose to policy makers amendments to the existing institutional configurations.

But it is the case that English is taking over, and that poses a big problem for the Régulation *School.*
The question is not only the language – more and more regulationists do publish in English – but the acceptance into an academic network of significant importance. For example, in collaboration with Pascal Petit, since the mid-70s, I've been working on modeling and estimating increasing returns to scale. When the increasing returns to scale hypothesis came into vogue, we were never quoted, because we did not belong to the core of the profession. It only becomes important when a US economist like Paul Romer starts working on increasing returns to scale and promoting endogenous growth models. So it is not a question of language, but a question of networks. It is very costly to be radical, because by definition, you are always speaking to a minority.

Where in other parts of the world has the Régulation *School had impact?*
The *régulation* approach had an early impact on some Latin American countries, such as Mexico, Brazil, Chile, Venezuela or Argentina, because some Latin American economists working in Paris were directly involved in the emergence of the *régulation* approach. This is the case for Carlos Ominami (1986) in Chile and Ricardo Hausmann (1981) for Venezuela, Jaime Aboites for Mexico (1989) or Luis Miotti (1994) for Argentina. It was thus adopted by some heterodox economists, since it integrates the domestic social relations with the insertion into the world economy. It helps to understand what the specific problems in the country are, instead of simply comparing the national economy with the view of neoclassical economics as found in US textbooks. Lately, the strongest relations with the *Régulation* School have been with Argentina, where there was the tradition of Prebisch and CEPAL. Since 1976, Argentina experienced a series of crises, which *régulation* theory is especially designed to investigate. With the collapse of the currency board, the Washington consensus has been drastically revised in Argentina and non-orthodox economists have allied in order to deliver a diagnosis of the 2001 crisis (Boyer and Neffa, 2004) and investigate new development strategies (Boyer and Neffa, 2007). The regulationists have been the catalyst of these collective efforts.

A second community has seized the opportunity provided by the French regulationist School. A faction of the Japanese Marxist tradition, the Uno

School (Hirata, 1993) has adopted the regulationist approach in order to understand the specificity of the Japanese capitalism, in contrast with the American model. This has extended the relevance of the approach not only to Japan but to other Asian countries such as Taiwan and South Korea (Inoue, 1994), and it is part of the process of progressive generalization by the multiplicity of long-run historical studies.

Let's talk a bit more about the Régulation *School. It gives a major focus to Fordism as the dominant form of economic systemic organization in the US and related economies for several decades after World War II. However, it also recognizes alternatives such as Toyotism in Japan (Boyer and Yamada, 2000), Uddevallism in Sweden, and others. All these seem to relate to the automobile industry. Can you talk about these alternatives, and are they all suffering the same crisis as is Fordism as you describe in your book,* After Fordism *(Boyer and Durand, 1997)?*

Let us decompose your question in three separate components. Firstly, the concept of Fordism has been misread by authors that considered it as a typical sectoral or even micro analysis of the productive systems of the car industry. Actually, Fordism is an accumulation regime in which mass production and mass consumption are synchronized by some major institutional forms. A capital labor compromise was built upon the exchange of the acceptance by workers of Fordist division of labor against an indexing of real wage increases.

Consequently, the productive system was delivering increasing returns to scale. Finally, a limited foreign competition was allowing an inward-looking accumulation regime. The reference to the car industry was only an allegory, not the core of a typical macroeconomic analysis.

Second, comparative analyses have shown that the American and French configurations were finally rather specific and not at all universal. The analysis of the Japanese productive system, the original transformations in Sweden of the social democratic model applied to production still increased the variety of productive systems and accumulation regimes (Boyer and Freyssenet, 2002). Thus, a large fraction of the regulationist research has contributed to the emerging literature about the diversity of capitalisms (Amable, 2003), as well as productive organizational forms.

Thirdly, each accumulation regime or productive model experiences specific structural crisis. Instead of blaming the imperfection of the relevant configurations, the impact of adverse exogenous shocks, or even the irrationality of actors, the *régulation* approach has coined the concept of endo-metabolism. The very success of a *régulation* mode progressively alters the parameters of the accumulation regime, up to a threshold that triggers the shift from equilibrium to another or from structural stability to instability. But the mechanisms are specific for each regime. Under Fordism, social struggles about income distribution and the productivity slow-down largely explain the structural crisis. Toyotism was perceived as a follower of Fordism, but it encountered major obstacles by its very success: major tension in the wage–labor nexus and destabilizing role of the financialization of the Japanese economy due to the very success of Toyotism, as a source of growing trade surplus. The very promising Uddevalla model ran into trouble when confronted with the transformations of the social democratic model, after a major banking crisis.

Do you see a systemic change in Japan after the 1990 collapse?
Clearly, the bursting out of the bubble of the 1980s has generated a structural crisis, in the sense that almost all institutional forms had to be adjusted to the new financial and international context. But given the highly specific functioning of the Japanese political system, it has proved quite difficult to solve the banking crisis and reform State interventions in order to promote a new growth regime (Boyer and Yamada, 2000). Therefore, far from being the repetition of the American Great Depression, the Japanese lost decade has exhibited an unexpectedly long period of institutional flux and uncertainty. In this respect, one notes an intellectual proximity with the Institutional Complementarity Approach proposed by Masahiko Aoki (2001; 2007).

You have written about the seven paradoxes of capitalism (1996). In that writing, you pose a number of capitalist alternatives for the world economy. Can you talk about those?
In the 1990s I realized the variety of institutional forms across nations. Instead of assessing the distance with respect to a canonical market economy idealized by a general equilibrium model, the regulationist agenda has pointed out the variety of complementarities of various institutional forms across OECD countries. These different architectures not only shape the short-term reaction to external shocks but also the pattern of innovation and economic specialization. A first taxonomy was first proposed by Amable et al. (1997) and then extended by Amable (2003):

- In *market-led capitalism*, such as the US, the usual reaction is to look for market mechanisms and the related regulatory agencies.
- The second method is to internalize within the firm the emerging externalities. For instance, in the *meso corporatist capitalism*, internal mobility of the workers used to be a key variable in reaction to external shocks. This is the Japanese or Korean approach, with their *keiretsu* and *chaebol* as key actors.

- In *social democratic capitalism*, well organized workers and firms recurrently negotiate social compromises. Therefore, institutional and organizational changes emerge out of renegotiation of previous arrangements, via the search of consensus. This is the case in many Northern European countries, such as Sweden, Finland and Denmark.
- In *state-led capitalism*, generally people don't like markets, as is the case in France, and firms don't want to adopt the corporatist strategy. Thus, the State has to take the lead. This is the continental model, more or less centralized and efficient, that is observed in a centralized form in France, more decentralized in Germany, and more clientelist in Italy. This is a public-led model.
- The fifth model is the Southern European model, in which you have a legacy of a paternalistic State and a family-centered welfare. It is in a sense a variant of the continental public-led European model.

All these configurations are constantly evolving in reaction to the transformations of the international environment, technical change and the shift in political alliance. This is a recurring theme in all regulationist research. For instance, most American economists were thinking that the German system was decaying, whereas some institutionalists were pointing out its structural stability (Hall and Soskice, 2001). Actually, via a series of marginal reforms (Boyer, 2006), the German economy is now again the first exporter in the world, because it has been specializing in the kind of machine tools and high quality consumer goods that the rest of the world, including China and India, is asking for.

You've been on the governing board of the Society of the Advancement of Socio-Economics. How does it relate to the Régulation *School? What has been the influence of economic sociologists such as Veblen (1919) or economists such as Schumpeter (1954) on this approach?*
Since the launching of the research program of the *Régulation* School, the economists involved have looked for complementarities with related social sciences. In search for an alternative to the neoclassical conception of substantive rationality, they have been using the concept of habitus from Pierre Bourdieu. They have been using the methods and the findings of Ecole des Annales and extending them to the contemporary period. More recently, they have been very much interested by the impact of political processes upon the emergence and viability of major institutional forms (Palombarini, 2001).

Therefore, my participation in SASE is continuing this strategy in order to find out alliances and complementarities with other contemporary research programs: economic sociology, in its two variants (American and European), comparative and historical institutional analysis, political economy and of course economic history. Joint books have been edited in order to capture some of the key features of contemporary capitalism (Boyer and Hollingsworth, 1995). The relations with the old American institutionalism, including Veblen (Villeval, 2002) and Commons (Théret, 2002) are less developed but existing. Concerning Schumpeter, the *Régulation* School has tried to combine an evolutionary approach of technology along with a political economy analysis of institutional forms (Coriat and Dosi, 2002) but the interest has focused much more on *The Theory of Evolution* (1911) than the later Schumpeter of *Capitalism, Socialism and Democracy* (1954). By the way, some regulationists, such as Pascal Petit, play an active role in the EAEPE and try to mix technological and institutional analyses.

In your 2004 book, The Future of Economic Growth, *you have suggested that the anthropogenic model is the future of economic organization. Can you talk about that?*
While looking for followers of Fordism, I carefully analyzed the likelihood of an ICT-led growth regime and a knowledge economy. Quite surprisingly, beneath the surface, I found that for a century, there has been a general trend in the differential growth of healthcare, education, training and leisure activities. Significant contemporary financial disequilibria are closely related to the rise of such an anthropogenetic model, that is, the production of mankind by mankind. My feeling is clear: what most analysts perceive as ad hoc problems and transitory disequilibria are de facto related to the emergence of this model, simultaneously in the developed and developing world.

This diagnosis has important consequences concerning the respective role of markets and State in the regulation, in the American sense, of the anthropogenetic sectors. Far away from ideologies, international comparisons recurrently show that collectively organized healthcare systems are simultaneously more efficient and fairer than typical market-centered organizations. But quite ironically, most European governments are groping along a marketization of health and education, whereas collectively financed and organized systems are one of the greatest assets of the European Union.

Some (Thom, 1975; Lordon, 1997) have argued that catastrophe theory can help understand economic issues, but in your writings, you seem to have resisted this argument.
No, quite on the contrary I may have anticipated the use of catastrophe in order to interpret the brutal shift from a high employment to a low

employment associated with the crisis of Fordism. In a model co-authored with Yves Balasko (Balasko and Boyer, 1980) we show that with the co-existence of two technologies exhibiting respectively increasing and decreasing returns to scale, a marginal shift in the demand could trigger a brusque discontinuity in economic activity. This is a reply to the quite trivial approach of real business cycles: they require a large exogenous shift in order to explain the transition from growth to recession or depression. In a sense, Frédéric Lordon (1997) has proposed another source of non-linearity – that is a logistic for productivity increases as a function of market size – interacting with a Godwin type model of income distribution and accumulation. This was followed by an equivalent strategy applied to the issue of globalization by Donatella Gatti (2000). Globalization may first enhance economic activity and then up to some threshold reduce it. Unfortunately, the test for heterodox macro modeling has been eroded under the aegis of the so-called "micro foundations of macroeconomics", which was in fact the adoption of Walrasian economics by almost all the economics profession. Ironically, the French establishment represented by Edmond Malinvaud reacted quite negatively to this new paradigm, stating that "marginal impact could only produce marginal outcomes" and that "I would know if several macroeconomic equilibria were really existing".

Where does the Régulation *School fit with the Post-Autistic movement (Guerrien, 2002)?*

The *Régulation* School basically agrees with the demand of the Post-Autistic movement since in a sense its research agenda is in line with the demands of rebel students and a (small) fraction of the economists. First, they ask for more diversity in terms of approaches, methodology and political economy orientations. Second, they are interested in more historically grounded analysis, that is a return to a significant volume of teaching concerning economic history and history of economic doctrines, theories and methodologies. Third, they want economists to deal with contemporary problems instead of abstract and a-temporal analysis. You might recognize some of the key orientations of the regulationist research program.

The problems have been diagnosed, but unfortunately the solutions have not been implemented: vocal students ask for radical changes but professors are the decision makers of last resort. They decide about the content of the curricula, and they tend to follow their own orientations in terms of research and clearly most of them were unable to teach the sub-disciplines concerned: history, political economy, contemporary economic policies. Therefore, some talented people are leaving economics to go into other more interesting fields such as management, law, economic sociology.

Consequently, the ills previously diagnosed have only marginally been cured. Currently, the first years of study of economics is not learning about economics but about mathematical tools required to formalize afterwards neoclassical theories. Mathematics is used as a selecting device in order to detect the talented students, potentially able to become professional economists. It is no surprise that the failure rate of first years is impressive.

But isn't France one of the great centers of mathematical economics?
Yes of course, because traditionally France has a strong cohort of talented mathematicians. In economics, engineers from Grandes Ecoles have turned mathematical economists or simply economists. If internationally the name of the game of the profession is to formalize, no doubt that the French education system produces a significant number of talented world class economists. But it is not a reason for imposing a heavy and unfriendly training in mathematics for anyone entering economic curricula. In my view it is a very bad strategy to say that one must study math before one can study economics. We should simultaneously learn theory and policy. One cannot teach Debreu to thousands of students. Math should not be used as a selective device.

How influential has the Régulation *School been in influencing policy in France? Was it not influential on the 8th 5-Year Plan in the early 1980s through its long association with the CGP, the main planning body?*
Given the institutional connections between CEPREMAP and CGP, the findings of the *Régulation* School have permeated towards some policy makers via the drafting of special reports and the participation in commissions and working groups. Another diffusion went through the channel of general public opinion and the teaching of economics in secondary schools via textbooks. Furthermore most French politicians have heard about the diagnosis concerning Fordism and its crisis. It was specially so for some leaders of the French socialist party. When Lionel Jospin created the Conseil d'Analyse Economique he appointed Michel Aglietta, Alain Lipietz and myself among a quite eclectic bunch of economists of all persuasions.

But there is a dark side to our relations with politics. Back in 1981, when Mitterrand became president, for purely political reasons his strategy was to ally with the Communist party in order to reduce its influence; it is the reason why the government decided to nationalize. This was not at all the kind of policy supported by the *Régulation* School. The research has shown that the issue of private/public property is orthogonal to the search for alternatives to Fordism. We argued that with the opening up of the French economy, the extra public spending would mainly benefit Germany. When asked what to do, we argued that France needed an incomes policy and an ambitious reform of the wage–labor nexus towards a new distribution of productivity between skill formation, work duration, wage and social benefit in order to govern a long and painful transition. This was probably too technocratic, since the pure political logic won: the Left decided to nationalize, to have a Keynesian re-inflation in a single country. Of course the related macroeconomic failure ended up in a complete reversal of economic policy in 1983 with a long-lasting austerity period.

From this episode we learned a central lesson: in the phrase "economic policy", the most important term is not economic, it is policy. Since then, Bruno Théret, Stefano Palombarini and Bruno Amable have been investigating the impact of political processes upon economic policy formation and especially institutional reform. This is one of our major agendas.

There is a movement to combine CEPREMAP with other research institutes. Is this a threat to the heterodox traditions that CEPREMAP has housed, such as the Régulation *School, Marxist economics, and ecological economics? And is the push toward Americanization behind that threat?*
The answer is definitely yes, since the American academic system now is the benchmark. This is a response to the globalization of the economics profession. It is necessary to keep brilliant French students who prefer to go to American universities and to attract others within a fierce European competition. It is important to recruit the best researchers and hence a much more differentiated salary policy in favor of the very best. Consequently, in such excellence centers, the teaching language is English. Still more, the curriculum has to exactly mimic the international standards, that is the American ones, with a lag of approximately a decade. Such an adaptation has taken place. There was the fusion of the researchers working in the three research centers, CERAS, DELTA and CEPREMAP. CEPREMAP (it now means CEntre Pour la Recherche EconoMique et ses APplications) has been transformed into a funding agency in order to promote the diffusion of academic research. The doctoral program "Analyse et Politique économique" has been redesigned in order to (try) to compete with London and Toulouse Schools, among others.

The consequences for non-mainstream research have been quite clear: dissolution of the regulationist team has removed our financial autonomy and discarded our specific research. We proposed a larger theme, the political economy of institutional change, with the hope that some other economists, even rational choice oriented, could join it. But the answer we got was "no, this does not exist in American economics departments". So our agenda is downplayed at every point. We are tolerated as a small part of economic history, which is really just swept under the carpet. It is a dramatic change and it is not isolated. We are probably the end of the French exceptionalism in economics. The Paris School of Economics wants just to compete with the rest of the world on the same terrain and no longer to innovate. But industrial organization theory and history suggests that by definition if you compete with the leader on the same ground, you lose.

How did the change come about?
At least three forces have coalesced. For technocratic reasons, CNRS, one of the major sources of funding for French research, has pushed for the constitution of large entities by the fusion of geographically or thematically close teams. Some young and modernist economists, who had long been struggling among them to take the lead in the concentration of Parisian research, agreed to respond positively to the CNRS pressure and shared accordingly the power and financing. Last but not least, the review of the Social Science Index, reinforced by the Shanghai ranking of universities, convinced the French establishment that "big is beautiful". Paradoxically marketing has become much more important than strategic choices concerning possible comparative institutional advantages of French academia. Possible breakthroughs and originality are no longer even considered.

To what extent are differences between US and European economics due to political differences rather than intellectual differences?
There is a wonderful comparative study about the styles in political economy and economic theorizing (Fourcade-Gouringhas, 2001). She argues that you have as many branches of political economy as national trajectories, shaped by the style of State interventions in the economy. Because political economy depends on the process of the formation of capitalism, the same analytical tools may have opposite consequences. In France, for instance, the State has been the main user and sometimes the originator of modern economic analysis: sophisticated microeconomic tools have been built not by firms for analyzing consumer behavior but by economic administration for the optimal management of public utilities, such as electricity and transportation. Thus, the tools that in the US are used to prove that the market allocates scarce resources efficiently are used in France in order to design and monitor markets and justify public intervention. Of course this is now more common with asymmetric information markets hypothesis, but this interpretation was already dominant back in the 1960s.

   Thus, in France, we don't think that the market is naturally efficient. On the contrary, it seems to be very difficult for English-speaking countries to understand that the State has been a large organizer and modernizer of the French economy, including using microeconomic theory. For example, why don't we have shortages in electricity in France like they have in California? In part, it is because we had economists like my microeconomics teacher, Marcel Boiteux, a very clever microeconomist, who was in charge of the nationalized electric company, EDF. Back in the 1960s he designed incredibly sophisticated models which told how to price public utilities in order to mimic competitive markets even in the case of monopoly. For French economists, it is not at all contradictory to talk about an efficient State. The deep logic of the State is to promote efficiency. Today, we learn micro as the founding block of macroeconomics and criticism of public intervention. What a strange evolution!

Given the pressure of a universal standard, what can be done?
A strategy would be that European economists would assemble and work out an alternative way for research and teaching in economics. But the drama of Europe is that it does not exist as an entity. In the academic world, each national community is mainly tied to the United States, or to some extent the United Kingdom. The European economists want to emulate the American Economic Association. The benchmark is always the US academic system.

Textbooks are United States textbooks with European examples added. European research is rarely homegrown in response to specific problems and the universities aim at producing US-style economists. What we should be doing is creating our own benchmarks for research and teaching, and thus the mobility of economists across Europe would progressively consolidate this new academic model.

There are a number of very specific methods of evaluating research developing in Europe. Britain has the Research Assessment Exercise (RAE); in the Netherlands and Spain, there are specific lists of journals being used to rate people's research. We've heard rumors that they are thinking of such a system for France. Can you speak about that?
In the past, assessment was ad hoc. At the university level, the evaluation system was so ad hoc that it seemed to be designed just to allow people to promote their own students. Therefore at the central level for entering CNRS or to be entitled to be hired by any university, two commissions were in charge of filtering the applications. Thus some competition was introduced. Two decades ago, I served on them. People were supposed to read all the papers and were making their own judgments, and there was no journal list. It was not that bad. Then you could detect a very bright

person working outside mainstream approaches and she/he could enter the career.

Now, with the increased pressure to publish, the growing numbers of PhDs, the internationalization of the profession and the Information and Communication Technologies facilities, the recruitment committees trust more and more the assessment provided by the number of articles published and the ranking of the related journals. Basically, people don't read the work any more. The ranking largely reflects the United States system so anyone who follows a different path ranks low. Of course each scientific community is struggling in order to promote its own favorite journals in the list and ranking of publications, but the pressure towards adoption of typical international standards is quite strong. On one side this system brings more clarity and "objectivity" into the academic system, but on the other side I am fearful about what this means for diversity and innovation. It might be efficient in the short to medium run, but in the long run it might erode inventiveness and diversity. People used to use their time reading, thinking and discussing with colleagues, and publication was the outcome. Now they use their time optimizing their effort to maximize the rank of the reviews they publish, and adapt the content of their research accordingly. Procedures and form outweigh the search for content and relevant theorizing.

One of us has proposed that Europe adopt a list of journals that includes journals open to broader views; would that help?
This is exactly the process taking place in CNRS, traditionally interested in promoting interdisciplinary research, for instance economic history, economic sociology and new areas of research. For instance, *Revue de la Régulation* has been admitted in the ranking of recognized reviews. But CNRS is in a weak position under the threat of being transformed into a mere funding agency. Furthermore, the top students ask for a typical US training; they want what will move them ahead, so there is strong pressure to not use a separate European standard. Today, a French economist, in order to get an adequate salary, needs an appointment at both a university and a research institute. Because the research institutes use US standards, this places enormous pressures for them to follow the US standards of research.

What do you see as the future of economics over the next 25 or so years?
It may actually dissolve as an integrated scientific discipline. I perceive three major tendencies:

- First, one observes a *balkanization* of the profession according to the issues, the domains, the techniques and the nature of social demand.

By the way, this extreme division of labor makes the evaluation of research more and more difficult and is why most academic authorities trust the assessment of each research community and only put a hierarchy upon their respective journals and reviews.

- Second, a high degree of *professionalization* is built upon the use of more and more refined techniques, for instance in econometrics or simulations. Financial analysis of markets seems to have totally divorced from previous financial theory since high profile mathematicians and statistical physicists have created a brand new sub-discipline, in high demand given the mathematization of contemporary economies.
- Third, the influence of new social demands from quite powerful economic actors and the primacy of techniques and expertise over the elaboration of economic concepts seem to imply a kind of *loss of substance of economics*. PhD students in economics tend to become specialists in data analysis according to a quite inductive and ad hoc approach with fewer and fewer links with explicit and formal modeling. Just an example: I attended a PhD seminar recently, the theme of which was "The influence of social norms upon the diffusion of obesity". No economic hypothesis was even mentioned but an intensive use of panel data analysis was the core of the research.

Thus, the economic content of more and more PhDs in economics is near zero. My first fear is about the dissolution of economics. Economics will become the analysis of complex data sets, whatever the data set. My second fear is that we won't have much need for typical economists. We will have many more technical experts and very few high theorists. This would imply a shrinking of the profession and its complete re-composition into new competences.

What do you think of the complexity work economists are doing in places like Santa Fe?
I am quite sympathetic to the Santa Fe project. My next paper is precisely using a model borrowed from statistical physics in order to understand the evolution of the quality criteria that governs the competition in the wine industry in France over one century. I am returning to my physics roots. This can be a promising avenue since it might explain the emergence of economic configurations out of the interactions between heterogeneous actors. Nevertheless, it faces two major difficulties. First, to do these models requires competences that economists do not possess and therefore they have to ally with physicists who do not necessarily have mastery of the basic concepts and reasoning of economists. This is for instance the

case for a quite interesting theory of viability (Aubin, 1991): nice dynamic patterns but not any reference to the role of prices! Second, generally you cannot derive analytical results since you have to make many simulations and risk inferences about the origins of changing configurations. Therefore, I feel that these approaches will experience many difficulties in order to compete against simpler, often false, but analytically grounded formalizations by conventional economists. They may succeed in finance or spatial theory but not necessarily in macro theory for instance, because the models with heterogeneous agents are too complex to be able to be explicit about where the results come from. So the teaching of economics may well continue to rely on simple models, essentially false but easier to master intellectually. This is already the drama of contemporary macroeconomic theory. I hope that this quite pessimistic prognosis will be proven false by a renaissance of our profession.

PART III

Reflections

12.   János Kornai

This interview took place in Budapest, Hungary on 30 July, 2008

What is your overall reaction to this project?
I was happy to hear about the project and to read parts of the first volume (Colander et al., 2004a) and portions of this one. I welcome your enthusiastic efforts to give an overview of heterodoxy out of mainstream, and to try and structure the ideas. There are certain characteristic elements of your project where I share your views, and we are in complete agreement, some on which I have no view, and then there are other issues where I believe you are leaving out certain aspects of contemporary economics, which I find important. The fact that you don't discuss them can be a sign that you don't find them important. There is little sense in discussing issues where I have no view or those issues where we agree. Thus, I hope we will spend much of the discussion on the disagreements, especially regarding matters you have left out of your presentation.

Where I agree is in your description of the American economics profession. There, I'm both an insider and an outsider. I spent 18 years teaching at Harvard in the United States – from 1986 to 2002. I had taught at Princeton, Stanford and Yale before that. I agree with your description of the self-perpetuating, oligopolistic mechanism that reproduces itself. The world of ideas in American economics is not a monopoly, but there is a very powerful core that does not reflect a fair competition of ideas. So there we are in full agreement.

I agree with you that Europe, instead of enhancing its own history is focusing too much on imitating the American pattern, and is becoming a second United States program. Also, I agree with your view that we need more diversity. Here it is not just agreement, but strong agreement.

What did we leave out?
You are urging all heterodoxies of the world to unite, and then everything from central Europe, from the Soviet Union and the post-Soviet region, and from China, everything east of the former Iron Curtain, is treated as non-existing.

There are hundreds and hundreds of economists, sociologists and political scientists in the Eastern part of the world, including China. They have been thinking about certain problems for decades. There are hundreds of voices, and you do not listen to these voices.

I am afraid referring to language difficulties would not excuse the exclusion. There were remarkable publications in English, written by authors of the ignored region. And there are various books and papers written by Western scholars who specialized in comparative economics, comparative politics, Sovietology, transitology etc., reporting on the discourse in that part of the world. I was surprised by these two volumes. I am meeting here the two authors of an excellent book, *Comparative Economics in a Transforming World Economy* (2004), written by Rosser and Rosser, profoundly studying alternative systems and providing clear analysis of the big issues related to systems. The same persons forget about their own work incorporated in the Rosser and Rosser volume, while editing the present volume

I have almost no disagreement with the other interviews. Nevertheless, I got the impression that we are not on the same wave-length with the subjects of the other interviews. We do not address the same issues. The "excitement" felt by your other partners and by me and my colleagues is caused by quite different puzzles. Your concept of "heterodoxy" or non-mainstream is so unconstrained that it might become an almost empty concept. Like "non-linear" or "non-Muslim". Club of all out-layers? I am not sure that we, economists working in formerly communist countries, fit in well here. You have a dinner of French cuisine, and you serve, just for the sake of larger variety also Chinese dumplings and Hungarian goulash.

In this context let me make a few remarks related to my own contributions. What you left out from your overview of heterodox approaches is my whole life's work (Kornai, 1971, 1980, 1992, 2000, 2007, 2008a). I don't want to give the impression that my concern is out of vanity. The fact that you wanted to talk to me means that you feel some respect for my work. So I am not hunting for your personal respect.

I feel uneasy because you are skipping over what is happening in the

Eastern debates of intellectual life – and that is not compensated by the fact that some people know my name and by the chance to have a conversation with you. Sometimes I feel like Tarzan felt when he was invited to a dinner of British gentlemen in the Tarzan movie. I am coming from the jungle and I know how to use a knife and fork and therefore I am acceptable. It's flattering to be at the dinner, but I am there with mixed feelings.

What came to me as I read through your interviews is how little I know the people you interview, and I suspect, they don't know me or my work. I have obviously met some of them, but it has not involved an ongoing relationship.

We were hoping that you would give voice to those issues. That was one of the motivations for this interview.
I respectfully disagree with that kind of division of labor – I would present the intellectual contributions of our region, while you and your colleagues, the advocates of heterodoxy, did not even try to integrate these contributions into your own thinking, or work hard for the incorporation of these ideas into our common new general approach.

Perhaps the editors and the subjects of the other interviews seem to have a split personality. How is it possible that you absolutely understand the importance of diversity and then miss such an important point? There is a whole way of thinking that is different from mainstream economics in the discourse "East of the Iron Curtain", and you don't recognize it in this volume.

Is the issue that is missing a discussion of systems and what you call the system paradigm?
Let me give you an indirect answer. In Western teaching, it is quite common to discuss a line of thought: Pareto (1896–97), Barone (1908), Lange (1936), Hayek (1940), and debates about socialism around 1930–1940 come up. And then it more or less ends. But the debate continued for 50 or 60 years or more and is still going on! That is not part of the standard discussion on "the debate on socialism".

Let us consider this phenomenon in a wider context. There is an ongoing debate for more than a century on systems. That became an important intellectual tradition, an influential school of thinking. It starts with Marx (1867), then Mises (1920) and Hayek (1944), Schumpeter (1942), Polányi (1944), and the German theorist of the social market economy, Walter Eucken (1940). I would place my own contributions about the socialist system in this intellectual current. The names just mentioned do not share the same political views, but they share a common interest in certain great puzzles: what are the inherent properties of alternative socio-political-economic systems. My point is that you miss this whole current of heterodoxy. I believe that a serious discussion of this line of thinking about great systems belongs to the broad picture of non-mainstream economics. It's not that the economists just mentioned don't know about the standard ideas, such as the law of supply and demand. It is that they are interested in a different set of questions, namely the great questions of world history. What are the pros and cons of capitalism? What are the pros and cons of socialism? Is there a third way? These are issues, clearly different from the set of questions studied by mainstream economics. You miss the whole line of heterodox thought that focuses on those issues.

One possible response to our leaving it out might be that socialism is essentially dead. We don't necessarily hold that, but it could be a defense for us. The second is that we are indirectly capturing that difference. One of the ideas that has been popping up in our interviews is that in the US there is stronger emphasis on markets and individual decision-making, and in Europe there is more of a focus on the social market economy and group decision-making. This difference shows up in terms of different research approaches that we believe the interviews captured. That difference in research approach captures different views on what society should be.

I find it highly oversimplified to say that the Soviet Union collapsed, and therefore the whole controversy over capitalism versus socialism is not interesting any more. Even if socialism would be dead forever, it would be still interesting because it is part of history. Studying history is important even if it deals with dead systems, dead regimes, dead ideas and dead people. We are the last generation that experienced that debate about socialism.

It is also not true that all socialist countries have disappeared. Cuba and North Korea are still living in a socialist system, and they are causing a lot of headaches in world politics. China still calls itself a communist country. And then think about Latin America! There are countries that are trying to create a new socialism. So I don't think the argument that the intellectual discourse about socialism is passé holds up.

Furthermore, there are issues that are on the agenda all over the world, including developed market economies that show some similarities to the problems experienced during the reform movements in the socialist region. I'm involved with the health sector reform, and I feel quite at home in doing so, given that the health sector is a hybrid form of public and private. The same issues about centralization and decentralization, planning and market, fixed or flexible prices, shortage and surplus, waiting lines and rationing, legal operation, black and grey markets, that concerned us in the socialist era exist today in the health sector. All the big questions debated in the controversies about market socialism, come up again in the discourse about reforming the health sector in the USA, in Western Europe, Eastern Europe or Russia. So the issues remain; in that sense socialism is not dead.

Let us say that we agree; your charge is reasonable, and we are glad you raised the issues.
There are a number of general issues that I would like to talk about that relate to your project. One is interdisciplinary issues, a second is mathematics, a third is publication of semi-finished products, and the last is the underlying philosophy of economics, which is one of the central problems of orthodox economics.

Let us ask first about your discussion of publication of semi-finished work. What are your views here?
Arriving at an understanding of something is a mental process that typically goes through various stages. A simplified understanding of the issue would involve first seeing a problem, and recognizing it. Then you come to a tentative answer expressed not precisely, but vaguely, and then you sharpen your understanding. Finally, you might arrive at a precise answer to the problem. I enjoy the first parts of understanding most, and I leave to others to do the last stage. I have the strongest admiration for those who do the first. The first one is the most important. Almost all important discoveries of social science start in a non-precise form, and then become more exact and precise.

What is the key to creativity?
There is psychology and there is social setting involved. I think it involves curiosity and open-mindedness – a skeptical attitude that you put question marks to a sentence where others put a full stop. It involves looking at problems that have been considered by many others with a fresh eye. Of course you need an intellectual talent, but many with intellectual talent are not necessarily original. Your first attempts at finding an answer are often vague, but you understand that there is an interesting problem there. Maybe your answer is wrong, but you understand that it is important.

Keynes wouldn't be able to publish anything today. He would at best be able to have an obscure blog on the internet. All respectable journals would reject his work.

I don't want a uniform rule. Some journals may have highly polished papers. But we do not get sufficient guidance for reading due to the almost infinite supply of working papers. There is just too much there on the internet. I think what we need are 10 or so distinguished and respectable journals, each with a different criterion of acceptance: relevance and originality, instead of refinement and polish. These editors should not rely mechanically on referee reports, and they should avoid conditional acceptances. So, I would like to see editors helping me to find pathbreaking new ideas, half-finished but relevant thoughts in these kinds of journals. Keynes was an editor of the *Economic Journal* for a while. We need more journals like they used to have – where the editor takes full responsibility, even with mistakes.

There is also another aspect calling for new journals and new editorial principles. We need journals that will publish serious interdisciplinary social science papers.

What role do you think environment plays?
I think the present situation in American economics is really problematic in this regard. If you have an interesting idea, but are not able to write it down in an absolutely precise mathematical model, or you are not able to formulate it as a testable hypothesis that can be tested by economic analysis. But if you work on a problem that is basically already solved, and you make a little twist on that, that includes the latest mathematics, then you do well. However, it is not really contributing a lot to knowledge. This is especially hard in social science, where much of theory is not subject to experiments.

What is your view of the rise of experimental economics?
It helps in solving certain problems, but not in solving other problems. Let me demonstrate my reservation with the issues we are discussing here. You cannot experiment with reforms very easily, and the policy is not repeatable, as the nearly tragic situation with the Hungarian health reform shows (Kornai, 2008b.) At the real system level you cannot do experiments.

I am worried by the world-wide tendency to suggest uniform prescriptions for the whole world. Quite a few reform-minded policy-makers want to decentralize in a centralized way, introduce by fiat market-oriented reforms. They tell people – you must use the market. It's a market economy created by command – you instruct people to act like market individuals.

Let reforms develop from the bottom up. Reforms should be tried at provincial and local levels when possible. This way a country, and at a higher level, the whole world is serving as a laboratory for experiments. We are able to do serious comparative studies, analyzing the advantages and disadvantages of a large set of different changes in various countries, regions, municipalities. The study of real-life mutations can lead to more reliable conclusions than artificial experiments in an artificial environment.

To sum up: I have respect for experimental economics if it is limited to what it can truly shed light on. But, unfortunately, that isn't always the most important set of problems.

What objections do you have to modern economics?
I disagree with those who say that economists have the unconditional obligation of specifying the preferences of an agent. This framework of so-called microfoundations is regarded as an undisputable condition of any work to be taken seriously. I would be more tolerant. If the researcher is able to say something about the decision-makers' preferences, that's fine. But I would not impose this approach on every researcher; I would not prescribe it as a mandatory component of every piece of theoretical work. One can say a meaningful scientific proposition simply by analyzing impact and reaction. If I know the relationship between impact and reaction, I can say meaningful things, without having to know what the driving force of the micro agent is. When I look at the core axioms of orthodoxy, I find that here is where I disagree. It seems that any time you do not say what the goal of the agent is, your analysis is considered ad hoc, and cannot be taken seriously. Mathematically that leads to various optimization techniques, which is fine, but optimization is not an absolute requirement of economic science. In each social science it might be sufficient to know that there is a repetitive pattern. What this means is that you don't need the so-called microfoundations to do good science for example in macroeconomics. The question is whether the model is convincing, fits real experience well and leads to workable conclusions, and now whether it has microfoundations.

The issue is not only relevant for macro; it is also relevant for micro. For example, in my book with Béla Martos on *Non-Price Control* (Kornai and Martos, 1981) we tried to do that. All one needs is response functions. In the paper published in *Econometrica* (Kornai and Martos, 1973) and later on in our book we used differential and difference equations to describe the motion of economic systems. The system relied on non-price signals like change of inventories or change of the backlog of orders. Our models lead to interesting conclusions in spite of the fact that they did not specify the preferences or objectives of the decision-makers.

One of the worst properties of much standard analysis is the assumption that the governments have a maximand. Governments are very complicated institutions. Apart from rhetoric they do not maximize anything. Politics is full of mutually conflicting, inconsistent goals, and therefore full of hesitation, vacillation, ups and downs. Creating a consistent government objective function makes the model alien to real political decision-making and therefore almost irrelevant.

What's your view of mathematics in economics?
I am a great fan of using mathematics. It has an extremely important place
in all kinds of thinking. But I find it highly damaging to make the use of
mathematics mandatory in writing a serious respectable paper. There are
certain issues that can be handled by mathematics and there are certain
issues that cannot. There is some positive correlation between relevance
and inapplicability of mathematics. The more difficult the question, the
less it can be mathematized. I'm not talking about rigor. One can be
rigorous in prose. Rigor is to a large extent a question of the precision
and clarity of definitions, as well as the precision and transparency of the
argumentation. You can have a mathematical model with all the precise
proofs of theorems and it can be absolutely sloppy because the fundamental concepts are not well defined. I am for more rigor, but I see rigor
differently than some other members of our profession. I see rigor mainly
as the crystal-clear understanding of the problem and the fundamental
concepts. I seriously object to the monopoly or close-to-monopoly of
mathematics as a tool of scientific analysis that seems to exist in the economics profession.

*Some economists in Western Europe seem to be pushing a relatively narrow
view of what is going on in American economics. An idea in our earlier book
was that some of the leading US economists at the highest levels of the mainstream, such as Kenneth Arrow, are much more open than many Western
European economists seem to think and that in parts of Western Europe they
are following a much more narrow-minded version of economic orthodoxy.
What is the situation for Eastern Europe? Is it following the narrow version,
or a more open version?*
Unfortunately, I see the first as being the case. In order to survive in the
world-wide profession, several colleagues here in this region think they
have to do that. They are even more servile than Western Europeans.
However, I should also say that I am not in a position to have a reliable
overview. I haven't reviewed all the Eastern European literature or studied
what is going on in teaching. I have bits and pieces of information. I am
regarded as a bit of an outsider here as well as in Western Europe and in
the United States, even though many in Eastern Europe regard me as their
teacher.

For Eastern Europe, my impression is that there are two clusters of
economists, where I define an economist as someone who is teaching in
an economics department. I will talk about two clusters, and there are, of
course, individuals outside of these clusters.

One group includes middle-aged and older economists who started their
career under the communist era and now they are either retrained formally

or self-restrained. They like to study easier subjects. They find institution-alism highly attractive. For a former Marxist, that is easier to learn. In any case, they didn't arrive at heterodoxy after a long struggle with theory the way someone like Duncan Foley (1982) or Steven Marglin (1974) did, but instead they went directly to institutionalism. Karl Polanyi is popular with many in this group, especially here in Hungary.

The other group is typically younger, and the dominant core of this group has received their PhD in the United States and is well trained in current mainstream economics. Some of them are very good and they move back and forth between their home country and the rest of the world. They are interchangeable with United States economists. They are not interested in anything special for this part of the world. They are interested in publishing papers in leading journals, because they want to become respectable members of the profession. They are what you call global economists. They work on problems that the tools can handle – small problems.

There are power struggles between these two groups about positions and money, and I am not a real fan of either one. The second group regards the first group as uncivilized, uneducated, dilettantish, and amateurish, publishing what they consider to be grotesque. But what gets lost by the younger group is any thinking about specific issues that we face.

In your most recent books, you stress the value of an interdisciplinary approach (Kornai, 2008a). You complained about "guest star" economists who came in and didn't know anything about the local conditions, but made advice anyway. Does this seem to be the same problem with the new group?
I should start by repeating that I only have a small sample. But from this small sample, my sense is that they don't worry about big issues – they worry about finding a small problem that they can model, which will lead to a publishable article.

Much of the public debate nowadays in Eastern Europe is uncivilized and uneducated. It is filled with empty political slogans. Our profession isn't trained for these debates. Economists get no training in how to relate economics to ethics, philosophy, psychology, or sociology, which are very important aspects of policy. A young economist trained in the United States learns from his teachers: if one says about a problem that it is an ethical issue, then here is the end of the task of the economist, and he is not obliged to say anything else. "The ethical aspect of a problem is not our business; it should be left to philosophers or priests." I think that is just a cheap excuse. It is the economist's task at least to clarify the ethical implication of the positive findings and especially of the prescription and policy recommendations. This is the minimum, and even that requires some training in moral reasoning. In addition, I like the economists who are ready to reveal their own values and link their recommendations to a clearly stated value system. But that is an addition which I would not necessarily require from everybody.

To do policy, you need a much broader training than economists get. Everything that you say in this volume about complexity is relevant from that point of view.

Do you believe that transdisciplinary education can be achieved through educational reform, or through greater cooperation of already trained specialists? Did the older group have the luxury of a broader education?
I don't want to suggest a uniform recipe for that. I don't mind if certain economists are only economists in a narrow sense. But others need at least one course in philosophy and ethics, and another course in sociology or political science or both during their graduate studies, to allow them to work intelligently with other social scientists. This would include economists who would be involved in policy issues. If the economists read on their own, they don't need the courses. Marx, Hayek and Schumpeter all read broadly, and went far beyond economics. Broad education is needed for young people who intend to enter politics, or decision-making at a higher level.

I would also like to see academic cooperation between disciplines. An institute like ours is an excellent place for that. That is one of the roles for our Institute for Advanced Study. I had a focus group here on the problem of honesty and trust. We had economists, political scientists, sociologists, historians and lawyers. It was quite interesting.

Earlier you said that there was a difference between Eastern European economists and Chinese economists? How do Chinese economists differ from other economists?
There are more Western-trained Chinese economists than Western-trained Eastern Europeans. There is a difference, however. Some of these Chinese economists are thinking about really fundamental issues, whereas I don't see that with Western-trained Eastern European economists. They are thinking specifically about what makes China different from the West and from the rest of the Communist world. They think about history and culture.

These Chinese economists are closer to my idea of a general social scientist than are Western-trained Eastern European economists (Kornai and Qian, 2008). This makes their work more interesting to me than much of what I read of the younger economists here in Eastern Europe. Chinese economists are making some original contributions. I'm not arguing that it is an either–or. As in the past in Eastern Europe, the Chinese economists face the problem of self-censorship, as certain topics are forbidden to discuss openly, particularly in Chinese language publications. There are different life strategies which are morally acceptable according to my own value system. If you want to be a dissident and risk your individual freedom, that is highly respectable. But I can fully understand also people who are keeping silent about certain issues regarded as political taboos by the political leadership and are active in another area of the public good. I have special respect for those who are really reconsidering the basic issues of economics.

Some consider Chinese reforms to have been influenced by your work.
Better to ask Chinese colleagues about that. What is factually certainly true: *Economics of Shortage* (Kornai, 1980) sold over 100 000 copies in China. I am amazed how many people in China have told me they were influenced by the book. Some have told me that they were my students, including even policy-makers at the central and local level.

Doesn't the Chinese path of reforms go against your view that a Third Way is not stable over time (Kornai, 1990; 1992)?
There is no system that is neither capitalism nor socialism. The hybrid form prevailing in China can find a place in the large box that I call capitalism. Capitalism is a very large box, with many variations that are different in various countries and change over time. I see it as a system with a dominance of private property, but not necessarily exclusively with private property. In China, the system evolved gradually. It wasn't structured after any economist's paper, and they have not worried about workers' management or cooperatives or the other sorts of things that Third Way advocates in Europe have often focused on. The emergence of private property started in agriculture. The agricultural reform was not followed by spectacular campaigns of privatization. They just gave the green light to the entry of private entrepreneurs, small and medium-sized business. This way the private sector increased rapidly. And then there were also certain very special forms of creating private business entities. One of these forms was the creation of town and village enterprises. At the beginning they were officially called collective companies, communal property. But in fact it was jointly owned by the community of the town and village which received part of the revenues, by the management and perhaps the employees of the firm, and also by the local mayor and the party secretary. It happened quite a few times that the mayor of a town simply took over the local firm, and he was very motivated to make it work. There is a large diversity in the form of sharing of profits and ultimately in the sharing of real (not nominal but real) ownership.

If you apply strict Western legal and moral standards, a large part of the Chinese ownership arrangements could be regarded as corruption. The mayor or the party apparatchik gets a part of the profit! I find this type of legalized corruption a way of weakening the resistance of the former cadre of leaders. If you don't want civil war between supporters of capitalism and opponents of capitalism, you must allow the clever members of the ruling elite to become interested in the change in the system. Therefore it is a good idea to allow a Chinese general and mayor to get something out of that. It may be morally disgusting, but it is probably necessary to oil the process of change. Maybe it is more a matter of having a second best rather than a third way.

In your memoirs (Kornai, 2007), which are very interesting, you describe how you came from a sophisticated and cultured Jewish family. Many in your family died during the Nazi rule. How did you personally escape?
I was 16 when the Nazis invaded. Half a million people were murdered in a few weeks, including my father, who before Hitler took power had worked as a lawyer for German companies and did not think he would be victimized. I was in Budapest, where there were not mass deportations, although I served for a few weeks in a slave labor camp, and then escaped. I describe my story in more detail in my memoirs. It was the fortunate result of the coincidence of luck, risk-taking and right instincts on my part (I was 16 at the time!), and benevolence of some people who helped me, particularly a group of Jesuits in Budapest.

In the 1950s you were a supporter of orthodox Stalinist views. Was this in some way a reaction against Nazism?
Certainly, it was one of the components as I saw Stalin as saving Hungary from the Nazis, but I don't think that was the only cause. There were other factors. I was attracted by Marxism as a universal answer to everything. I was non-religious, and was looking for a *Weltanschauung*. Marxism offers that. Another factor was that I was opposed to the pre-war economic system which had kept masses of people in deep poverty. Finally, I liked being part of a collective, belonging to a group, and the Communist Youth Movement provided that, with many intelligent people belonging to it. Later I became much more individualistic. But after the war, I was looking to be part of a broader movement.

You rose rapidly as a journalist, which was aided by your excellent knowledge of German. Was that an important part of your initial training in economics? Has that affected your views?
Yes, I think that the practical views I got as a journalist helped me understand how a communist system actually works. I learned to get

information by talking to people. This has implications for methodology. Economics cannot be only a science of analyzing data. Economists must talk to people. It's not the same as doing a survey, but it is important to actually talk to the people in the field you are studying, with workers and managers in firms about how they actually make decisions. I learned a lot as a reporter, but my interpretation of what I learned was wrong. Later on I put on quite a different interpretation, much like the change that happens in an Escher painting that shows one thing when looked at a certain way and something else when looked at another, as seen on the cover of Rosser and Rosser (2004).

I was privileged during that period to attend meetings of the economics committee of the ruling Politburo, which was led by the Number Two figure in the government. I saw him make important decisions in a strong way and much admired him for that. However, later I would come to be disturbed at how he did this without consulting with others, without gaining input from people affected by these decisions.

How did you come to move away from your orthodox Stalinist views?
I was not moved by rational argument. I was aware of the rational arguments against it but did not react to these arguments. My change came from the emotional and ethical side. A former colleague of mine, an enthusiastic Communist, told me how he was cruelly tortured to make false confessions by another enthusiastic Communist, whom I knew, and who was a nice person, not a sadist or anything, because it was ordered by the party. Then I finally began to understand that cruelty, torture, prosecution and punishment of innocent people was a systemic problem, not due to the personal characteristics of the people running the system.

I had thought of dissidents as enemies of the people, but when I realized that people were making forced false confessions, were lying, then I realized that everything else we were told could be lies. The whole edifice of my convictions, beliefs and norms was destroyed. Then I began to read with an open mind, and I started to see things in a different way. It took two or three years, but over those years I changed. The Hungarian Revolution of 1956 also contributed to my inner urge to go along this road of change.

How did you move from a journalist to an economist?
In 1955 a group of journalists, including me, were fired from our job by the Politburo because we organized a rebellious meeting attacking the communist leadership. When I was removed from journalism for political reasons, I was made a research assistant at half the pay in the Institute of Economics of the Hungarian Academy of Sciences. Eventually I became

a full-time junior research fellow, and started to write my PhD thesis on overcentralization. It was not a normative book; it was a positive book on how a communist system works. I used tables and data. My main source was conversations with medium-level technocrats, the so-called "red executives".

We got closer to the day of the Revolution. The official defense of my thesis became a public event, almost a mass rally, seen as part of the revolutionary movement, with my advocacy of decentralization. A few weeks later, at the very first day of the Revolution I was commissioned by the new revolutionary government to elaborate specific economic policy proposals. The idea was that my proposals would be included in the speech of the Prime Minister when he was going to present his program to Parliament. I started to do the job, worked very hard for several days, but then I felt I was not able to prepare a meaningful, well-elaborated, consistent program for the revolutionary regime. It was heart-breaking, but I just did not feel capable of finishing the job, and gave it up.

After the Revolution was overthrown by the Soviet invasion, the same director of the Economics Institute, who praised me before the Revolution, publicly condemned me as a traitor of socialism and Marxism, and I was fired from the academy. Nevertheless the book was published first in Hungarian in 1957 and later in English by Oxford University Press (Kornai, 1959). So while I got condemned in Hungary, I got high praise in the English and American press. Because of the accusations against my book, my connections with certain illegal conspiracies, and also because I was one of the organizers of a movement aiding the families of arrested dissidents, I was harassed by the Hungarian KGB. Some of my friends were killed, or sentenced to long prison terms, some emigrated, while others would join the new regime.

Why didn't you leave Hungary?
Because I am Hungarian.

In 1963, you were recalled to the Academy, and you were allowed to go to the West. What was your reaction to the West, and what led you to write Anti-Equilibrium *(Kornai, 1971)?*
I enjoyed the consumer society. Beside the pleasures it presented for me also intellectual problems. It suggested that the communist system was failing in important ways. The inspiration for *Anti-Equilibrium* came from my comparing the two systems. For example, I was thinking about the following questions. What are the components of the system that can be changed? Can you introduce the market, while maintaining public

ownership and the political structure? Can you maintain planning and have markets?

In reading Western textbooks, such as the famous one by Paul Samuelson (1961), I found that they didn't have a good understanding of communism. They didn't answer my questions.

I then read Debreu's *Theory of Value* (1959) about general equilibrium theory. I admired his use of mathematics, but found that I wasn't satisfied with the questions he was asking, such as his focus on welfare theorems. Even the western discussions of the socialist calculation debate were too Walrasian, such as the arguments of Oskar Lange. This dissatisfaction led to *Anti-Equilibrium*, especially after I consulted with my old co-author on mathematical topics, Tamás Lipták. After having gotten divorced from my first love, Marxism, it was much easier to divorce from the second love, neoclassical orthodoxy.

Would you say that Anti-Equilibrium *was a forerunner of later complexity ideas?*
I think it might be. But that is not for me to say. Since you are pushing me, I will try to be honest. I think it was a forerunner of complexity economics because it emphatically raised the question that prices are not the only signal that matters. It was also a forerunner of challenging standard utility theory, ideas advocated by Kahneman and Tversky (1982) that have become behavioral economics, problems about information and rationality in the economy. It was a forerunner of many things – maybe too many things. Although it was praised by Kenneth Arrow and Tjalling Koopmans and I guess some graduate students read it at that time, I think the work has been almost completely forgotten now.

How did you come to your most famous idea of the soft budget constraint, which receives a clear statement in your 1980 book, The Economics of Shortage?
The core of the idea came up much earlier, particularly in a paper in Hungarian on profit-sharing in some firms (Kornai, 1958). This early paper described the phenomenon of profit-motivated public firms asking for compensation of losses due to unforeseen external conditions. I also discussed the paternalistic relation between state and firm, comparing it to the relationship between father and son. The son is wasting money, getting in financial trouble, and then the father must help him out. The son is expecting the father's helping hand, and that motivates him in irresponsible spending.

However, I didn't use the name 'soft budget constraint' in my early work. I used it in a lecture course on socialist systems presented at Stockholm University in 1975 for the first time. The term was very important to help people get to understand the idea. If I were writing a 'how to do' book for American economists on how to succeed as an academic economist, I would say that you should coin a term that is close to one learned in introductory economics.

Self-irony aside, I am happy that the concept and the theory of the soft budget constraint became widely known. And I am less happy, because the impact of the soft budget constraint syndrome is still not sufficiently recognized. There are many economists who are ready to admit that the soft budget constraint is a characteristic trouble in socialist economies, and during the post-socialist transition. I believe the issue is more general. There are many intermediate and hybrid forms in the world economy with these problems. Regular market economies, which never went through a socialist phase, are full of soft budget constraint phenomena (Kornai et al., 2003). Bailouts of banks and other firms in Western market capitalist economies are clear examples.

When the transition came, you wrote a book, The Road to a Free Economy *(Kornai, 1990). In your most recent book,* From Socialism to Capitalism *(Kornai, 2008a), you stated that some of your views in that earlier book were not correct. How have your views changed?*
I didn't expect the big recession associated with the transformation. I was far too optimistic about how easy the transition would be. To a certain degree, I now see that it was inevitable, but had we expected it, some of the changes could have been more cautious. We moved too quickly in some issues. The Chinese seem to be learning from our mistakes. They are being much more cautious, privatizing gradually to avoid allowing an institutional vacuum to appear.

Did not your advice help in Hungary, especially with regard to hardening the budget constraint?
This may be, as has been reported in some sources (Rosser and Rosser, 2004). We did insist on payment for privatization of state-owned enterprises and a firm foundation for our banking system (Kornai, 1993). However, it was also somewhat easier for Hungary, given our long period of a more market-oriented and decentralized system during the socialist period. But we could not avoid all the problems that the other countries in Eastern and Central Europe experienced.

What do you see as the future of economics over the next 25 years?
My premonition is that it will become part of an integrative social science. Economics has moved far beyond the narrow confines of economics.

Unfortunately, I don't see much encouragement of originality. We need to encourage new movements in the way that happens in the art world, with new exhibitions and new galleries, new outlets. We need new associations and new journals with strong editors that can provide these new outlets and new publicity in order to achieve this broader and more integrated social science.

13. Reinhard Selten

This interview took place in his office at the University of Bonn on 1 August, 2008

Do you have any comments on the chapters and interviews that we sent you?
I had an opportunity to read one of the interviews. I was overall impressed and thought what I have read was very well done. Very interesting to read, so far there is nothing that I disagree with. I'm impressed.

Let's start out with some autobiographical information.
I was born on October 5, 1930 in Breslau in Lower Silesia. At that time it was part of Germany and only German was spoken. After the war Breslau became part of Poland and its name was changed to Wrocław. I didn't want to visit the city because I thought people speaking a foreign language, in this case Polish, it would feel awkward and I would feel not at ease. But later, this is after I won the Nobel Prize, I went to visit. I was surprised once I was there. There was still enough familiarity where I could find my way around. I got a guide and we went around to my childhood places. Of the four, one survived, but one street had vanished.

I was surprised by the attitude of the people; they had a strong identification with historical Lower Silesia, even though they were Polish. There was a feeling of local continuity. I was surprised – the population changed but the feeling of the place did not change that much. They had rebuilt the old Rathaus and other old houses in their original style. This was done in the time of communism already, but communists suppressed any attempt to know more about the German history of the place. However, after the downfall of communism the Polish people living there became very curious about the past, maybe because it was a forbidden subject matter under communism. They now feel a local historical continuity. In the university there are now pictures of all Silesian Nobel laureates, including me.

Your father was Jewish and your mother Protestant. How did you survive the World War II years?
There were many of these privileged mixed marriages then. The Nazis felt at first that it would cause too much dissent if they broke up such marriages, but as the war went on things got worse. My family wasn't associated with any particular religion, but given the political situation they decided to have me baptized as a Protestant. My father died in 1942, and the Holocaust was later. So my father did not go into a concentration camp. He was put into a Jewish hospital and they didn't have adequate or enough medical equipment, which contributed to his death.

It was difficult under Hitler to be a half-Jewish boy. I had to leave school at the age of 14. I had no professional opportunity. I was hoping at the time to get an apprenticeship and learn a trade, but the only position open to me was that of an unskilled worker. My older brother learned a trade. I believe he had two choices and became a transport merchant. They needed a lot of transport merchants during the war (*laughter*). In January 1945 they told us to leave Breslau as the city was going to be fortified. We were able to get on one of the last trains before all the outbound trains were stopped. I remember it took several days and we had to go through Germany. It was difficult. We became refugees. We first went to Saxonia and then to Austria.

Once in Austria, I did not want to beg, but our money was worthless. Farmers did sell a little food, so it was a kind of begging. I got a job working on a farm but I was a pretty bad farmer, more of a city boy. I did get better at some things on the farm. Today you use machines, but then you had to rely on your hands. I became good at haymaking using rakes, but I was very bad at weeding.

Let's move on to your formal education.
I started school again in 1946 and I became interested in mathematics in high school. It took a lot of walking to get to school and then to walk back home. To keep my mind busy I would think about mathematical problems. Besides developing my ability in mathematics, the walking also led to a lifelong love for hiking. I was educated in mathematics at the University of Frankfurt am Main from 1951 to 1957, until I finished my "Diplom"

which is roughly equal to your master's degree. Then I became a research assistant of Professor Heinz Sauermann at the economics department at the University of Frankfurt am Main. However I still wrote a PhD thesis in mathematics on "valuation of n-person games". My advisor was Professor Ewald Burger, to whom I owe very much. I received my PhD in 1961 and my Habilitation in economics in 1968. I am now professor emeritus at the University of Bonn, Germany.

This institution in Germany of having to do a Habilitation after getting one's PhD may be disappearing as a professional requirement. Do you approve of this?
I think that it is a good thing that it is going. The Habilitation was a more advanced monograph beyond the PhD dissertation. Things have changed with dissertations these days. When I did mine it was like doing a monograph; now dissertations are collections of three papers.

How did you become interested in economics?
Early on at the university I was interested in psychology and economics and took some courses in those subjects. I learned experimental techniques from psychologists and was particularly interested in gestalt psychology, which was a forerunner of cognitive psychology. This actually started when I was in high school. Also in high school I became aware of game theory from an article in *Fortune* magazine. As a student of mathematics I read von Neumann and Morgenstern's famous book (von Neumann and Morgenstern, 1944). Later I participated in a student seminar by Ewald Burger and he offered me the chance to write a master's thesis in cooperative game theory. This thesis along with my PhD thesis had the aim of axiomatizing a value for games in extensive form. This led me to see the perfectness problem before others, I believe. After I received my master's, I started to work with Heinz Sauermann at Frankfurt. I worked for him for 10 years. I initially was asked to work on the application of decision theory to the theory of the firm, but I proposed to Heinz Sauermann to run an oligopoly experiment and he supported me in this.

Your first publication in 1959 was on oligopolies and experimental economics, with some calling you the father of European Experimental Economics. How did you get involved with this?
Yes, this was my first publication. It was written with Heinz Sauermann and it was titled "An Oligopoly Experiment" (Sauermann and Selten, 1959). When we began doing economic experiments at Frankfurt, all this was new. No such area or field existed before. What helped was my desire to learn some psychology while I studied mathematics. This allowed me

to be acquainted with experimental techniques. I also listened to some lectures by the gestalt psychologist Edwin Rausch. This made it natural for me to think about an experimental approach to oligopoly.

Given my studies in mathematics I was interested in game theory and at that time in oligopolies. I was interested in its application and the link between oligopolistic behavior and rationality. I believed that game theory would provide a different approach to oligopolistic behavior, which led to my thinking of experiments.

In 1958 I became aware of Herbert Simon's work on bounded rationality (Simon, 1957). I was doing all this at the same time – game theory, studying oligopoly, learning experimental techniques. I felt Simon's worked fitted right in. With Heinz Sauermann we came up with an aspiration adaptation theory of the firm which was published in 1962 (Sauermann and Selten, 1962). In 1961 I went to Pittsburgh and visited Simon and his colleagues. Since then I have been very much involved with bounded rationality and moved from armchair thinking to experimental work.

Did you know of Vernon Smith's work during this time?
No, but I did look at Chamberlin's work (Chamberlin, 1948), and I was influenced by his work. I wanted to run similar market experiments. Smith I learned of later. He came out with his seminal paper on the double oral auction in 1962. Let me mention that Austin Hogatt published an experimental paper on oligopoly in 1959 (Hoggatt, 1959).

Do you see a difference between the experimental work in economics that is going on in Europe as compared to what is being done in the United States?
In the beginning there were substantial differences. American researchers wanted to supply an experimental foundation for rational economic theory. In Germany we took a more behavioral approach. For us the main task was the observation and explanation of boundedly rational behavior in economically interesting laboratory situations. Our experiments were often exploratory rather than directed at testing prespecified hypotheses.

In the second half of the 1970s these differences began to become less and less pronounced. Disagreements about methodological issues still exist, but they are much less geographically concentrated.

Your game theoretic work on perfectness and on equilibrium selection is based on strong rationality assumptions. Can you explain how this relates to your emphasis on bounded rationality?
I started out as a naive rationalist, that is as somebody who thinks that people must act rationally. Herbert Simon opened my eyes to the fact that human economic behavior is only boundedly rational. Nevertheless

I continued to be interested in the question of how absolute rationality should be defined in game theory. In my view this is an important philosophical question, even if absolute rationality is beyond the cognitive capabilities of real human beings. Moreover the absolutely rational solution of a game can serve as a benchmark for the evaluation of experiments. The comparison of observed behavior with the benchmark provides insight into the structure of bounded rationality.

The issue of bounded rationality has occupied a lot of my thinking. In 1962 Heinz Sauermann and I published a paper on aspiration adaptation (Sauermann and Selten, 1962). This paper is an attempt at proposing a general theory of bounded rationality, but it is purely speculation. Only recently did we succeed in obtaining experimental evidence for some basic aspects of aspiration adaptation theory, but this work is still unpublished.

Rational decision and game theory and bounded rationality are different research programs. I have worked on both. I spent at least as much effort on bounded rationality as on game theory but my game theoretic work was more successful.

A third research program is evolutionary game theory. In his PhD thesis, John Nash offered two interpretations of game equilibrium, one of them is similar to the modern biological one. The game is played repeatedly with random matching by a mass population of players and then by learning a state of affairs will evolve in which all pure strategies used are optimal. The second interpretation presupposes completely rational behavior in a one-shot game, where everybody acts to optimize against everyone else, correctly predicting the optimal behavior by everybody else.

It seems that you are presenting Nash as the father of evolutionary game theory, but some have said that you are the real father of evolutionary game theory.
This is not true. I gave it a mathematical form that made it professionally digestable for game theorists (Selten, 1980). The original paper was written by the biologists Maynard Smith and Price (1973), and it was badly written. It has two different definitions of an evolutionarily stable strategy. It was written in a style that no game theorists would read it.

The University of Bielefeld was the perfect place for me at that time to study these matters. It took an interdisciplinary approach. This interdisciplinary approach allowed me to do research linking biology with game theory. A biologist named Henrich said to me: "I have a student that I will send to you". The student was a young mathematician, Peter Hammerstein, and he made me aware of evolutionary stability. He now has a chair in Berlin. Maynard Smith and Price had a paper with strange and difficult notation, and I just translated it to normal mathematics and proved a theorem. I became interested from then on in biological game theory (Selten and Hammerstein, 1984). This led me into developing evolutionary stability in extensive games, which really explained the ideas of Maynard Smith and Price (Selten, 1983). I also wrote a paper with Avi Shmida on theoretical models of pollination of flowers by bees (Selten and Shmida, 1991). The Center for Interdisciplinary Research had some money left over for a conference and Peter Hammerstein asked the professor he was working for to apply for it. In this way he had the opportunity to organize the first international conference on evolutionary stability in 1978.

You liked Bielefeld because of its interdisciplinary focus, but you came here to Bonn because they provided you an opportunity to establish an experimental laboratory with computers?
Yes, maybe an example of bounded rationality on my part. When I got the offer from Bonn in 1984 I asked what do I want to do? I wanted a laboratory and to build it up in three years. This was the first economic experimental lab in Europe. I got another offer from Bielefeld, but it was too little and too late. They would give me the money in one year. I couldn't spend it all at once and wanted to take the time needed to put the lab together correctly.

In his interview with us, Ernst Fehr said he felt there was more long-term support for experimental and behavioral research in Europe (or at least in Switzerland) than in the US. Would you agree with him about this?
Yes. There is support. Long-term support is important, particularly at the beginning. I didn't want to build up the laboratory very quickly when I started. Experiments were much more difficult and uncertain at that time. And I wanted to start slowly. There was so much to learn and develop. Now the methods are much more advanced. This was a major attraction of coming to Bonn. They provided the support I needed within the time frame I believed was necessary. I liked the interdisciplinary approach of Bielefeld, but I wanted to build my own lab for experimental economics. They were willing to do that. Here our work is focused on experimental economics. We have the goal of developing a descriptive branch of decision and game theory that takes Simon's work on bounded rationality seriously.

Although you have occasionally visited temporarily in American academic institutions such as Princeton and Berkeley, you have remained in German universities as your main base since your Habilitation: The Free University

of Berlin (1969–72), Bielefeld University (1972–84), and the Rheinische Friedrich-Wilhelms University in Bonn since 1984. Were you offered a job in the US? Were you tempted? Why did you decide to stay in Europe?
I did receive some offers from the United States, but because of lifestyle I decided to stay in Europe. I was at Berkeley for one year, 1967 to 1968, as a visiting professor, and they asked me to stay. The pay was very much higher there than what I was getting here. Also Stanford might have given me support. But it was a lifestyle choice that made me decide to stay in Europe. At the time I was in the US I did not drive a car, and so it would have been very difficult for me to get around. I like to hike, and what I saw in California was empty areas where you don't see anybody when you hiked in the mountains. I like the middle mountains as we call them here. The landscapes of middle Europe are what I wanted, but things are changing. Europe is becoming more Americanized, and America is becoming more Europeanized.

Also the university departments in Europe were more diverse in those days. When I was a student each economics professor spoke his own language, or jargon, and had his own philosophy. The history of thought was all that they could agree on.

What are your thoughts of the Americanization of European economics? Do you think it is happening, and do you see it as something positive or negative?
Yes, and I think overall it is something positive. In former times here economics was more like philosophy, although I like philosophy. But that has changed and because of the American influence economics in Europe has become more and more mathematical. Economics should be a science based on empirical and experimental evidence, I believe. I'm trying to do that with developing a theory of bounded rationality. I have seen some revolutions in economics during my time. One was the introduction of mathematics after the war, which was very important.

Prior to 1972 you published only in German, but then switched mostly to English (Harsanyi and Selten, 1972). Why?
When I was young it was necessary to publish in German, if I wanted to become a professor at a German university. The older professors did not read English. They had learned French when they were young, since then this was the dominant language. Only later did English become the international language of science.

Jonathan Pool and I have constructed a game theoretic model of foreign language learning decisions (Selten and Pool, 1991). People learn foreign languages in order to be able to communicate with other people who could not be reached otherwise. Casual empiricism suggests that it is not the number of native speakers but rather the language income, that is the sum of the incomes of all native speakers which is important here. At the moment English has the highest language income and this explains its position as the dominant medium of international communication. However, this may change in the future.

I started publishing in English in order to get international recognition. The first thing I published in English was my dissertation on game theory. Though I don't want to see the end of local customs and regional languages, there are advantages to an international language. I would prefer Esperanto being the international language as it has no native speakers and is thus neutral. My wife and I met as advocates of using Esperanto. I think that it might replace English some day in that role.

Let's go back to some of your more important work. You were awarded the Nobel Memorial Prize in Economic Sciences with John Nash and John Harsanyi for your discovery of the concept of subgame perfect equilibrium, codified in your 1965 paper. How did you come to develop this idea?
The idea of subgame perfectness has its roots in my experimental work. In the early 1960s I ran experiments on a dynamic oligopoly game with demand inertia. The situation described by the model seemed to be interesting and I wanted to see what happens in this situation. The experimental game had some features like indivisibilities of investment and different interest rates for positive and negative accounts which seemed to be realistic, but prevented an adequate analytical approach to it. Later I developed a simplified version which permitted a non-cooperative solution by backward induction, but I soon realised that this was not the only equilibrium of the game. Nevertheless I thought that the backward induction equilibrium is the only natural one and the notion of subgame perfectness formalized this intuition. The definition of subgame perfectness was only a small part of my paper of 1965 on oligopoly with demand inertia.

Subgame perfectness opened the possibility to construct and to analyse multi-stage game models. Thereby many interesting economic problems could be attacked, first in the area of industrial organization, but later also in many other areas. As far as I know the first English language paper in this literature was my article on "a simple model of imperfect competitions where 4 are few and 6 are many" from 1973.

Is this the time that you first met John Harsanyi, when you worked with him and other prominent game theorists for the US Arms Control and Disarmament Agency?
I met him first in Princeton at a game theory conference in 1961. In 1965 I met him again at the first international workshop on game theory at Jerusalem. Game theory was still a small and relatively new field.

Only 17 people participated in this workshop. John Harsanyi presented his new theory of games with incomplete information and there were heated discussions on this topic. My longlasting cooperation with John Harsanyi began at this workshop. Soon afterwards I joined a group of game theorists and mathematical economists hired by Harold Kuhn's and Oskar Morgenstern's research firm Mathematica for doing work on a project for the Arms Control and Disarmament Agency. The group did not produce anything of practical value for the agency, but it did make important theoretical advances. John Harsanyi and I worked on bargaining under incomplete information and eventually published a paper on this subject in *Management Science* (Harsanyi and Selten, 1972). The most notable result was the work by Aumann, Moschler and Stearns on repeated games with incomplete information.

In your paper on the chain store paradox (1978) you throw doubt on the behavioral relevance of subgame perfect equilibrium. Did this agitate you?
When I discovered the chain store paradox in 1972 I was very much disturbed. I had an upset stomach for two weeks. Up to then my understanding of bounded rationality was based on the idea that the complexity of most real decision problems makes it too difficult to compute the fully rational solution. However, in the case of the chain store paradox the fully rational analysis is very easy, but nevertheless fails to be convincing. In the role of the chain store you feel strongly inclined to deter entry in the beginning. Nevertheless rational analysis yields the conclusion that it makes no sense to deter entry in the last period and it follows by backward induction that you cannot deter entry even in the first period. The cooperative choice is always the only rational one for the chain store. Nevertheless I felt that playing against agents as rational as myself, I would still try to deter entry in the role of the chain store. It was painful for me to face my own lack of rationality in the chain store game. Finally I made my peace with this by developing the three-level theory of decision making explained in my paper on the chain store problem.

Some view your 1986 paper with your student, Rolf Stoecker, as the definitive experimental disproof that economic agents engage in backward induction, an idea that you are also credited with as part of the subgame perfection concept. Would you agree that this paper should be viewed in this way?
The results of this experiment confirmed the three-level theory of decision making. Decisions can be made on three levels. The first level is routine. We don't think, we just do something suggested by behavioral tendencies formed by prior routine learning. The second level is the level of imagination. Decisions on this level are based on imagined scenarios describing

plausible chains of events following possible actions. Human decision makers cannot vividly imagine more than a few periods ahead. This means that backward induction works by imagination in a few periods before the end, but not before.

The third level is the level of rational analysis. However, rational analysis of complex interactive decisions is often impossible. Therefore most strategic decisions are made on the level of imagination, or even on the routine level. A decision problem will activate either the routine level, or the routine level and the level of imagination, or all three levels. A pre-decision determines one of these three activation patterns. Every activated level suggests a decision and then a post-decision determines which one of them will be taken.

If a decision has been reached on the level of rational analysis, it is not necessarily taken. Pre-decision and post-decision are themselves routine decisions formed by a stochastic mechanism below consciousness. Rational analysis will not always produce a decision which turns out to be superior by hindsight. Therefore rational analysis will often not be trusted. A further reason for lack of trust in rational analysis is that thinking is not always flawless. Experience can easily favor the level of imagination. In this way one can understand that decision makers are reluctant to follow the rational recommendation for the chain store game even if they fully understand the logic of the backward induction argument. One has to come to terms with the fact that this applies not only to other people but also to oneself.

Where do Simon's rules of thumb come in?
The concept of a rule of thumb is not central to the theory of bounded rationality. In everyday language a rule of thumb is a simple way to find an approximately right answer to a computational problem, for example by replacing π by 22/7. This presupposes that there is a correct answer to which the approximately right one can be compared. However, apart from rare exceptions, real decision problems are more difficult.

Simon emphasized the procedural character of bounded rationality. The decision maker does not try to optimize an objective function. Instead of this he makes use of decision procedures involving a finite number of steps leading to the final decision. The rationality lies in the selection of the next step and not in a preference order over outcomes.

You have a reputation for publishing in non-refereed outlets because of disliking changing papers to satisfy referees. Is the refereeing process at journals a way that orthodox ideas are maintained against new challenges to them?
Yes, this is often the case. I recently had an important paper where a referee was violently against the new ideas in the manuscript. He not

only recommended rejection but also said that the paper should not be published in any journal! I should not have sent the manuscript to this reputed journal, but I leave the decision about where to send a paper to my co-authors. Today a young researcher in Europe needs publications in US-based journals.

You have served as president of the European Economic Association. Do you see it as serving more as an agent of the Americanization of European economics or as a base for the development of an independent European approach to economics?
I don't see it as an agent of Americanizing Europe, but as an association that can do something to improve economics in Europe. That is how I look at the Association. But I don't see that there is something like a European approach.

Are national traditions more important?
Not necessarily. There should be a global economics. There is a tendency in the United States to forget that outside of America important research is done. Too often only American economists are cited. The US has a big population and spends much more for scientific research per capita, than European countries do. For this reason the United States is now the center of science. More Americans receive the Nobel Prize than scientists from any other country.

Where do you see the university structure in Germany going and how will this affect economic research there? Are changes you see in Germany parallel to or different from trends you see in the rest of Europe?
At the moment the German universities are in a period of structural change. In Germany almost all universities are public state universities. Up to recently "the" state exerted detailed budgetary control, but now a number of states passed new university laws which permit autonomy within a global budget. This is certainly an improvement.

The Federal government has organized a competition among the universities for additional research money. This "excellence initiative" has given substantial temporal financial support to some universities. Bonn received an "excellence cluster for cooperative research in mathematics and economics". This additional money is welcome, but what is really needed, is much higher long-term financial support of higher education.

What do you see as the future of economics over the next 25 years?
Three areas of research have been of special significance in my life as an economist: 1) game theory and its applications; 2) experimental economics;

and 3) bounded rationality. When I began to do game theory, this field was very small and did not get much recognition among economists, but now everything is full of game theory. When I did my first experiments, there was not yet a field of experimental economics, but now the use of experimental methods in economics is fully established. However, unlike game theory and experimental economics, the theory of bounded rationality has not yet reached the mainstream.

In the last decades experimental economics has done much for a better understanding of motivation. We know now that fairness and reciprocity are important motivational forces. However, theorists try to deal with such other-directed motives by putting unusual arguments into the utility function, like in the inequity aversion theory by Fehr and Schmidt (1999). In my view this approach is mistaken. The interaction of different motivational forces cannot be adequately described as the result of utility maximization. As Herbert Simon emphasized, bounded rationality is procedural. A boundedly rational decision procedure involves a number of steps. Each step is reasonable, but nothing is optimized by the procedure.

I think that future economics needs to focus on bounded rationality. Important progress has been made since Herbert Simon's seminal work (1957) in this area. I expect an acceleration of the rate of progress in the near future and I hope that the theory of bounded rationality will reach the mainstream within my lifetime.

Bibliography

Aboites, Jaime (ed.) (1989), *Industrialización y desarrollo agrícola en México*, México DF: Plaza y Valdés/UAM.

Agliari, Anna, Gian-Italo Bischi and Laura Gardini (2002), "Some methods for the global analysis of dynamic games represented by non-invertible maps", in Tönu Puu (ed.), *Oligopoly Dynamics: Models, and Tools*, Heidelberg: Springer-Verlag, pp. 111–46.

Agliari, Anna, Carl Chiarella and Laura Gardini (2006), "A re-evaluation of the adaptive expectations in light of global dynamic analysis", *Journal of Economic Behavior and Organization*, **60**, 526–52.

Agliari, Anna, Laura Gardini and Tönu Puu (2000), "The dynamics of a triopoly Cournot game", *Chaos, Solitons and Fractals*, **12**, 2531–60.

Aglietta, Michel (1974), "Accumulation et régulation du capitalisme en longue période, Exemple des Etats-Unis (1870–1970)", PhD thesis, Université de Paris-I (Sorbonne).

Aglietta, Michel (1976), *Régulation et Crises du Capitalisme*, Paris: Calmann-Lévy.

Ahn, S.K. and Reinsel G.C. (1990), "Estimation for partially nonstationary multivariate autoregressive models", *Journal of the American Statistical Association*, **85**, 813–23.

Albin, Peter S. with Duncan K. Foley (1998), *Barriers and Bounds to Rationality: Essays in Economic Complexity in Interactive Systems*, Princeton: Princeton University Press.

Althusser, Louis Pierre (1971), "Ideology and ideological state apparatuses" (English translation by Ben Brewster), *Lenin and Philosophy and Other Essays*, New York: Monthly Review Press, pp. 127–86.

Amable, Bruno (2003), *The Diversity of Modern Capitalism*, Oxford: Oxford University Press.

Amable, Bruno and Stefano Palombarini (2005), *L'Economie Politique n'est pas une Science Morale*, Paris: Raisons d'Agir.

Amable, Bruno, Rémi Barré and Robert Boyer (1997), *Les Systèmes d'innovation à l'ère de la Globalisation*, Paris: Economica.

Anderson, T.W. (1951), "Estimating linear restrictions on regression coefficients for multivariate normal distributions", *Annals of Mathematical Statistics*, **22**, 327–51.

Anufriev, M. and C.H. Hommes (2009), "Evolution of market heuristics", *Knowledge Engineering Review*, forthcoming.

Aoki, Masahiko (1990), "Towards an economic model of the Japanese firm", *Journal of Economic Literature*, **26**(1), March, 1–27.

Aoki, Masahiko (2001), *Toward a Comparative Institutional Analysis*, Cambridge, MA: MIT Press.

Aoki, Masahiko (2007), *The Japanese Economy after the Flux Decade: Where Will Changes in Company Structure Lead?*, Paris: Cournot Centre for Economic Studies, *Prisme*, **10**, September.

Arthur, W. Brian, Steven N. Durlauf and David A. Lane (1997), "Introduction", in W.B. Arthur, S.N. Durlauf and D.A. Lane (eds), *The Economy as an Evolving Complex System II*, Reading, MA: Addison-Wesley, pp. 1–14.

Aubin, Jean-Pierre (1991), *Viability Theory*, Boston: Birkhauser.

Aumann, Robert J. (1974), "Subjectivity and Correlation in Randomized Strategies", *Journal of Mathematical Economics*, **1**, 67–96.

Ayres, Clarence E. (1932), *Huxley*, New York: Norton.

Balasko, Yves and Robert Boyer (1980), "Technical progress and employment", mimeo *CEPREMAP*, December (revised version, February 1983).

Barone, Enrico (1908), "Il ministro della produzione nello stato colletivista", *Giornale degli Economisti*, September/October, pp. 267–93. English translation, "The ministry of production in the collectivist state" (1935), in F.A. Hayek (ed.), *Collectivist Economic Planning*, London: Routledge, pp. 245–90.

Barro, Robert J. and Xavier Sala-i-Martin (1995), *Economic Growth*, New York: McGraw-Hill.

Bateman, Bradley W. (2007), "Engineering trouble: a review essay", *Journal of Economic Behavior and Organization*, **62**, 484–92.

Battiston, Stefano, Domenico Delli Gatti, Mauro Gallegati, Bruce Greenwald and Joseph Stiglitz (2007), "Credit chains and bankruptcy propagation in production networks", *Journal of Economic Dynamics and Control*, **31**, 2061–84.

Beckmann, Martin J. and Tönu Puu (1985), *Spatial Economics: Potential, Density, and Flow*, Amsterdam: North-Holland.

Beckmann, Martin J. and Tönu Puu (1990), *Spatial Structures*, Heidelberg: Springer-Verlag.

Bénassy, Jean-Pascal (1975), "Neo-Keynesian disequilibrium theory in a monetary economy", *Review of Economic Studies*, **42**, 503–23.

Bénassy, Jean-Pascal, Robert Boyer and R.M. Gelpi (1979), "Régulation des economies capitalistes et inflation", *Revue Économique*, **30** (3), 397–441.

Berndt, Christian (2003), "Territorialized key words and methodological nationalism", *European Urban and Regional Studies*, **10**, 283–95.

Bertalanffy, Ludwig von (1962), *General Systems Theory*, New York: George Braziller.

Binmore, Ken and Avner Shaked (2010), "Experimental economics: where next?", *Journal of Economic Behavior and Organization*, **73**(1), 87–100.

Bischi, Gian-Italo, Laura Gardini and Michael Kopel (2000), "Analysis of global bifurcations in a market share attraction model", *Journal of Economic Dynamics and Control*, **24**, 855–79.

Bischi, Gian-Italo, Laura Gardini and Christian Mira (2006), "Basin fractalization generated by a two-dimensional family of Z1-Z3-Z1 maps", *International Journal of Bifurcations and Chaos*, **16**, 647–69.

Blum, Lenore, Felipe Cucker, Michael Shub and Steve Smale (1998), *Complexity and Real Computation*, New York: Springer-Verlag.

Bolton, Gary E. and Axel Ockenfels (2000), "ERC: a theory of equity, reciprocity, and competition", *American Economic Review*, **90**(1), 166–93.

Boulding, Kenneth (1966), "The economics of the coming spaceship earth", in H. Jarret (ed.), *Environmental Quality in a Growing Economy*, Baltimore: Johns Hopkins University Press.

Boulding, Kenneth E. (1978), *Ecodynamics: A New Theory of Societal Evolution*, Beverly Hills, CA: Sage Publications.

Boulding, Kenneth E. (1981), *Evolutionary Economics*, Beverly Hills, CA: Sage Publications.

Bowles, Samuel and Robert Boyer (1988), 'Labor discipline and aggregate demand: a macroeconomic model', *American Economic Review*, **78**, 395–400.

Bowles, Samuel, Robert Boyd, Ernst Fehr and Herbert Gintis (2005), *Moral Sentiments and Material Interests*, Cambridge, MA: MIT Press.

Bowles, Samuel, David M. Gordon and Thomas E. Wesskopf (1983), *Beyond the Waste Land*, New York: Doubleday.

Boyer, Denis, Robert Boyer and Gilles Laferté (2007), "La connexion des réseaux comme facteur de changement institutionnel: l'exemple des vins de Bourgogne", PSE Working Paper No. 2007–42, Paris School of Economics, available at: http://www.pse.ens.fr/document/wp200742.pdf.

Boyer, Robert (1975), "Modalités de la régulation d'économies capitalistes dans la longue période: Quelques formalisations simple", CEPREMAP Working Paper, Paris.

Boyer, Robert (1990), *The Regulation School: A Critical Introduction* (translated by Craig Charney), New York: Columbia University Press (originally in French, 1981).

Boyer, Robert (1996), "The seven paradoxes of capitalism: or is a theory of modern economies still possible?", CEPREMAP Working Paper 9620, Paris.

Boyer, Robert (2002), "Introduction" (English translation by Carolyn Shread), in Robert Boyer and Yves Saillard (eds), *Régulation Theory: The State of the Art*, London: Routledge, pp. 1–10 (originally in French, 1995).

Boyer, Robert (2004), *The Future of Economic Growth: As New Becomes Old* (English translation), Cheltenham, UK and Northampton, MA, USA: Edward Elgar (originally in French, 2003).

Boyer, Robert (2006), "What is the future for codetermination and corporate governance in Germany?", in Jens Beckert, Bernhard Ebbinghaus, Anke Hassel and Philip Manow (eds), *Transformationen des Kapitalismus. Festschrift für Wolfgang Streeck zum sechzigsten Geburtstag*, Frankfurt and New York: Campus Verlag, pp. 135–57.

Boyer, Robert and Jean-Pierre Durand (1997), *After Fordism* (English translation by Sybil Hyacinth Mair), Basingstoke, UK: Macmillan (originally in French, 1993).

Boyer, Robert and Michel Freyssenet (2002), *The Productive Models*, Basingstoke and New-York: Palgrave MacMillan, Gerpisa.

Boyer, Robert and J. Rogers Hollingsworth (eds) (1997), *Contemporary Capitalism: The Embeddedness of Institutions*, Cambridge: Cambridge University Press.

Boyer, Robert and Jacques Mistral (1978), *Accumulation, Inflation, Crises*, Paris: Presses Universitaires de France (in French).

Boyer, Robert and Julio Neffa (eds) (2004), *La Crisis Argentina (1976–2001): una Vision desde la Theorias Institucionalistas y Regulacionistas*, Madrid and Buenos Aires: Editorial Mino y Davila.

Boyer, Robert and Julio Neffa (eds) (2007), *Salida de Crisis y Estrategias alternativas de Desarollo. La Experiencia Argentina*, Madrid and Buenos Aires: Editorial Mino y Davila.

Boyer, Robert and Yves Saillard (eds) (2002), *Regulation Theory: The State of the Art*, London: Routledge.

Boyer, Robert and Toshio Yamada (eds) (2000), *Japanese Capitalism in Crisis*, London: Routledge.

Bramwell, Anna (1989), *Ecology in the 20th Century*, New Haven: Yale University Press.

Braudel, Fernand (1973a), *Capitalism and Material Life: 1400–1800* (English translation by Miriam Kochan), New York: Harper and Row (originally in French, 1967).

Braudel, Fernand (1973b), *The Mediterranean and the Mediterranean World in the Age of Philip II* (English translation by Sian Reynolds), New York: Harper and Row (originally in French, 1949).

Brock, William A. and Cars H. Hommes (1997), "A rational route to randomness", *Econometrica*, **65**, 1059–95.

Brock, William A. and Cars H. Hommes (1998), "Heterogeneous beliefs and routes to chaos in a simple asset pricing model", *Journal of Economic Dynamics and Control*, **22**, 1235–74.

Brock, William A., Cars H. Hommes and Florian O.O. Wagener (2005), "Evolutionary dynamics in markets with many trader types", *Journal of Mathematical Economics*, **41**, 7–42.

Brock, William A., Cars H. Hommes and Florian O.O. Wagener (2009), "More hedging instruments may destabilize markets", *Journal of Economic Dynamics and Control*, **33**, 1912–28.

Brock, William A., W. Davis Dechert, Blake LeBaron and José Scheinkman (1996), "A test for independence based on the correlation dimension", *Econometric Reviews*, **15**, 197–235.

Brousseau, Vincent and Alan Kirman (1993), "The dynamics of learning in n-person games with the wrong N", in Ken Binmore, Alan P. Kirman, and Piero Tani (eds), *Frontiers of Game Theory*, Cambridge, MA: MIT Press.

Brundtland, Gro Harlem (ed.) (1987), *Our Common Future: Report of the World Commission on Economic Development*, Oxford: Oxford University Press.

Bullard, Robert D. (2000), *Dumping in Dixie: Race, Class, and Environmental Quality*, Boulder, CO: Westview Press.

Burkhart, Judith, Ernst Fehr, Charles Efferson and Carel van Schaik (2007), "Other-regarding preferences in a non-human primate: common marmosets provision food altruistically", *Proceedings of the National Academy of Sciences*, **104**, 19762–6.

Bush, Robert R. and Frederick Mosteller (1955), *Stochastic Models and Learning*, New York: Wiley.

Callari, Antonio (2005), "Interrogating the 'new pluralism' in economics: views from left field", paper presented at *Eastern Economic Association*, 5 March, New York.

Campbell, Donald T. (1965), "Variation, selection and retention in sociocultural evolution", in H.R. Barringer, G.I. Blanksten and R.W. Mack (eds), *Social Change in Developing Areas: A Reinterpretation of Evolutionary Theory*, Cambridge, MA: Schenkman, pp. 19–49.

Cassel, Gustav (1918), *Theoretische Sozialökonomie*, Leipzig: C.F. Winter, English translation, 1923, *The Theory of Social Economy*, London: T.F. Unwin.

Chaitin, Gregory J. (1987), *Algorithmic Information Theory*, Cambridge: Cambridge University Press.

Chamberlin, Edward (1948), "An Experimental Imperfect Market", *Journal of Political Economy*, **56**, 95–108.

Chiarella, Carl, Roberto Dieci and Laura Gardini (2002), "Speculative behaviour and complex asset price dynamics: a global analysis", *Journal of Economic Behavior and Organization*, **49**, 173–97.

Chomsky, Noam (1959), "On certain formal properties of grammars", *Information and Control*, **2**, 137–67.

Clark, John Maurice (1918), "Economics and modern psychology" parts I and II, *Journal of Political Economy*, **26**(1–2), January–April, 1–30, 136–66.

Coase, Ronald H. (1988), *The Firm, the Market, and the Law*, Chicago: University of Chicago Press.

Coats, A.W. Bob (ed.) (2000), *The Development of Economics in Western Europe since 1945*, London: Routledge.

Colander, David (ed.) (2000), *The Complexity Vision and the Teaching of Economics*, Cheltenham, UK and Northampton, MA, USA: Edward Elgar.

Colander, David (ed.) (2006), *Post Walrasian Macroeconomics: Beyond the Dynamic Stochastic General Equilibrium Model*, New York: Cambridge University Press.

Colander, David (2007), *The Making of an Economist Redux*, Princeton: Princeton University Press.

Colander, David (2009), *The Making of A European Economist*, Cheltenham, UK and Northampton, MA, USA: Edward Elgar.

Colander, David and Terry Plum (2004), "Efficiency, journal publishing and scholarly research", Middlebury College Department of Economics, Working Paper, 2004–19.

Colander, David, Richard P.F. Holt and J. Barkley Rosser, Jr. (2004a), *The changing face of economics: Conversations with Cutting Edge Economists*, Ann Arbor: University of Michigan Press.

Colander, David, Richard P.F. Holt and J. Barkley Rosser, Jr. (2004b), "The changing face of mainstream economics", *Review of Political Economy*, **18**(4), 485–99.

Colander, David, Richard P.F. Holt and J. Barkley Rosser, Jr. (2007–08), "Live and dead issues in the methodology of economics", *Journal of Post Keynesian Economics*, **30**(2), Winter, 303–11.

Colander, David, Peter Howitt, Alan Kirman, Axel Leijonhufvud and Perry Mehrling (2008), "Beyond DSGE models: toward an empirically based macroeconomics", *American Economic Review*, **98**(2), May, 236–40.

Colander, David, Hans Föllmer, Armin Haas, Michael Goldberg, Katarina Juselius, Alan Kirman, Thomas Lux and Brigitte Sloth (2009), 'The financial crisis and the systemic failure of academic economics', *Critical Review*, **21**(2–3), 249–67.

Cooley, Charles Horton (1902), *Human Nature and the Social Order*, 1st edn, New York: Scribner's.

Copic, Jernej, Mathew O. Jackson and Alan Kirman (2009), "Identifying community structures from network data via maximum likelihood methods", *The B.E. Journal of Theoretical Economics*, **9**(1) (Contributions), Article 30.

Coriat, Benjamin and Giovannni Dosi (2002), "Evolution and regulationary theory: similarities and differences", in Robert Boyer and Yves Saillard (eds), *Regulation Theory: The State of the Art*, London: Routledge, pp. 306–11.

Costanza, Robert (1980), "Embodied energy and economic valuation", *Science*, **210**, 1219–24.

Crutchfield, James (1994), "The calculi of emergence: computation, dynamics and induction", *Physica D*, **75**, 11–54.

Cunningham, William (1892a), "The relativity of economic doctrines", *Economic Journal*, **2**(1), March, 1–16.

Cunningham, William (1892b), "The perversion of economic history", *Economic Journal*, **2**(3), September, 491–506.

Dahl, M. and Alan Kirman (1994), "Economic research in Europe", *European Economic Review*, **38**, 505–22.

Daly, Herman (1968), "On economics as a life science", *Journal of Political Economy*, **76**, 392–406.

Daly, Herman (1972), *Toward a Steady State Economy*, San Francisco: W.H. Freeman.

Dardi, Marco and Mauro Gallegati (1992), "Alfred Marshall on speculation", *History of Political Economy*, **24**, 571–94.

Darwin, Charles R. (1859), *On the Origin of Species by Means of Natural Selection, or the Preservation of Favoured Races in the Struggle for Life*, 1st edn, London: Murray.

Davis, John B. (2006), "The turn in economics", *Journal of Institutional Economics*, **2**, 1–20.

Dawes, Christopher, James Fowler, Tim Johnson, Richard McElreath and Oleg Smirnov (2007), "Egalitarian motives in humans", *Nature*, **446**, 794–6.

Day, Richard H. (1994), *Complex Economic Dynamics, Volume I: An Introduction to Dynamical Systems and Market Mechanisms*, Cambridge, MA: MIT Press.

Day, Richard H. (2007), "The complex problem of modeling economic complexity", in Massimo Salzano and David Colander (eds), *Complexity Hints for Economic Policy*, Milan: Springer, pp. 58–68.

Debreu, Gérard (1959), *Theory of Value: An Axiomatic Analysis of Economic Equilibrium*, New York: Wiley.

Debreu, Gérard (1974), "Excess demand functions", *Journal of Mathematical Economics*, **1**, 15–23.

Dechert, W. Davis (ed.) (1996), *Chaos Theory in Economics: Methods, Models and Evidence*, Cheltenham, UK and Northampton, MA, USA: Edward Elgar.

Dehez, Pierre and Omar Licandro (2007), "Interview with Jacques Drèze", in Paul A. Samuelson and William A. Barnett (eds), *Inside the Economist's Mind: Conversations with Eminent Economists*, Malden, MA: Blackwell, pp. 278–306.

Delli Gatti, Domenico and Mauro Gallegati (1996), "Financial market imperfections and irregular growth cycles", *Scottish Journal of Political Economy*, **43**, 146–58.

Delli Gatti, Domenico, Mauro Gallegati and Laura Gardini (1993), "Investment confidence, corporate debt and income fluctuations", *Journal of Economic Behavior and Organization*, **22**, 161–87.

Delli Gatti, Domenico, Mauro Gallegati and Alan P. Kirman (eds) (2000), *Interaction and Market Structure: Essays on Heterogeneity in Economics*, Heidelberg: Springer-Verlag.

Delli Gatti, Domenico, Corrado Di Guilmi, Mauro Gallegati and Gianfranco Giulioni (2007), "Financial fragility, industrial dynamics, and business fluctuations in an agent-based model", *Macroeconomic Dynamics*, **11**, 62–79.

Delli Gatti, Domenico, Mauro Gallegati, Gianfranco Giulioni and Antonio Palestrini (2003), "Financial fragility, patterns of firm entry and exit, and aggregate dynamics", *Journal of Economic Behavior and Organization*, **51**, 79–97.

Delli Gatti, Domenico, Edoardo Gaffeo, Mauro Gallegati, Gianfranco Giulioni and Antonio Palestrini (2008), *Emergent Macroeconomics: An Agent-Based Approach to Business Fluctuations*, Milan: Springer.

Dequech, David (2007–08), "Neoclassical, orthodox, mainstream, and heterodox economics", *Journal of Post Keynesian Economics*, **30**(2), Winter, 279–302.

Destanne de Bernis, Gérard (1975), "Les limites de l'analyse en termes d'équilibre générale", *Revue Économique*, **26**, 884–930.

Dosi, Giovanni, Giorgio Fagiolo and Andrea Roventini (2005), "Animal spirits, lumpy investment, and business cycles", *LEM Paper Series*, Sant' Anna School of Advanced Study, Pisa, Italy.

Duménil, Gérard and Dominique Lévy (1988), "Theory and facts: what can we learn from a century of history of the US economy?", paper presented at the Conference on Regulation Theory, Barcelona.

Dumontier, Jacques (1970), *Les Agents économiques. Eléments d'économique*, Vol. 1. Paris: Dunod.

Dumontier, Jacques (1971), *Les Agents économiques. Les Structures économiques*, Vol. 2. Paris: Dunod.

Easterlin, Richard A. (1995), "Will raising the incomes of all increase the happiness of all?", *Journal of Economic Behavior and Organization*, **27**, 35–47.

Elster, Jon (1989), *The Cement of Society – A Study of Social Order*, Cambridge, UK: Cambridge University Press.

Eucken, Walter (1940), *Die Grundlagen der Nationalökonomie*, Heidelberg: Springer, English translation, 1951, *The Foundations of Economics*, Chicago: University of Chicago Press.

Ezekiel, Mordecai (1938), "The cobweb theorem", *Quarterly Journal of Economics*, **52**, 255–80.

Falk, Armin, Ernst Fehr and Urs Fischbacher (2003), "On the nature of fair behavior", *Economic Inquiry*, **41**, 20–26.

Favereau, Olivier (1993), "Théorie de la régulation et économie des conventions: Canevas pour une confrontation", *La Lettre de la Régulation*, **7**, 1–3.

Fehr, Ernst (1985), "Die selbstverwaltete Unternehmung – eine effiziente Alternative zum Kapitalisumus?", *Ökonomie und Gesellschaft*, **3**, 276–332.

Fehr, Ernst (1991), "Cooperation, harassment and involuntary unemployment?", *American Economic Review*, **80**, 624–30.

Fehr, Ernst and Colin Camerer (2007), "Social neuroeconomics – the neural circuitry of social preferences", *Trends in Cognitive Science*, **11**, 419–27.

Fehr, Ernst and Armin Falk (2002), "Psychological foundation of incentives", Schumpeter lectures at the European Economic Association meeting 2001, *European Economic Review*, **46**, 687–724.

Fehr, Ernst and Simon Gächter (2000a), "Fairness and retaliation – the economics of reciprocity", *Journal of Economic Perspectives*, **14**, 159–81.

Fehr, Ernst and Simon Gächter (2000b), "Cooperation and punishment in public goods experiments", *American Economic Review*, **90**, 980–94.

Fehr, Ernst and Simon Gächter (2002), "Altruistic punishment in humans", *Nature*, **415**, 137–40.

Fehr, Ernst and Herbert Gintis (2007), "Human motivation and social cooperation", *Annual Review of Sociology*, **33**, 43–64.

Fehr, Ernst and Lorenz Götte (2007), "Do workers work more if wages are high? – Evidence from a randomized field experiment", *American Economic Review*, **97**, 298–317.

Fehr, Ernst and Klaus Schmidt (1999), "A theory of fairness, competition and cooperation", *Quarterly Journal of Economics*, **114**, 817–68.

Fehr, Ernst and Klaus Schmidt (2010), "On inequity aversion: a reply to

Binmore and Shaked", *Journal of Economic Behavior and Organization*, **73**(1), 101–8.

Fehr, Ernst, Urs Fischbacher and Michael Kosfeld (2005), "Neuroeconomic foundations of trust and social preferences", *American Economic Review, Papers and Proceedings*, **95**, 346–51.

Fehr, Ernst, Simon Gächter and Georg Kirchsteiger (1997), "Reciprocity as a contract enforcement device", *Econometrica*, **65**, 833–60.

Fehr, Ernst, Oliver Hart and Christian Zehnder (forthcoming), "Contracts as reference points: experimental evidence", *American Economic Review*.

Fehr, Ernst, Georg Kirchsteiger and Arno Riedl (1993), "Does fairness prevent market clearing? an experimental investigation", *Quarterly Journal of Economics*, **108**, 437–60.

Feldman, Allan M. and Alan Kirman (1973), "Fairness and envy", *American Economic Review*, **64**, 995–1005.

Fischbacher, Urs, Christina M. Fong and Ernst Fehr (2009), "Fairness, errors and the power of competition", *Journal of Economic Behavior & Organization*, **72**(1), October, 527–45.

Foley, Duncan K. (1982), "Realization and accumulation in a Marxian model of the circuit of capital", *Journal of Economic Theory*, **28**, 300–319.

Föllmer, Hans (1974), "Random economies with many interacting agents", *Journal of Mathematical Economics*, **1**, 51–62.

Fourcade-Gouringhas, Marion (2001), "Politics, institutional structures and the rise of economics: a comparative study", *Theory and Society*, **30**(3) (June), reprinted in Richard Swedberg (ed.) (2005), *New Directions in Economic Sociology*, London: Routledge.

Friedman, Daniel and John Rust (eds) (1993), *The Double Auction Market – Institutions, Theories and Evidence*, Reading, MA: Addison-Wesley.

Frydman, R. and M. Goldberg (2003), "Imperfect knowledge expectations, uncertainty adjusted UIP and exchange rate dynamics", in P. Aghion, R. Frydman, J. Stiglitz, and M. Woodford (eds), *Knowledge, Information and Expectations in Modern Macroeconomics: In Honor of Edmund S. Phelps*, Princeton, NJ: Princeton University Press.

Frydman, R., and M. Goldberg (2008), *Imperfect Knowledge Economics: Exchange Rates and Risk*, Princeton, NJ: Princeton University Press.

Frydman, R., M. Goldberg, S. Johansen and K. Juselius (2008), "Imperfect knowledge and a resolution of the purchasing power parity puzzle", Working Paper, Center on Capitalism and Society, Columbia University, and University of Copenhagen.

Fua, Giorgio and Mauro Gallegati (1996), "An annual chain index of Italy's 'Real' Product, 1861–1989", *Review of Income and Wealth*, **42**, 207–24.

Fudenberg, Drew and Eric Maskin (1986), "The folk theorem in repeated games with discounting or incomplete information", *Econometrica*, **54**, 533–54.

Gallegati, Mauro (1990), "The spread of Alfred Marshall's economics in Italy, 1885–1925", in R. McWilliams Tullberg (ed.), *Alfred Marshall in Retrospect*, Aldershot, UK and Brookfield, VT, USA: Edward Elgar, pp. 133–51.

Gallegati, Mauro and Alan Kirman (eds) (1999), *Beyond the Representative Agent*, Cheltenham, UK and Northampton, MA, USA: Edward Elgar.

Gallegati M. and J.E. Stiglitz (1992), "Stochastic and deterministic fluctuations in a non-linear model with equity rationing", *Giornale degli economisti ed annali di economia*, no. 51, 97–108.

Gallegati, Mauro, Laura Gardini, Tönu Puu and Irina Sushko (2003), "Hicks's trade cycle revisited: cycles and bifurcations", *Mathematics and Computers in Simulation*, **63**, 505–27.

Gallegati, Mauro, Steve Keen, Thomas Lux and Paul Ormerod (2006), "Worrying trends in econophysics", *Physica A*, **370**, 1–6.

Gallegati, Mauro, Alan Kirman and Matteo Marsili (eds) (2003), *The Complex Dynamics of Economic Interaction*, Berlin: Springer.

Gardini, Laura, Iryna Sushko and Ahmad Naimzada (2008), "Growing through chaotic intervals", *Journal of Economic Theory*, 143, 541–57.

Garnett, Robert F., Jr. (2005), "Whither heterodoxy?" *Post-Autistic Economics Review*, 30 October, issue 34, article 1.

Garnett, Robert F., Jr. (2006), "Paradigms and pluralism in heterodox economics", *Review of Political Economy*, **18**, 521–46.

Gatti, Donatella (2000), *Compétences, Organisations et Coordinations dans une Economie d'Innovation. Une analyse comparative du Chômage pour quatre Pays de l'OCDE*, EHESS Thesis, Paris, December.

Gaunersdorfer, Andrea, Cars H. Hommes and Florian O.O. Wagener (2008), "Bifurcation routes to volatility clustering under evolutionary learning", *Journal of Economic Behavior and Organization*, **67**, 27–47.

Georgescu-Roegen, Nicholas (1960), "Economic theory and agrarian economics", *Oxford Economic Papers*, **28**, 1–40.

Georgescu-Roegen, Nicholas (1971), *The Entropy Law and the Economic Process*, Cambridge, MA: Harvard University Press.

Gérard-Varet, Louis-André, Robert Jordan and Alan P. Kirman (1990), "A model of temporary equilibrium with stochastic quantity rationing", in Jean J. Gabszewicz, Jean-François Richard and Laurence A. Wolsey (eds), *Economic Decision Making: Games, Econometrics and Optimisation (Contributions in Honour of Jacques H. Drèze)*, Amsterdam: North-Holland.

Giampietro, M., K. Mayumi, and J. Martinez Alier (2000), "Blending new insights from complex systems thinking with old insights from biophysical analyses of the economic process", *Population and Environment*, **22**, 97–108.

Goodwin, Richard M. (1947), "Dynamic coupling with especial reference to markets having production lags", *Econometrica*, **15**,181–204.

Gordon, David (2005), "Fadonomics", *Ludwig von Mises Institute*, 2 June, available at http://www.mises.org/story/1828.

Gramsci, Antonio (1996), "Americanism and Fordism" (English translation), Prison Notebook No. 22, in *Prison Notebooks*, New York: Columbia University Press, originally in Italian, 1934.

Grandmont, Jean-Michel (1998), "Expectations formation and stability in large socio-economic systems", *Econometrica*, **66**, 741–81.

Grandmont, Jean-Michel, Alan Kirman and Wilhelm Neuefeind (1974), "A new approach to the uniqueness of equilibrium", *Review of Economic Studies*, **41**, 289–291.

Granger, C.W.J. (1983), "Co-integrated variables and error-correcting models", unpublished UCSD Discussion Paper 83–13, University of California, San Diego.

Green, Jerry R. (1972), "On the inequitable nature of core allocations", *Journal of Economic Theory*, **4**, 132–43.

Guerrien, Bernard (2002), "Is there anything worth keeping in standard microeconomics?", *Post-Autistic Economics Review*, **12**, 15 March.

Gumowski, Igor and Christian Mira (1980), *Dynamique Chaotique*, Toulouse: Cépadues Editions.

Güth, Werner, Rolf Schmittberger and Bernd Schwarze (1982), "An experimental analysis of ultimatum bargaining", *Journal of Economic Behavior and Organization*, **3**(4), 367–88.

Haeckel, Ernst (1866), *Generelle Morphologie der Organismen*, Berlin: G. Reimer.

Hahn, Frank H. (1982), "The Neo-Ricardians", *Cambridge Journal of Economics*, **6**(4), December, 353–74.

Haken, Hermann (1983), *Synergetics: Non-equilibrium Phase Transitions and Social Measurement*, 3rd edn, Berlin: Springer-Verlag.

Hall, Charles A.S., Cutler J. Cleveland and Robert Kaufman (1986), *Energy and Resource Quality: The Ecology of the Economic Process*, New York: Wiley-Interscience.

Hall, Peter A. and David Soskice (2001), *Varieties of Capitalism, The Institutional Foundations of Comparative Advantage*, Oxford: Oxford University Press.

Hanna, Susan, Carl Folke and Karl-Göran Mäler (eds) (1996), *Rights to Nature: Ecological, Economic, Cultural, and Political Principles of Institutions for the Environment*, Washington, DC: Island Press.

Harsanyi, John C. (1962), "Bargaining in Ignorance of the Opponent's Utility Function", *Journal of Conflict Resolution*, 6, 29–38.

Harsanyi, John C. and Reinhard Selten (1972), "A generalized Nash solution for two-person bargaining games with incomplete information", *Management Science*, **18**, 141–201.

Harsanyi, John C. and Reinhard Selten (1988), *A General Theory of Equilibrium Selection in Games*, Cambridge, MA: MIT Press.

Hausmann, Ricardo (1981), "State landed property, oil rent and accumulation in Venezuelan economy", PhD thesis, Cornell University.

Hayek, Friedrich A. (1940), "Socialist calculation: The 'competitive' solution", *Economica*, **7**, 121–49.

Hayek, Friedrich A. (1944), *The Road to Serfdom*, Chicago: University of Chicago Press.

Hayek, Friedrich A. (1948), *Individualism and Economic Order*, Chicago: University of Chicago Press.

Hayek, Friedrich (1988), *The Fatal Conceit: The Errors of Socialism*, Stanford: Hoover Institution.

Heemeijer, P., C.H. Hommes, J. Sonnemans, and J. Tuinstra (2009), "Price stability and volatility in markets with positive and negative expectations feedback: an experimental investigation", *Journal of Economic Dynamics and Control*, **33**(5), 1052–72.

Henrich, Joseph, Robert Boyd, Samuel Bowles, Colin Camerer, Ernst Fehr and Herbert Gintis (2004), *Foundations of Human Society – Economic Experiments and Ethnographic Evidence from Fifteen Small Scale Societies*, Oxford: Oxford University Press.

Henrich, Joseph, Robert Boyd, Samuel Bowles, Herbert Gintis, Ernst Fehr, Colin Camerer and Richard McElreath (2001), "In search of Homo Economicus: behavioral experiments in 15 small scale societies", *American Economic Review Papers and Proceedings*, **91**, 73–8.

Hicks, John R. (1939), *Value and Capital*, Oxford: Clarendon Press.

Hicks, John R. (1950), *A Contribution to the Theory of the Trade Cycle*, Oxford: Oxford University Press.

Hildenbrand, Werner and Alan Kirman (1973), "Size removes inequity", *Review of Economic Studies*, **40**, 305–19.

Hildenbrand, Werner and Alan Kirman (1976), *Introduction to Equilibrium Analysis*, Amsterdam: North-Holland.

Hildenbrand, Werner and Alan Kirman (1988), *Equilibrium Analysis*, Amsterdam: North-Holland.

Hirata, Kiyoaki (1993), *Société Civile et Régulation*, Tokyo: Iwanami Shoten.

Hodgson, Geoffrey M. (1974), "Marxian epistemology and the transformation problem", *Economy and Society*, **3**(4), November, 357–92.

Hodgson, Geoffrey M. (1982), *Capitalism, Value and Exploitation: A Radical Theory* Oxford: Martin Robertson.

Hodgson, Geoffrey M. (1982–83), "Worker participation and macroeconomic efficiency", *Journal of Post Keynesian Economics*, **5**, 266–75.

Hodgson, Geoffrey M. (1989), "Post-Keynesianism and institutionalism: the missing link", in John Pheby (ed.), *New Directions in Post Keynesian Economics*, Aldershot, UK and Brookfield, VT, USA: Edward Elgar, pp. 94–123.

Hodgson, Geoffrey M. (1991), *After Marx and Sraffa: Essays in Political Economy*, London: Macmillan.

Hodgson, Geoffrey M. (1993a), "The Mecca of Alfred Marshall", *Economic Journal*, **103**(2), March, 406–15.

Hodgson, Geoffrey M. (1993b), "Institutional economics: surveying the 'old' and the 'new'", *Metroeconomica*, **44**(1), February, 1–28.

Hodgson, Geoffrey M. (1997), "The fate of the Cambridge capital controversy", in Philip Arestis and Malcolm C. Sawyer (eds), *Capital Controversy, Post Keynesian Economics and the History of Economic Theory: Essays in Honour of Geoff Harcourt*, London and New York: Routledge, pp. 95–110.

Hodgson, Geoffrey M. (1998), "The approach of institutional economics", *Journal of Economic Literature*, **36**(1), March, 166–92.

Hodgson, Geoffrey M. (2001), *How Economics Forgot History: The Problem of Historical Specificity in Social Science*, London and New York: Routledge.

Hodgson, Geoffrey M. (2003), "How did economics get into such a state?" in Fullbrook, Edward (ed.), *The Crisis in Economics: The Post-Autistic Movement: The First 600 Days*, London and New York: Routledge, pp. 143–6.

Hodgson, Geoffrey M. (2004), *The Evolution of Institutional Economics: Agency, Structure and Darwinism in American Institutionalism*, London and New York: Routledge.

Hodgson, Geoffrey M. (2005), "Characterizing institutional and heterodox economics – a reply to Tony Lawson", *Evolutionary and Institutional Economics*, **2**, 213–23.

Hodgson, Geoffrey M. and Thorbjørn Knudsen (2004), "The complex evolution of a simple traffic convention: the functions and implications of habit", *Journal of Economic Behavior and Organization*, **54**(1), 19–47.

Hodgson, Geoffrey M. and Thorbjørn Knudsen (2006), "Why we need a generalized Darwinism: and why a generalized Darwinism is not enough", *Journal of Economic Behavior and Organization*, **61**(1), September, 1–19.

Hodgson, Geoffrey M. and Harry Rothman (1999), "The editors and

authors of economics journals: a case of institutional oligopoly?",
Economic Journal, **109**(2), February, F165–F186.

Hoffman, Elizabeth, Kevin McCabe, Keith Shachat and Vernon Smith
(1994), "Preferences, property rights and anonymity in bargaining
games", *Games and Economic Behavior*, **7**(3), 346–80.

Hoggatt, Austin C. (1959), "An experimental business game", *Behavioral
Science*, **4**, 192–203.

Hommes, Cars H. (1991), *Chaotic Dynamics in Economic Models: Some
Simple Case-Studies*, Groningen: Wolters-Noordhoff.

Hommes, Cars H. (1993), "Periodic, almost-periodic and chaotic dynamics
in Hicks' nonlinear trade cycle model", *Economics Letters*, **41**, 391–7.

Hommes, Cars H. (1994), "Dynamics of the cobweb model with adaptive
expectations and non-linear supply and demand", *Journal of Economic
Behavior and Organization*, **24**, 315–35.

Hommes, Cars H. (1995), "A reconsideration of Hicks' nonlinear trade
cycle model", *Structural Change and Economic Dynamics*, **6**, 435–59.

Hommes, C.H. (1998), "On the consistency of backward looking expectations: the case of the cobweb", *Journal of Economic Behaviour and
Organization*, **33**, 333–62.

Hommes, Cars H. (2002), "Modeling the stylized facts in finance through
simple nonlinear adaptive systems", *Proceedings of the National
Academy of Sciences USA*, **99**, 7221–8.

Hommes, Cars H. (2006), "Heterogeneous agent models in economics
and finance", in L. Tesfatstion and K.L. Judd (eds), *Computational
Economics, Volume 2: Agent-Based Computational Economics*,
Amsterdam: Elsevier Science B.V., pp. 1109–86.

Hommes, Cars H. (2009), "Bounded rationality and learning in complex
markets", in J.B. Rosser, Jr. (ed.), *Handbook of Complexity Research*,
Cheltenham, UK and Northampton, MA, USA: Edward Elgar, pp.
87–123.

Hommes, Cars H. (2010), "The heterogeneous expectations hypothesis:
some evidence from the lab", CeNDEF Working Paper, University of
Amsterdam, January.

Hommes, Cars H. and J. Barkley Rosser, Jr. (2001), "Consistent expectations equilibria and complex dynamics in renewable resource markets",
Macroeconomic Dynamics, **5**, 180–203.

Hommes, Cars H. and Helena E. Nusse (1989), "Does an unstable Keynesian
unemployment equilibrium in a non-Walrasian dynamic macro model
imply chaos?", *Scandinavian Journal of Economics*, **91**, 161–7.

Hommes, Cars H. and Helena E. Nusse (1990), "Resolution of chaos
with application to a modified Samuelson model", *Journal of Economic
Dynamics and Control*, **14**, 1–19.

Hommes, Cars H. and Helena E. Nusse (1991), "'Period Three to Period Two' bifurcation for piecewise linear models", *Journal of Economics*, **54**, 157–69.

Hommes, Cars H. and Gerhard Sorger (1998), "Consistent expectations equilibria", *Macroeconomic Dynamics*, **2**, 287–321.

Hommes, Cars H. and Florian O.O. Wagener (2009), "Complex evolutionary systems in behavioral finance", in T. Hens and K.R. Schenk-Hoppé (eds), *Handbook of Financial Markets: Dynamics and Evolution*, North Holland: Elsevier, pp. 217–76.

Hommes, Cars H., Helena E. Nusse and András Simonovits (1995), "Cycles and chaos in a socialist economy", *Journal of Economic Dynamics and Control*, **19**, 155–79.

Hommes, Cars H., Joep Sonnemans, Jan Tuinstra and Henk van de Velden (2005), "Coordination of expectations in asset pricing experiments", *Review of Financial Studies*, **18**, 955–80.

Hommes, Cars H., Joep Sonnemans, Jan Tuinstra and Henk van de Velden (2007), "Learning in cobweb experiments", *Macroeconomic Dynamics*, **11**, 1938–70.

Hommes, Cars H., Joep Sonnemans, Jan Tuinstra and Henk van de Velden (2008), "Expectations and bubbles in asset pricing experiments", *Journal of Economic Behavior and Organization*, **67**, 116–33.

Hoover, K., S. Johansen and K. Juselius (2008), "Allowing the data to speak freely: the macroeconometrics of the cointegrated vector autoregression", *American Economic Review*, **98**, pp. 251–5.

Horgan, John (1997), *The End of Science: Facing the Limits of Knowledge in the Twilight of the Scientific Age* (paperback edition), New York: Broadway Books.

Hornborg, A., J. Martinez Alier, and J.R. McNeil (eds) (2007), *Rethinking Environmental History: World-System History and Global Environmental Change*, Lanham, MD: Alta Mira Press.

Hotelling, Harold (1929), "Stability in competition", *Economic Journal*, **39**, 41–57.

Howarth, Richard B. and Richard B. Norgaard (1992), "Environmental valuation under sustainable development", *American Economic Review*, **82**, 473–7.

Inoue, Yasuo (1994), "Trajectoires nationales d'industrialisation de la Corée du Sud et de Taïwan", *Japon in Extenso*, no. 32.

Israel, Giorgio (2005), "The science of complexity: epistemological problems and perspectives", *Science in Context*, **11**, 1–31.

James, William (1890), *The Principles of Psychology*, 2 vols, 1st edn, New York and London: Holt and Macmillan.

Jansson, AnnMari (ed.) (1984), *Integration of Economy and Ecology: An*

Outlook for the Eighties, Stockholm: Asko Laboratory, University of Stockholm.

Jensen, Keith, Joseph Call and Michael Tomasello (2007), "Chimpanzees are rational maximizers in an ultimatum game", *Science*, **318**, 107–9.

Johansen, S. (1983), "Some topics in regression", *Scandinavian Journal of Statistics*, **10**, 161–94.

Johansen, S. (1988a), "The mathematical structure of error correction models", *Contemporary Mathematics*, 80, 359–86.

Johansen, S. (1988b), "Statistical analysis of cointegration vectors", *Journal of Economic Dynamics and Control*, **12**, 231–54.

Johansen, S. (1995), *Likelihood-Based Inference in Cointegrated Vector Autoregressive Models*, Oxford: Oxford University Press.

Johansen, S. (2006), "Confronting the economic model with the data", in D. Colander (ed.), *Post Walrasian Macroeconomics*, Cambridge: Cambridge University Press, pp. 287–300.

Johansen, S. and A. Hald (1983), "On de Moivre's recursion formulae for the duration of play", *International Statistics Review*, **51**, 239–53.

Johansen, S. and K. Juselius (1990), "Maximum likelihood estimation and inference on cointegration – with applications to the demand for money", *Oxford Bulletin of Economics and Statistics*, **52**, 169–210, reprinted in J. Campos, N.R. Ericsson and D.F. Hendry (eds.) (2005), *General-to-Specific Modelling*, Vol I, Cheltenham, UK and Northampton, MA, USA: Edward Elgar, pp. 512–53.

Johansen, S. and K. Juselius (1992), "Testing structural hypotheses in a multivariate cointegration analysis of the PPP and UIP for UK", *Journal of Econometrics*, **53**.

Johansen, S. and K. Juselius (1994), "Identification of the long-run and the short-run structure. An application to the ISLM model", *Journal of Econometrics*, **63**, 211–44.

Johansen, S. and K. Juselius (2006), "Extracting information from the data: a European view on empirical macro", in D. Colander (ed.), *Post Walrasian Macroeconomics*, Cambridge: Cambridge University Press, pp. 301–34.

Johansen, S. and S. Keiding (1981), "A family of models for the elimination of substrate in the liver", *Journal of Theoretical Biology*, **89**, 549–56.

Johansen, S. and A.R. Swensen (1999), "Testing rational expectations in vector autoregressive models", *Journal of Econometrics*, **93**, 73–91.

Johansen, S., R. Mosconi and B. Nielsen (2000), "Cointegration analysis in the presence of structural breaks in the deterministic trend", *Econometrics Journal*, **3**(2), 216–49.

Johansen, S., K. Juselius, R. Frydman and M. Goldberg (2009), "Testing hypotheses in an I(2) model with applications to the persistent long swings in the Dmk/$ rate", forthcoming in *Journal of Econometrics*.

Juselius, K. (1991), "Long-run relations in a well defined statistical model for the data generating process. Cointegration analysis of the PPP and the UIP conditions for Denmark and Germany", in J. Gruber (ed.), *Econometric Decision Models: New Methods of Modeling and Applications*, New York: Springer Verlag.

Juselius, K. (1994), "On the duality between long-run relations and common trends in the I(1) and the I(2) case: an application to aggregate money holdings", *Econometric Reviews*, **13**(2), 151–78.

Juselius, K. (1995), "Do the purchasing power parity and the uncovered interest rate parity hold in the long run? An application of likelihood inference in a multivariate time series model", *Journal of Econometrics*, **69**(1), 211–40.

Juselius, K. (1996), "An empirical analysis of the changing role of German Bundesbank after 1983", *Oxford Bulletin of Economics and Statistics*, **58**, 791–817.

Juselius, Katarina (1999), "Models and relations in economics and econometrics", *Journal of Economic Methodology*, **6**(2), 259–90.

Juselius, Katarina (2001), "European integration and monetary transmission mechanisms: the case of Italy", *Journal of Applied Econometrics*, **16**, 341–58.

Juselius, K. (2006), *The Cointegrated VAR Model: Methodology and Applications*, New York: Oxford University Press.

Juselius, K. (2009), "The PPP puzzle. What the data tell when allowed to speak freely", Chapter 8 in T.C. Mills and K. Patterson (eds), *Palgrave Handbook of Empirical Econometrics*, Basingstoke, Palgrave Macmillan.

Juselius, K. and M. Franchi (2007), "Taking a DSGE model to the data meaningfully", *Economics – The Open-Access, Open-Assessment E-Journal*, No. 2007–4.

Kahneman, Daniel and Amos Tversky (1982), *Judgment under Uncertainty: Heuristics and Biases*, New York: Cambridge University Press.

Kapp, K. William (1963), *Social Costs of Business Enterprises*, 2nd edn, London: Asia Publishing House.

Keiding, S., N.J. Christensen, S.E. Damgaard, A. Dejgård, H.L. Iversen, A. Jacobsen, S. Johansen, F. Lundquist, E. Rubinstein and K. Winkler (1983), "Ethanol metabolism in heavy drinkers after massive and moderate alcohol intake", *Biochemical Pharmacology*, **32**, 3097–102.

Keynes, John Maynard (1935), *The General Theory of Employment*, London: Macmillan.

Kirman, Alan (1971), "Optimum tariffs in a general equilibrium model of trade", PhD thesis, Princeton University, H.W. Kuhn, Supervisor.

Kirman, Alan (1975), "Learning by firms about demand conditions", in Richard H. Day and Theodore Groves (eds), *Adaptive Economic Models*, New York: Academic Press.

Kirman, Alan (1983), "Communication in markets: a suggested approach", *Economics Letters*, **12**, 101–108.

Kirman, Alan (1989a), "The intrinsic limits of economic theory: the emperor has no clothes", *Economic Journal*, **99**(395), 126–39.

Kirman, Alan (1989b), "L'importance des réseaux en Economie", *Mathématique et Informatique pour les Sciences Humaines*, **106**, 5–15.

Kirman, Alan (1992), "What or whom does the representative individual represent?", *Journal of Economic Perspectives*, **6**(2), 117–36.

Kirman, Alan (1993), "Ants, rationality and recruitment", *Quarterly Journal of Economics*, **108**, 137–56.

Kirman, Alan (1995), "The behaviour of the foreign exchange market", *Bank of England Quarterly*, 15 August, pp. 286–93.

Kirman, Alan (1997), "The economy as an evolving network", *Journal of Evolutionary Economics*, **7**, 339–53.

Kirman, Alan and M. Dahl (1994), "Economic research in Europe", *European Economic Review*, **38**, 505–22.

Kirman, Alan and Wilson Schmidt (1965), "Key currency burdens: the UK case", *National Banking Review*, September.

Kirman, Alan and D. Sondermann (1972), "Arrow's theorem, many agents and invisible dictators", *Journal of Economic Theory*, **5**, 308–35.

Kirman, Alan and Nicolaas Vriend (2000), "Evolving market structure: a model of price dispersion and loyalty for the Marseille fish market", in Domenico Delli Gatti, Mauro Gallegati and Alan Kirman (eds), *Interaction and Market Structure*, Heidelberg: Springer-Verlag.

Kirman, Alan, C. Oddou and Shlomo Weber (1986), "Stochastic communication and coalition formation", *Econometrica*, **54**, 129–38.

Kirman, Alan, Gerard Weisbuch and Dorothea Herreiner (2000), "Market organization and trading relationships", *The Economic Journal*, **110**, 411–36.

Kolmogorov, A.N. (1965), "Three approaches to quantitative definition of information", *Problems of Information Transmission*, **1**, 4–7.

Kornai, János (1958), "Kell-e Korrigálni a Nyereségrészesedést?" ("Should the practice of profit sharing be corrected?"), *Közgazdasági Szemle*, **7**, 720–34.

Kornai, János (1959), *Over Centralization in Economic Administration*, London: Oxford University Press.

Kornai, János (1971), *Anti-Equilibrium: On Economic Systems Theory and the Tasks of Research*, Amsterdam: North-Holland.

Kornai, János (1980), *The Economics of Shortage*, Amsterdam: North-Holland.

Kornai, János (1990), *The Road to a Free Economy: Shifting from a Socialist System – the Example of Hungary*, New York: Norton.

Kornai, János (1992), *The Socialist System: The Political Economy of Communism*, Princeton: Princeton University Press.

Kornai, János (1993), "The evolution of financial discipline under the post socialist system", *Kyklos*, **46**, 315–36.

Kornai, János (2000), "What the change of the system from socialism to capitalism does and does not mean", *Journal of Economic Perspectives*, **14**(1), 27–42.

Kornai, János (2007), *By Force of Thought: Irregular Memoirs of an Intellectual Journey*, Cambridge, MA: MIT Press.

Kornai, János (2008a), *From Socialism to Capitalism: Eight Essays*, Budapest and New York: Central European University Press.

Kornai, János (2008b), "Coffee and tea: some comments on reforming the system of health insurance in Hungary", *Acta Oeconomica*, **58**(2), 239–61.

Kornai, János and Tamás Liptak (1965), "Two-level planning", *Econometrica*, **33**, 141–69.

Kornai, János and Béla Martos (1973), "Autonomous control of the economic system", *Econometrica*, **41**, 509–28.

Kornai, János and Béla Martos (eds) (1981), *Non-Price Control*, Amsterdam: North-Holland.

Kornai, János and Yingyi Qian (eds) (2008), *Market Socialism: In the Light of the Experience of China and Vietnam*, London: Palgrave Macmillan.

Kornai, János, Eric S. Maskin and Gérard Roland (2003), "Understanding the soft budget constraint", *Journal of Economic Literature*, **41**, 509–28.

Kuhn, Thomas S. (1962), *The Structure of Scientific Revolutions*, Chicago: University of Chicago Press.

Lange, Oskar (1936), "On the economic theory of socialism", *Review of Economic Studies*, **4**, 53–71.

Laury, Susan K., James Walker and Arlington Williams (1995) "Anonymity and voluntary provision of public goods", *Journal of Economic Behavior and Organization*, **27**, 365–80.

Lavoie, Don (1989), "Economic chaos or spontaneous order? Implications for political economy of the new view of science", *Cato Journal*, **8**, 613–35.

Lawson, Tony (1997), *Economics and Reality*, London and New York: Routledge.

Lawson, Tony (2006), "The nature of heterodox economics", *Cambridge Journal of Economics*, **30**, 483–505.

Levitt, Steven D. and John A. List (2007), "What do laboratory experiments measuring social preferences reveal about the real world?", *Journal of Economic Perspectives*, **21**(2), 153–74.

Lewis, Alain A. (1985), "On effectively computable realizations of choice functions", *Mathematical Social Sciences*, **10**, 43–80.

Lipietz, Alain (1977), *Le Capital et son Espace*, Paris: Maspéro.

Lipietz, Alain (1979), *Crise et Inflation, Pourquoi?* Paris: Maspéro.

Lipietz, Alain (1986), "New tendencies in the international division of labor: regimes of accumulation and modes of regulation", in A.J. Scott and M. Storper (eds), *Production, Work, and Technology*, London: Allen & Unwin.

Lipietz, Alain (1993), *Vert-Espérance: L'Avenir de L'Écologie Politique*, Paris: La Découverte.

List, John A., Robert Berrens, Alok Bohara and Joe Kerkvliet (2004), "Examining the role of social isolation on stated preferences", *American Economic Review*, **94**(3), 741–52.

Lordon, Frédéric (1993), "*Irrégularités des trajectoires de croissance, évolutions et dynamiques non-linéaires. vers une schématization de l'endométabolisme*", thesis, EHESS, Paris.

Lordon, Frédéric (1997), "Endogenous structural change and crisis in a multiple time-scales growth model", *Journal of Evolutionary Economics*, **7**, 1–21.

Lösch, August (1940), *Die Räumliche Ordnung der Wirtschaft*, Jena: Gustav Fischer. English translation, 1954, *The Economics of Location*, New Haven: Yale University Press.

Loewenstein, George, Leigh Thompson and Max Bazerman (1989), "Social utility and decision making in interpersonal contexts", *Journal of Personality and Social Psychology*, **57**, 426–41.

Lubrano, Michael, Luc Bauwens, Alan Kirman and Camelia Protopopescu (2003), "Ranking European economic departments: a statistical approach", *Journal of the European Economic Association*, **1**, 1367–401.

Lutz, F.A. (1940), "The structure of interest rates", *Quarterly Journal of Economics*, **55**, 36–63.

Malinvaud, Edmond (1977), *Theory of Unemployment Reconsidered*, Oxford: Basil Blackwell.

Mantegna, Rosario N. and Eugene Stanley (2000), *An Introduction to Econophysics: Correlation and Complexity in Finance*, Cambridge, UK: Cambridge University Press.

Mantel, Rolf (1974), "On the characterization of aggregate excess demand", *Journal of Economic Theory*, **7**(3), 348–53.

Marglin, Steven A. (1974), "What do bosses do? The origins and functions of hierarchy in capitalist production", *Review of Radical Political Economics*, **6**(2), 60–102.

Mariátegui, José Carlos (1996), *The Heroic and Creative Meaning of Socialism: Selected Essays*, edited and translated by Michael Pearlman, Atlantic Highlands, NJ: Humanities Press International.

Markose, Sheri M. (2005), "Computability and evolutionary complexity: markets as complex adaptive systems (CAS)", *Economic Journal*, **115**, F159–F192.

Markowitz, Harry (1952), "Portfolio selection", *Journal of Finance*, **7**, 77–91.

Marshall, Alfred (1890), *Principles of Economics: An Introductory Volume*, 1st edn, London: Macmillan.

Marshall, Alfred (1892), "A reply to 'The Perversion of Economic History' by Dr. Cunningham", *Economic Journal*, **2**, 507–19.

Martinez Alier, J. (1971), *Labourers and Landowners in Southern Spain*, London: St. Anthony's College Publications, Allen and Unwin (originally published in Spanish, 1968).

Martinez Alier, J. (1977a), *Haciendas, Plantations and Collective Farms (Agrarian Class Societies: Cuba and Peru)*, London: Frank Cass (Spanish editions published 1972 and 1974).

Martinez Alier, J. (1977b), "El pacto de la Moncloa: lucha syndical y nuevo corporativismo", *Cuadernos de Ruedo Ibérico*, nos. 59–60, 32–51.

Martinez Alier, J. (1983), "Sharecropping: some illustrations", in T. Byres (ed.), *Sharecropping and Sharecroppers*, London: Frank Cass, pp. 94–106.

Martinez Alier, J. (1987), *Ecological Economics: Energy, Environment and Society*, Oxford: Blackwell, revised paperback editions, 1990, 1993; originally in Catalan, *L'ecologia i l'economia: Història d'unes Relacions Amagades*, Edicions, **62**, Barcelona, 1984).

Martinez Alier, J. (2001), "Mining conflicts, environmental justice, and valuation", *Journal of Hazardous Materials*, **86**,153–70.

Martinez Alier, J. (2002), *The Environmentalism of the Poor: a Study of Ecological Conflicts and Valuation*, Cheltenham, UK and Northampton, MA, USA: Edward Elgar.

Martinez Alier, J. and J.M. Naredo (1979), "La noción de 'fuerzas productivas' y la cuestion de la energia", *Cuadernos de Ruedo Ibérico*, nos. 63–66, 71–90.

Martinez Alier, J. and M. O'Connor (1996), "Ecological and economic distribution conflicts", in R. Costanza, J. Martinez Alier and O. Segura (eds), *Down to Earth: Theory and Applications of Ecological Economics*, Washington: Island Press.

Martinez Alier, J. and Leah Temper (2007), "Is India too poor to be green?", *Economic and Political Weekly*, 28 April, 1489–92.

Marx, Karl (1867), Capital, *Volume I: A Critical Analysis of Capitalist Production*, originally in German, English translation, 1974, London: Lawrence & Wishart.

Marx, Karl and Friedrich Engels (1975), *Cartas Sobre las Ciencias de la Naturaleza y las Matemáticas*, Barcelona: Anagrama.

Mas-Colell, Andreu (1985), *The Theory of General Economic Equilibrium: A Differentiable Approach*, Cambridge, UK: Cambridge University Press.

Maynard Smith, John and George R. Price (1973), "The logic of animal conflicts", *Nature*, **246**, 15–18.

McCloskey, Deirdre N. (2003), "Notre Dame Loses", *Eastern Economic Journal*, **29**, 309–15.

McNeill, John R. (2000), *Something New Under the Sun: An Environmental History of the Twentieth-Century World*, New York: W.W. Norton.

Mill, John Stuart (1843), *Ratiocinative and Inductive Logic*, London: Longmans Green.

Miotti, Luis E. (1994), *Argentine: Fragilité de l'accumulation et Options de la Régulation*, Paris: Armond Collin.

Mira, Christian and Laura Gardini (2009), "From the box-within-a-box bifurcations organization to the Julia set Part I", *International Journal of Bifurcation and Chaos*, **19**, 281–327.

Mirowski, Philip (1989), *More Heat than Light: Economics as Social Physics, Physics as Nature's Economics*, Cambridge: Cambridge University Press.

Mirowski, Philip (2002), *Machine Dreams*, Cambridge: Cambridge University Press.

Mirowski, Philip (2007), "Markets come to bits: evolution, computation, and markomata in economic science", *Journal of Economic Behavior and Organization*, **63**, 209–42.

Mises, Ludwig von (1920), "Die Wirtschaftrechnung im Sozialistischen Gemeinwesen", *Archiv für Sozialwissenschaft und Sozialpolitik*, **47**, 86–121, English translation, 1935, "Economic calculation in the socialist commonwealth", in F.A. Hayek (ed.), *Collectivist Economic Planning*, London: Routledge, pp. 87–130.

Morris-Suzuki, Tessa (1989), *A History of Japanese Economic Thought*, London: Routledge.

Müller-Armack, Andreas (1947), *Wirtshaftslenkung und Marktwirtshaft*, Hamburg: Verlag für Wirtschaft und Sozialpolitik.

Munda, Giuseppe (1995), *Multicriteria Evaluation in a Fuzzy Environment:*

Theory and Applications in Ecological Economics, Heidelberg: Physica-Verlag.

Nelson, Richard R. and Sidney G. Winter (1982), *An Evolutionary Theory of Economic Change*, Cambridge, MA: Harvard University Press.

Neumann, John von, edited by Arthur W. Burks (1966), *Theory of Self-Reproducing Automata*, Urbana: University of Illinois Press.

Neumann, John von and Oskar Morgenstern (1944), *The Theory of Games and Economic Behavior*, Princeton: Princeton University Press.

Nicolis, Grégoire and Ilya Prigogine (1977), *Self-Organization in Nonequilibrium Systems: From Dissipative Structures to Order through Fluctuations*, New York: Wiley-Interscience.

Nordhaus, William D. (2007), "A review of the Stern Review on the Economics of Climate Change", *Journal of Economic Literature*, **45**, 686–702.

Norgaard, Richard B. (1984), "Coevolutionary development potential", *Land Economics*, **60**, 160–73.

North, Douglas C. (1990), *Institutions, Institutional Change, and Economic Performance*, Cambridge, UK: Cambridge University Press.

Nunes, Paulo Augusto Lourenço Dias Nunes, Jeroen C.J.M. van den Bergh and Peter Nijkamp (eds) (2003), *The Ecological Economics of Biodiversity: Methods and Applications*, Cheltenham, UK and Northampton, MA, USA: Edward Elgar.

Ominami, Carlos (1986), *Le Tiers Monde dans la Crise*, Paris: Éditions La Découverte.

O'Neill, John (2007), *Markets, Deliberation and Environment*, London: Routledge.

Orléan, André (2006), "La sociologie économique et la question de l'unité des sciences sociales", *L'Année Sociologique*, **55**, 279–306.

Oxford English Dictionary (OED) (1971), *The Compact Edition of the Oxford English Dictionary, Volume A–O*, Oxford: Oxford University Press.

Palander, Tord F. (1935), *Beitrage zur Standortstheorie*, Uppsala: Almqvist & Wiksell.

Palander, Tord F. (1953), "On the concepts and method of the Stockholm School", *International Economic Papers*, **3**, 5–57.

Palombarini, Stefano (2001), *La Rupture du Compromis Social Italien*, Paris: CNRS Editions.

Pareto, Vilfredo (1896–97), *Cours d'Économie Politique Professé a l'Université de Lausanne*, Paris and Lausanne: Rouge, English translation by Ann Schwien (1971), *Manual of Political Economy*, New York: Kelly.

Passet, René (1979), *L'Économie et le Vivant*, Paris: Payot.

Pimentel, David, L.E. Hurd, A.C. Bellotti, M.J. Forster, I.N. Oka, O.D. Sholes and R.J. Whitman (1973), "Food production and the energy crisis", *Science,* **182**, 443–9.

Podolinsky, Serhii (1880), "Le socialisme et l'unité des forces fisiques", *Revue Socialiste,* June.

Poincaré, Henri (1880–1890), *Mémoire sur Les Courbes Défines par les Équations Différentielles I-VI, Oeuvre I*, Paris: Gauthier-Villars.

Polányi, Karl (1944), *The Great Transformation*, Boston: Beacon Press.

Pryor, Frederick L. (1995), *Economic Evolution and Structure: The Impact of Complexity on the US Economic System*, New York: Cambridge University Press.

Puu, Tönu (1964), "Studier i det Optima Tillgångsvalets Teori" ("Studies in the theory of choice of financial assets"), PhD Thesis, Uppsala: Almqvist & Wiksell.

Puu, Tönu (1966), "Les effets de substitution et d'expansion dans la théorie de la production", *Revue d'Économie Politique,* **74**, 57–91.

Puu, Tönu (1968), "Complementarity, substitutability and regressivity in the theory of production", in J. Paelink (ed.), *Recherches Récents sur la Fonction de Production*, Namur: Presses Universitaires Notre-Dame de la Paix, pp. 97–131.

Puu, Tönu (1969), "Causal versus teleological explanation in economics", *Scandinavian Journal of Economics,* **71**, 111–26.

Puu, Tönu (1979), "Regional modelling and structural stability", *Environment and Planning A*, **11**, 1431–38.

Puu, Tönu (1981), "Catastrophic structural change in a continuous regional model", *Regional Science and Urban Economics*, **11**, 317–33.

Puu, Tönu (1989), *Nonlinear Economic Dynamics*, Heidelberg: Springer-Verlag.

Puu, Tönu (1990), "On the unity of arts, crafts, and sciences", *Journal of Cultural Economics*, **14**, 19–34.

Puu, Tönu (1991), "Chaos in duopoly pricing", *Chaos, Solitons & Fractals,* **1**, 457–73.

Puu, Tönu (1995), "The chaotic monopolist", *Chaos, Solitons & Fractals,* **5**, 35–44.

Puu, Tönu (2003), *Attractors, Bifurcations & Chaos: Nonlinear Phenomena in Economics*, 2nd edition, Heidelberg: Springer-Verlag.

Puu, Tönu (2006), *Arts, Sciences and Economics: A Historical Safari*, Heidelberg: Springer-Verlag.

Puu, Tönu (2007), "The Hicksian trade cycle with floor and ceiling dependent on capital stock", *Journal of Economic Dynamics and Control*, **31**, 575–92.

Puu, Tönu, Laura Gardini and Irina Sushko (2005), "A multiplier-accelerator model with floor determined by capital stock", *Journal of Economic Behavior and Organization*, **56**, 331–348.

Rabin, Matthew (1993) "Incorporating fairness into game theory and economics", *American Economic Review*, **83**, 1281–302.

Rappaport, Roy (1967), *Pigs for the Ancestors: Ritual in the Ecology of a New Guinea People*, New Haven: Yale University Press, 2nd edn, 1985.

Rausch, Edwin (1952), *Struktur und Metrik figural-optischer Wahrehmung*, Frankfurt: Waldemur Kramer.

Richter, M.K. and K.C. Wong (1999), "Non-computability of competitive equilibrium", *Economic Theory*, **14**, 1–28.

Rissanen, Jorma (1989), *Stochastic Complexity in Statistical Inquiry*, Singapore: World Scientific.

Robbins, Lionel (1932), *An Essay on the Nature and Significance of Economic Science*, 1st edn, London: Macmillan.

Robinson, Joan (1933), *The Economics of Imperfect Competition*, London: Macmillan.

Roemer, John E. (1981), *Analytical Foundations of Marxian Economic Theory*, Cambridge: Cambridge University Press.

Rosser, J. Barkley, Jr. (1999), "On the complexities of complex economic dynamics", *Journal of Economic Perspectives*, **13** (4), 169–92.

Rosser, J. Barkley, Jr. (2004a), *Complexity in Economics, Volumes I–III: The International Library of Critical Writings in Economics (174)*, Cheltenham, UK and Northampton, MA, USA: Edward Elgar.

Rosser, J. Barkley, Jr. (2004b), "Epistemological implications of economic complexity", *Annals of the Japan Association for the Philosophy of Science*, **13**, 45–57.

Rosser, J. Barkley, Jr. (2009), "Computational and dynamic complexity in economics", in J.B. Rosser, Jr. (ed.), *Handbook of Research on Complexity*, Cheltenham, UK and Northampton, MA, USA: Edward Elgar, pp. 22–35.

Rosser, J. Barkley, Jr. and Marina V. Rosser (2004), *Comparative Economics in a Transforming World Economy*, 2nd edn, Cambridge, MA: MIT Press.

Rosser, J. Barkley, Jr., Carl Folke, Folke Günther, Heikki Isomäki, Charles Perrings and Tönu Puu (1994), "Discontinuous change in multilevel hierarchical systems", *Systems Research*, **11**(3), 77–93.

Salmon, M. (1982), "Error correction mechanisms", *The Economic Journal*, **92**, 615–29.

Samuelson, Paul A. (1947), *The Foundations of Economic Analysis*, Cambridge, MA: Harvard University Press.

Samuelson, Paul A. (1961), *Economics*, 5th edn, New York: McGraw-Hill.

Samuelson, Paul A. (1988), "The passing of the guard in economics", *Eastern Economic Journal*, **14**, 319–29.

Sargent, Thomas J. (1993), *Bounded Rationality in Macroeconomics*, Oxford: Clarendon Press.

Sauermann, Heinz and Reinhard Selten (1959), "Ein Oligopolexperiment", *Zeitschrift für de gesamte Staatswissenschaft*, **115**, 427–71.

Sauermann, Heinz and Reinhard Selten (1962), "Anspruchs-anpassungstheorie der Unternehmung", *Zeitschrift für Staatswissenschaft*, **118**, 577–97.

Schelling, Thomas C. (1969), "Models of segregation", *American Economic Review*, **59**(2), June, 488–93.

Schelling, Thomas C. (1971), "Dynamic models of segregation", *Journal of Mathematical Sociology*, **1**, 143–86.

Schmoller, Gustav (1900), *Grundriss der allgemeinen Volkswirtschaftslehre*, Part 1, Munich and Leipzig: Duncker und Humblot.

Schotter, Andrew R. (1985), *Free Market Economics: A Critical Appraisal*, New York: St Martin's Press.

Schumpeter, Joseph A. (1911), *Théorie de l'Evolution Economique. Recherche sur le Profit, le Credit, l'Intérêt et le Cycle de la Conjoncture*, French translation 1983, Paris: Dalloz.

Schumpeter, Joseph A. (1942), *Capitalism, Socialism, and Democracy*, New York: Harper and Row.

Schumpeter, Joseph A. (1954), *Capitalism, Socialism and Democracy*, 4th edn, London: Allen & Unwin.

Scott, James (1998), *Seeing Like a State: How Certain Schemes to Improve the Human Condition Have Failed*, New Haven: Yale University Press.

Selten, Reinhard (1965), "Spielstheoretische Behandlung eines Oligopolmodells mit Nächfrageträgheit – Teil I: Bestimmung des dynamischen Preisgleichgewichts", *Zeitschrift für die gesamte Staatswissenschaft*, **121**, 301–24.

Selten, Reinhard (1973), "A simple model of imperfect competition where 4 are few and 6 are many", *International Journal of Game Theory*, **2**, 141–201.

Selten, Reinhard (1975), "Reexamination of the perfectness concept for equilibrium points in extensive games", *International Journal of Game Theory*, **4**, 25–55.

Selten, Reinhard (1978), "The chain store paradox", *Theory and Decision*, **9**, 127–59.

Selten, Reinhard (1980), "A note on evolutionary stable strategies in asymmetric animal conflict", *Journal of Theoretical Biology*, **83**, 93–101.

Selten, Reinhard (1983), "Evolutionary stability in extensive two-person games", *Mathematical Social Sciences*, **5**, 269–363.

Selten, Reinhard and Joachim Buchta (1998), "Experimental sealed bid first price auctions with observed bid functions", in D. Budescu, I. Erev and R. Zwick (eds), *Games and Human Behavior: Essays in Honor of Amnon Rapaport*, Mahwah, NJ: Lawrence Erlbaum Associates, pp. 79–102.

Selten, Reinhard and Thorsten Chmura (2008), "Stationary concepts for experimental 2×2 Games", *American Economic Review*, **98**, 938–66.

Selten, Reinhard and Peter Hammerstein (1984), "Gaps in Harley's argument on evolutionarily stable learning rules and in the logic of 'tit for tat'", *The Behavioral and Brain Sciences*, **7**, 115–16.

Selten, Reinhard and J. Pool (1991), 'The distribution of foreign language skills as a game equilibrium', in Reinhard Selten (ed.), *Game Equilibrium Models IV: Social and Political Interaction*, vol. 4, Berlin: Springer, pp. 64–87.

Selten, Reinhard and Avi Shmida (1991), "Pollinator foraging and flower competition in a game equilibrium model", in R. Selten (ed.), *Game Equilibrium Models I*, Heidelberg: Springer-Verlag, pp. 195–246.

Selten, Reinhard and Rolf Stoecker (1986), "End behavior in sequences of finite prisoner's dilemma supergames", *Journal of Economic Behavior and Organization*, **7**, 47–70.

Selten, Reinhard, Michael Mitzkewitz and Gerald R. Uhlich (1997), "Duopoly strategies programmed by experienced players", *Econometrica*, **65**, 517–55.

Shannon, Claude and Warren Weaver (1948), *The Mathematical Theory of Communication*, Urbana: University of Illinois Press.

Simon, Herbert A. (1957), *Models of Man*, New York: Wiley.

Simon, Herbert (1962), "The architecture of complexity", *Proceedings of the American Philosophical Society*, **106**, 467–82.

Slutsky, Eugen E. (1915), "On the theory of the budget of the consumer", *Giornali degli Economisti*, **51**, 1–28, originally in Italian as "Sulla Teoria del Bilancio del Consumatore".

Smith, Vernon L. (1962), "An experimental study of competitive market behavior", *Journal of Political Economy*, **70**, 111–37.

Smith, Vernon L. (1982), "Microeconomic systems as an experimental science", *American Economic Review*, **72**, 58–77.

Solomonoff, R.J. (1964), "A formal theory of inductive inference Parts I and II", *Information and Control*, **7**, 1–22; 224–54.

Sonnemans, Joep, Cars H. Hommes, Jan Tuinstra and Henk van de Velden (2004), "The instability of a heterogeneous cobweb economy: a strategy experiment in expectation formation", *Journal of Economic Behavior and Organization*, **54**, 453–81.

Sonnenschein, Hugo F. (1972), "Market excess demand functions", *Econometrica*, **40**(3), 549–63.

Sorger, Gerhard (1998), "Imperfect foresight and chaos: an example of a self-fulfilling mistake", *Journal of Economic Behavior and Organization*, **33**, 363–83.

Stern, Nicholas (2007), *The Economics of Climate Change: The Stern Review*, New York and Cambridge: Cambridge University Press.

Stiglitz, Joseph E. (1993), "Post Walrasian and Post Marxian economics", *Journal of Economic Perspectives*, **7**(1), Winter, 109–14.

Stiglitz, Joseph (1998), "The private uses of public interests: incentives and institutions", *Journal of Economic Perspectives*, **12**(2), 3–22.

Sushko, Irina, Laura Gardini and Tönu Puu (2002), "Duopoly with piecewise linear discontinuous reaction functions", in Tönu Puu and Irina Sushko (eds), *Oligopoly and Complex Dynamics: Tools and Models*, Heidelberg: Springer-Verlag, pp. 147–70.

Théret, Bruno (2002), "Saisir les faits économiques: une lecture structuraliste génétique de la méthode Commons", RR Working Paper No. 2002–1, Histoire de la pensée économique series, available at http://web.upmfgrenoble.fr/lepii/regulation/wp/index.html#1.

Thom, René (1975), *Structural Stability and Morphogenesis: An Outline of a Theory of Models*, English translation, Reading, MA: Benjamin (originally in French, 1972).

Thomas, R. Brooke (1976), "Energy flow at high altitude", in Paul T. Baker and Michael A. Little (eds), *Man in the Andes: A Multidisciplinary Study of High-altitude Quechuas*, Stroudsburg, PA: Dowden, Hutchinson & Ross.

Thomas, Hugh (1961), *The Spanish Civil War*, London: Penguin (revised version published 2003).

Turing, Alan M. (1952), "The chemical basis of morphogenesis", *Philosophical Transactions of the Royal Society, B*, **237**, 37–72.

van den Bergh, Jeroen C.J.M. (ed.) (1999), *Handbook of Environmental and Resource Economics*, Cheltenham, UK and Northampton, MA, USA: Edward Elgar.

Veblen, Thorstein (1919), *The Place of Science in Modern Civilization*, New York: Huebsch.

Velupillai, Kumaraswamy (2000), *Computable Economics*, Oxford: Oxford University Press.

Velupillai, K. Vela (2005), "A Primer on the tools and concepts of computable economics", in K. Vela Velupilla (ed.), *Computability, Complexity and Constructivity in Economic Analysis*, Victoria: Blackwell, pp. 148–97.

Vernadsky, Vladimir I. (1924), *La Géochimie*, Paris: Alcan.

Villeval, Marie-Claire (2002), "Régulation theory among theories of institutions", in Robert Boyer and Yves Saillard (eds), *Regulation Theory: The State of the Art*, London: Routledge, pp. 291–8.

von Stackelberg, Heinrich F. (1934), *Marktform und Gleichgewicht (Market Structure and Equilibrium)*, Vienna: Springer.

Wicksell, Knut (1898), *Geldzins und Güterpreise*, Jena: Gustav Fischer (English translation, 1936, *Interest and Prices*, London: Macmillan).

Wiener, Norbert (1948), *Cybernetics, or Control and Communication in the Animal and the Machine*, New York: Wiley & Sons, 2nd edn (1961), Cambridge: MIT Press.

Williamson, Oliver E. (1975), *Markets and Hierarchies: Analysis and Anti-Trust Implications: A Study in the Economics of Internal Organization*, New York: Free Press.

Young, H. Peyton (1998), *Individual Strategy and Social Structure: An Evolutionary Theory of Institutions*, Princeton: Princeton University Press.

Index

Titles of publications appear in *italics*.